Pleasant Valley Revisited

This book is dedicated in
memory of
Robert D. Parker
6/10/1960 to 12/28/2015

By Zeke Crandall

This book is published by Zeke Crandall LLC., 6210 West Shaw Butte Drive, Glendale, 85304

All rights to this book in any form are strictly prohibited unless authorized by the author 2016 with all copyrights reserved.

The ISBN number is 978-0-9773784-7-0 and the book's copyright number through the United States Library of Congress is TXu0018130-80

Soft bound signed copies of Pleasant Valley Revisited are available for sale at discounted internet pricing on our website, www.arizonatales.com or by email, email address is zekecrandall46@hotmail.com.

Other published soft bound books that are Currently available by this author are, Arizona Tales, Arizona Train Robbers, The Simple Man, Ghost in the Desert, and The Power Affair and Pleasant Valley-Revisited, all through our website, email, Amazon and Kindle

Look for new books written by this author as well over 2016-2018 including, The Death Cave, Tonto Basin Pioneer, Arizona Tales Vol 2, The Angels & Spirits, Camel Project and Boxing Referee.

Thank you,
Zeke Crandall

Preface

The Author was at a gun show here in Phoenix at the fairgrounds in the summer of 2012. I had a table at which I were selling books. Late Saturday afternoon as I was working at my table a man came by and looked at my books. He picked up a copy of one of the two working manuscripts of future books that I had brought along, to show folks that there were other books, I was working on. One of those manuscripts was the book called *Pleasant Valley-Revisited.* The man looked up at me and said,

> *"Wow, how ironic, there is a Tewksbury in the building next to you and I think he would love to meet you. He is selling some of his guns and ammunition."*

I could not contain my excitement at the opportunity of meeting a living Tewksbury relative. I was so excited to meet this man that I asked my neighbor to watch my table while we went over to meet the man. As we walked through the crowd toward their table in the other building from a distance I recognized a lady straight ahead of us standing at a table in the back of the building, she looked just like pictures I had seen of Edwin Tewksbury. She a dark complexion, fine facial features and jet black hair, she stood out, so she was easy to spot. As we stopped at their table, I looked at the lady and said;

"You must be a Tewksbury!?"

She looked up at me and said;

"Yes! I am!"

Then the lady spoke and, and introduced me to the elderly white haired man standing next to her and said;

"This is my cousin Bill Brown. He is also a Tewksbury too."

Then she asked me how I knew she was a Tewksbury and I told her;

"I think because you look just like your great uncles, Edwin and James Tewksbury."

Then she said;

"Wow, you must know your stuff!"

I shook hands with her cousin, Bill Brown, while she helped a fellow buy one of Bill's guns that he had for sale. He told me that his cousin's name was Barbara Tewksbury. I told him that I was working on a manuscript about the feud, but that I still needed a lot of information to finish the book. He said that I had come to the right place and he gave me his business card; Bill Brown, Getaway Guns. He introduced me to his cousin and told me to give him a call to set up a time when I could come over to his home office and he would share any information I needed to complete the story, He also said he had a lot of pictures that could put faces to the family names of the folks in the story, pictures that I did not have. He said he was excited to meet me because it was his family that was involved in the events that made up the Pleasant Valley Feud and in my amazement, he told me that he was the family historian.. I could have stayed and talked with him all day, but I knew he was there to sell guns and I needed to sell books.

I called Bill the following Monday and made arrangements to meet him at his home for a visit where we could talk about his family and his research and from there we could go for lunch. When I got to his home we had a great first visit. It was like I had known him all my life. After I gave him a set of my books, we went into his office and he showed me most of his research. He let me pick out the articles and pictures that I wanted and we went to Staples and he allowed me to copy them and gave me permission to use them in my book. Then we went to lunch.

When I saw the picture of all of the Tewksbury men that was taken at the roping contest, I almost fell over. That picture not only showed that Arizona Charlie and Tom Horn knew each other but also that the story the bartender told me at the Palace Bar about Horn and Meadows gambling with Doc Holliday in Prescott in 1886 was absolute truth.

The pictures and information Bill provided me with that day revealed a lot of pertinent information that would be necessary for me to complete my story. Bill mentioned that he felt another good source that no other author had used would be Will Croft Barnes. Barnes wrote a book on his experiences as an Apache County Deputy Sheriff and that he was involved in the Pleasant Valley War and as far as he knew no other historian had read his book. I found Barnes' book, *Apaches and Longhorns* on the Amazon website. In the book Will Croft Barnes described living in the Arizona Territory in the mid to late 1800's as an army scout and a cattle rancher, and most of all, his memories of being a deputy sheriff. I couldn't afford to buy this out of print book at the time, but I did find it at the U. S. Library of Congress in a PDF format, which I downloaded free. I read the book from cover to cover and I cannot for the life of me figure out how other historians or writers have not used this very credible person as a source for the Pleasant Valley Feud. For gosh sake not only was he a deputy sheriff but he was also a recipient of the Congressional Medal of Honor, while serving

In the army, while stationed in the southwest.

Then, about six months later, I ran into Ellwood Metcalf at a neighborhood Subway restaurant. He was sitting across from me at a table and I made a comment about the cool, "Pink Floyd" shirt he was wearing and we struck up a conversation, because I happened to be wearing a "Pink Floyd' shirt as well.

Ellwood Metcalf told me that he has lived here in Arizona all of his life. I told him that I was an author and I was working on a book about the feud in and around Young, Arizona. I went on to tell him that I had personally met and befriended Bill Brown, who was the great grandson of John Tewksbury and John Rhodes. He mentioned he had read about a man who was also involved in the Pleasant Valley War by the name of Frederick Russell Burnham. He said the guy was amazing man who was very heavily involved in the feud. I told him that I had come across Burnham in my research, but all I knew was that he was a scout for General Crook and that he was the co-founder of the Boys Scout's program.

Ellwood told me that Burnham was involved in the range war and that he actually had written a book about his life in Arizona and in Africa. He told me that the book was called *"Scouting on Two Continents,"* and I needed to read it for sure.

I have since read the book and Ellwood Metcalf was right, Frederick Russell Burnham was an amazing man, and he definitely was involved in the Pleasant Valley War. Not only involved but Burnham was the first person to come forward that was with the Graham faction. His take on the feud is priceless.

I would also like to thank the folks at Sharlot Hall Museum and Archives in Prescott, Arizona as well as Wendy Goen, our Arizona State Historian and her staff at the Arizona State Archives for their diligent work keeping our Arizona historical records safe for all Arizonans and also for their help and patience as I spent countless hours over the last five years researching this book. And last but not least, I would like to thank L. J. Horton and Osmer Flake for their valuable writing.

A special thanks to Bill Brown and Ellwood Metcalf for heading me in the right direction, along with Will Barnes and his book, *"Apaches and Longhorns,"* whereby the author found valuable information about this range war. It is impossible for any historian to know all the facts but was able, with the help of Bill Brown, the Tewksbury family historian, Frederick Russell Burnham and Will Barnes, all of whom are very credible sources, to present my findings and as always leave it up to the reader to make their own decision.

After completing my research, it was obvious that the Pleasant Valley War aka The Tonto Basin War was in fact not a range war at all but a bitter feud between the Graham family and the Tewksbury family, but sheep did play a small part.

This author wondered where the notions originated that the Pleasant Valley War was a sheep versus cattle range war, as well as hearing that it was caused by a love affair between members of the two factions.

The author read the novel written by Zane Grey, *"To the Last Man,"* that he supposedly called the Pleasant Valley War, a love story in the midst of a cattle versus sheep war, but in the forward of the book, Grey states very plainly that he was not able to ascertain much information from survivors of either the Tewksbury or the Graham families, or their friends so he could write a factual story; so he simply wrote a book that he called a Pleasant Valley love story between Tewksbury woman and a Graham cowboy, which again, let me emphasize, was a fictional story, along with working the story around a cattlemen and sheep men range war. Over time this fictional story seemed to take on a life of its own even though it was a fictional story.

In fact, this true story has nothing to do with a love story, but bringing sheep to a valley that was primarily used to raise cattle definitely had something to do with regard to fueling an already heated rivalry between the families. Since no person from either the Tewksbury's or the Graham's were willing to talk to anyone, because he was in most cases looking into the eyes of a man who was involved in the feud. Zane Grey simply made up a great story that went viral and over the years became real to those folks that lived in and around Tonto Basin.

With respect to Zane Grey, whom I admire and who is one of my mentor's, it wasn't until 20 years after his book was published that the walls of silence around the war finally started to crumble with the passing of Tom Graham in 1892 and Edwin Tewksbury in 1904, and people started to come forward with their stories and experiences. The following is a quote by William Colcord, a neutral pioneer resident of Tonto Basin at the time of this feud says it all:

> *"Working with large herds of cattle gave some men a fever no doctor could ever cure, a burning desire to have a big herd of their own. They put their brands on too many calves that stuck by the wrong cows. Had to kill a man because he knew too much; killed another man, just because he had a leaky mouth; and pretty soon it was living by the gun, one day at a time. A few of them made it out alive but they never realized their dream."*

The cover of the book of the abandoned home in the town of Young, Arizona, that was taken by Brian &

Christina Nicks, my daughter and son-in-law. The back cover photo of was also taken by Brian and Christina from Arizona State Route 188 on our way out of the valley.

The author would also like to thank Joe Schuler for his diligent art work in creating both the back and front covers, and a special thanks to Jeff Foreman for reading the finished manuscript and making any changes he deemed necessary, and of course, the author would like to thank Kathy Porter for her diligent work in proofreading the original manuscript.

I would also like to thank Bill Brown, the Tewksbury Family Historian for providing the author with many historical letters, pictures and of course his grandmother, Bertha Tewksbury and his great grandmother Mary Ann Tewksbury- Rhodes, along with Don and Marian Hensley for showing us around Young and Pleasant Valley and letting my daughter Christina, son in law Brian Nicks and the author us stay with them at their place during the annual Pleasant Valley Days, a celebration, that occurs every year, held by the living relatives of the Tewksbury and Graham families on the third weekend of July, including in the festivities is a parade and roping contest, along with several other events including a dance on Friday evenings to kick-off the celebration weekend including all of the museums are open only on that weekend.

In this book, the author has taken a different direction than in my other books, presenting different versions and stories I found representing different views of this tragic feud, along with biographies of men involved in both sides of Graham's and Tewksbury factions.

In each chapter, there will be some of the same information presented, but there will be a ton of new facts as well. In the end of the book, the author will summarize the research. Every piece of the pie is very important because history is like a jigsaw puzzle. The more we can discover the clearer the picture becomes. Sadly, none of us were there so we can only rely on our research to bring out the best story possible and this author will present a lot of new information. As always, this author leaves the final decision up to the reader.

Below is a map of Tonto Basin including Pleasant Valley that was found on the National Parks website. The town of Young is in the Middle of Pleasant Valley.

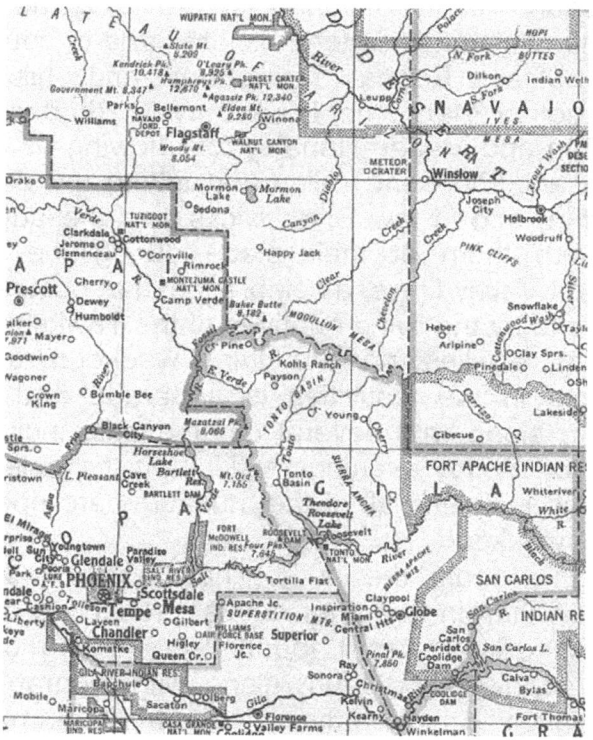

Chapter One
Northeast Arizona

In 1877 the first permanent settlers who arrived at Round Valley near the town of Payson, Arizona Territory were Mormon farmers and ranchers, and arrived in Arizona by wagon train. Their determined and courageous leaders were A.V. Greer and a man named Harris, who both traveled all the way from Texas, bringing with them wagons loaded with all the household goods needed to start a new life, including a herd of dairy cattle, hogs and chickens.

A year later the first Utah pioneers arrived, establishing the First Ward of the Latter Day Saints in the valley through which ran what they called The Little Colorado River. With the coming of the Mormons, that wild and unruly Little Colorado was tamed like a wild unbroken horse, slowly and painstakingly. Hardy, resourceful and persevering, other pioneers such as the Holden's, Eagar's, Crosby's, Wilbank's and Udall families built permanent homes, raised children, dug ditches and canals and built the dams necessary to irrigate their farms, gardens and orchards.

The peaceful village of Eagar, Arizona and the surrounding area, was named after the three Mormon Eagar brothers, who settled there in 1878, and was a quiet unassuming area. But the neighboring town of Springerville, Arizona some eighty miles away, became one of the wildest and most lawless towns in the Old West. The town was named after Harry Springer, an Albuquerque, New Mexico merchant who had a branch store there in the early days. Springerville was, for a time, a favorite hangout for cattle rustlers, horse thieves and fugitives on the lamb from all over the Southwest, until they moved onto nearby Show Low, Arizona, named for the poker game of the same name.

After the widely publicized Gunfight at the OK Corral in Tombstone on October 26, 1881, what was left of the notorious Clanton gang moved to Apache County, where lawmen were only conspicuous by their lack of presence in the area at that time. The surviving members of the Clanton family, Phin, Ike and Leonard, claimed a homestead on Coyote Creek east of Springerville, Arizona. They continued the pursuits, which their previous experience had prepared them, of trading horses and cattle of questionable ownership.

In addition to the Clanton brothers men of similar temperament, avocation and reputation moved into the area. The Smith gang moved east to the Mormon settlements from the town of Canyon Diablo in 1882 after the bridge construction was completed. They were one of the most ruthless gangs in all of the Southwest.

By early 1883, some of the toughest outlaws ever seen in the west who made up the population of Canyon Diablo,. drifted east to the Springerville area as well as south to Payson and Pleasant Valley, an area south of the Mogollon Rim, as it was the last of the Wild West frontiers. This was after the completion of the train bridge over Canyon Diablo by the Atlantic & Pacific railroad, and the subsequent hiring of a real town marshal. After robbing banks and stagecoaches in Arizona's booming mining towns around Tombstone, Globe and Superior, outlaw gangs would ride all day and night to their hideouts in and around the Springerville and White Mountains area.

The men of the Snyder-Cavanaugh Gang started a gun battle amongst themselves one afternoon. They were under the influence of too many alcoholic beverages. They got into a heated argument while dividing up the loot they had stolen the day before from an Atlantic & Pacific passenger train near Winslow in the Northeastern part of Arizona Territory.

Before the day was over, nine of them lay dead, conveniently on the hill behind the town of Eagar, Arizona's town cemetery. Making it easy to bury them and mark their graves.

The Westbrook brothers, who arrived from Colorado, were unscrupulous land jumpers and outlaws. They had murdered a Springerville, citizen by the name of James Hale in the town streets in 1885. When questioned about the dirty deed, they stated that they simply, wanted to see if a bullet would go through a Mormon.

Billy the Kid, and members of his gang called, "The Regulators," originally from New Mexico, also rode into the Springerville area from Canyon Diablo looking for a new place to hide, gamble, drink and of course carry on with prostitutes. For a time, outlaws had virtual control of the whole area. A.F. Barnes, no relation to Will Barnes, a Springerville was quoted,

> "I am no angel and have seen most of the tough towns in the west, but Springerville was the worst of them all."

In the Newspaper from St Johns, Arizona, on April 14, 1886, was published the following article:

> "Ike Clanton shot a Mexican and an unknown person burned Johnson's Hotel and Saloon. And Pete Slaughter discharged all of his bad men at once as soon as he arrived home from a trip to Texas, and that there has been in that town such an unusual reign of peace in that town that the people are growing fidgety and unsettled."

The Tenth Arizona Territorial Legislature created Apache County in 1879. The county started at the Utah Border on the north and follows along the Arizona/:New Mexico border and continued south to the Gila river. It is a narrow and long county about fifty miles wide at the largest point. Apache County encompasses 20,940 rugged square miles of high desert. Law enforcement at the time it became a county was in the hands of incompetent deputies and/or self-appointed vigilante gangs. The county government was in debt, corrupt and inefficient. Oddly enough, the first indictments served in the new county were not against murderers or thieves, but against the Graham and Tewksbury families, rival cattle ranching families, whose blood feud continued until the last man was dead, and became known as the Pleasant Valley War or the Tonto Basin War.

Law-abiding citizens, particularly the Mormon settlers, who had been prevented from holding public office by some of the corrupt county officials, elected Commodore Perry Owens as their new sheriff. The following article was published in a newspaper from St. Johns, Arizona a year after his election:

> *"The lawless element ran amok in Apache County, a reign of terror in the whole county. After Commodore Perry Owens was elected the new sheriff, Springerville was cleaned up almost immediately. The outlaws disappeared it seemed like overnight; having respect for Owens famed ability with a six-shooter."*

Commodore Perry Owens was born July 29, 1852 and died of natural causes on May 19, 1919. His father's name was Oliver H. Perry Owens. In honoring the memory of his father, his mother named their first son after him. Perry was born in Hawkins County, Tennessee, but raised on a farm in Liberty Township, Hendricks County, Indiana. He ran away from home at age thirteen to work on ranches in Oklahoma and New Mexico. Like all young men of his time Owens had no use for farming and wanted to be a cowboy. By his twenty first birthday Owens was a working cowboy on Hillard Roger's ranch outside Bartles, Oklahoma. In an interview given later in life, Owens admitted running with *"a gang of tough characters"* in his youth and was possibly involved in rustling, whiskey running and other depredations in the Indian Territory.

By 1881, Owens was working as a ranch foreman for James D. Houck and A. E. Hennings in the Arizona Territory. The story at the time was that Owens and another man with him were attacked by several Navajo braves, who were attempting to steal the horses Owens was guarding. He was said to have killed two warriors, earning him the nickname *"Iron Man"* for standing and fighting the savages. In truth, in September 1883, Owens was arrested by Indian Agent Dennis Matthew Riordan, for the murder of a young Navajo boy near James Houck's ranch in Navajo Springs, who he shot while the youth was trying to steal horses.

Owens was, subsequently, acquitted of the murder by the Apache County authorities. Owens had long red hair and had adopted the look of a typical cowboy as is perfectly clear in the famous photo which was taken in New Mexico during this time period. He wore his hair long in his youth, often curling it up underneath his hat, and he was popular with the ladies, who often made fun of his unusual name. Also, around this same time, he homesteaded a ranch outside Navajo Springs, Arizona building a small dugout cabin, a well, and stables for his livestock. Owens is said to have named his place the *"Z-Bar Ranch,"* this brand was t officially registered with the Apache County Recorder's Office.

Commodore Perry Owens accepted the nomination to run for the office of Sheriff of Apache County by the People's Party and enjoyed the support of the Apache County Stock Growers Association. In November 1886, Owens won the election and took office immediately. Though he had been elected by a margin of only 91 votes over Democratic candidate Tomas Perez, Owens was well liked within his jurisdiction, and often described as having a calm demeanor. Upon taking office in January 1887, Owens was entrusted with 14 bench warrants that had been left un-served by his predecessor, Jon "Don" Lorenzo Hubbell.

**Commodore Perry Owens
Photo found in our National Archives**

Included among the warrants were Mormon gunman Lot Smith, former Tombstone cattle rustler Ike Clanton, and another cattle rustler and horse thief by the name of Andy Cooper, an alias for Cooper Blevins, whom Owens once worked with on a cattle drive and knew very well. Owens knew that Cooper Blevins was a killer on the run from Texas. His first year in office was relatively normal, with nothing of consequence short of a few arrests of drunken cowboys and cattle rustlers in and around nearby Holbrook, Arizona, with only three reported shooting incidents in which he shot two men. Then on September 4, 1887 while in Holbrook, Owens tried to arrest Andy Cooper on the warrant he had been carrying for horse thievery. Cooper reported around town that he would not be taken alive and the ensuing gun battle between Sheriff Owens that took the life of Cooper along with two of his brothers and another cattle rustler that was with them at the time, brought national fame to Owens.

The Arizona Territory was a wild and crazy place at that time. The Atlantic and Pacific Railroad was extending its northern route across from St. Johns to Winslow and from there it was planned to go to Flagstaff, Williams, Ashfork and on to the Arizona border with California at Kingman.

The railroad ran into difficulties constructing the bridge over Canyon Diablo which lay thirty miles west of Winslow and almost thirty miles east of Flagstaff. It was an ambitious undertaking to be sure. The canyon is two hundred thirty feet deep and three hundred feet across. It is very steep and presented a major project for the railroad engineers. In fact, after completing the engineering process, which took about two years, it took another two years of construction to build the bridge it ended up ten feet short. It was engineering process that missed its target causing the railroad to delay the completion by another year while they appropriated the funds to complete the project.

The railroad created a construction town which was named after the canyon. It had one street that was a mile long. Lined on both sides were saloons, dance pavilions, bordellos and three restaurants, with the railroad workers living in tents. There was no law and order. Gambling, drinking, dancing, wild women as well as a lot of shooting and death were commonplace. So much so that the nearest hospital, located in nearby Winslow and operated by the railroad, stopped taking in gunshot patients within the year. There were more people killed in Canyon Diablo from 1878 to the completion of the bridge in 1882 than in Dodge City, Abilene, Kansas and

Tombstone combined.

The businessmen in Flagstaff finally decided it was bad for business to have such lawlessness, so they decided to hire a marshal. The first town marshal was hired at three o'clock one afternoon and was buried in the Canyon Diablo cemetery at nine o'clock that same night. The next marshal lasted thirty days and in his first week he killed twenty-two men trying to arrest them. He was fatally shot the first week of his second month on the job on a Sunday morning as he stepped into the street after eating his breakfast.

Canyon Diablo was a haven for some of the worst outlaws in the Southwest. Murderers, robbers and rustlers came from Texas to the Arizona and New Mexico Territories after Texas instituted the Texas Rangers. Before the Rangers the bad guys would simply leave one county where they were working their dirty deeds to hide out in an adjoining county. The local county Sheriff's only had jurisdiction in their counties, so they could only track them to the county lines. The Texas Rangers jurisdiction ended at the Texas state line. Consequently they made life miserable for the rustlers, train and bank robbers as well as killers, driving them further west into the Arizona and New Mexico Territories, where the only thing about law and order in these two Wild West territories was the absence of lawmen.

Chapter Two
Pleasant Valley Settlers

The first settlers in Pleasant Valley were stockmen, raising cattle, horses and other farm animals. Pleasant Valley as the crow flies is fifty miles east of Payson and twenty miles below the Mogollon Rim and sixty miles north of Globe. The valley can be reached by heading out east on State Route 260, once on top of the rim approaching Woods Canyon Lake, exit to the left, there is a dirt road sign, State Route 288, also named the Young Road, and is on the right side of highway 260 indicating the traveler must turn right from the main road in order to reach Pleasant Valley and the settlement of Young, Arizona.

From State route 260, Young is a drive of about twenty-two miles, of which the first twelve miles is a well maintained dirt road, easily driven by a car with the last eight miles of SR288 being paved into the business center of Young. The road is well maintained year round. There are a lot of ranch homes and barns on both sides of the road before one reaches the settlement of Young, which is in the middle of Pleasant Valley and has a couple of restaurants, a convenience store that also sells gasoline, museums, one saloon, and a couple of hotels and lodges. State Route 288 follows the original trail the settlers used to travel from Pleasant Valley to Payson and on the south side of the Valley, SR288 continues on the original trail to Globe, located about sixty miles from Young.

The Tewksbury's along with James Stinson, who was the largest cattle rancher in the valley with a herd of over twelve hundred head that grazed on his one hundred and sixty-acre parcel of land, along with five thousand acres of National Forest land that lay adjacent to his property. Stinson held a promissory grazing rights note from the government that gave him permission, even though he did not own the property, to fence in the whole five thousand acres of National Forest Land adjacent to his ranch.

Of course the other ranchers in the valley also held promissory grazing rights to another twenty-five thousand acres of National Forest Preserves but their rights did not allow them to fence it that land, as it was all considered free grazing land on that part of forest.

The first settler in Pleasant Valley was Al Rose, followed shortly by the other original settlers, James Stinson, William Middleton, James Roberts, J.D, Edwin and James Tewksbury, Tom and John Graham, W.H. Bishop, George Blaine, William Richards, the Houdon family, all four brothers, Mart Blevins and his five sons, including Cooper Blevins, aka Andy Cooper., Cooper changed his name due to the fact that he was on the run from the law in Texas where he was wanted for the charges of murder.

Each man was allowed a homestead of a 160 acre parcel of land by the U.S. Government. The land in Pleasant Valley was fertile, with many springs and creeks. It was a perfect place to raise stock. The meadows were full of bear grass, a wild grass that can grow up to two feet in height. This was prime land to raise cattle and horses, with every one hundred sixty acre parcel surrounded by U.S. National Forest Service land that again was available for every settler to use under the government free grazing laws.

Of course Pleasant Valley was also a great place for outlaws, gun fighters and gamblers that arrived from the nearby railroad town of Canyon Diablo once the construction of the bridge was completed in early 1883. The Atlantic & Pacific Railroad sold over a million acres of property on both sides of the tracks that ran all the way through the Arizona Territory to the Aztec Land & Cattle Company out of New York, whose office was located in Holbrook, Arizona.

Within six months of purchasing the land, Aztec brought in over half a million cattle to graze on its land, providing the rustlers plenty of cattle and horses to steal. Aztec was the holding company for the Hashknife Ranch, which had ranch houses spread across Northern Arizona in an ineffectual attempt to minimize the widespread rustling problem. Sadly, it was some of their own employees who were rustling from Aztec.

These slime ball outlaws had a sweet deal going. During the day they were working as Hashknife Cowboys, watching and rounding up cattle and horses, branding new calves. They had a place to lay their heads along with breakfast and dinner each night. Then after dinner they would rustle the cattle they were being paid to watch, drive them down the trail to Pleasant Valley and then on through the valley to the rugged Sierra Ancha Mountains which bordered the south portion of Pleasant Valley. They then would hide the stolen stock in the deep canyons, giving them time to rebrand the stock and allow the hair to grow over the old brand and allow the cattle to fatten up before going to market, leaving one or two men to guard the stolen stock and do whatever was needed to keep people away from the area.

It took about two weeks for the hair on the cattle and horses to grow out, hiding the old brand, the cattle were then sold to waiting buyers from New Mexico and well known cattle rustlers from Sulphur Springs Valley near Tombstone and who in turn sold the rustled, re-branded cattle to the Mexican Army making a tidy profit in each transaction.

So with the rustlers and their schemes, the abundance of so many gunmen and outlaws and, of course, the greed of the Graham's and James Stinson, the stage was set for trouble with a capital T.

In the earlier days, the Tewksbury and Graham families were friends and close neighbors. Tom

Graham's ranch house was within two miles of Edwin Tewksbury's ranch house, located on Cherry Creek. One of the Graham ranches was on nearby Marsh Creek and the other Graham ranch was on Spring Creek, both creeks running maybe three miles west of Cherry Creek. The three Tewksbury ranches were only two to three miles from each other's ranch houses. Scattered near these five ranches in Pleasant Valley were the ranches of Al and Ed Rose, William Middleton, W.H. Bishop, Jim Roberts and George Blaine. These ranches are all within a few miles in either direction along Cherry Creek. The Blevins' ranch being the farthest away as they settled on Canyon Creek, located about fifteen miles northeast of the Rose ranches.

There were running creeks and springs all over Pleasant Valley and the ground was fertile allowing every rancher to also plant several acres of vegetables. The Middleton's specialized in milk cows and their butter went for a dollar a pound which was an amazingly high price for the time. Word got about that the Middleton's milk and butter were worth every penny and folks came from all over the valley just to buy his fresh milk and amazing butter.

An Introduction to the Tewksbury Family:

James Dunning Tewksbury aka J.D., the father of John, Edwin and James was born in Boston. In 1849 he worked aboard a schooner that was on its way to San Francisco traveling down the east coast Atlantic Ocean to the tip of South America, then up the west coast of South and North America before anchoring in San Francisco.

After wandering around the California coast, the elder Tewksbury made his way to the gold fields around Sacramento to try his hand at mining for gold, on the Sacramento and American Rivers, hoping to strike gold and get rich. He worked placer mines along the rivers, but by the time he arrived in the gold fields the gold rush was already at an end having only lasted from 1849 to the end of 1851.

After wandering around the gold fields from 1851 to 1853 without much success J.D. settled down near the gold fields of Humbolt County in Northern California. Another reason he settled there may have been due to the fact that he met and fell in love with a beautiful Eel River Indian maiden from a nearby tribe. White women were very scarce in the West in those days. They were married and she gave birth to four boys, John, Edwin, James, Frank, and a daughter Elvira before she passed away. The exact dates are unknown to the author, but we know it was sometime before J. D. and his four grown sons & one daughter when they showed up in Globe, Arizona in 1879.

It was in Globe that J.D. met and married Lydia Crigger Shultes, his second wife, who had been married twice before marrying J.D. She also brought with her two sons, Walter and Parker, into the marriage. Both of who were just young children and along with Elvira and their younger half brother Frank, who had no part in the feud that was to come. From Globe in January of 1880, J.D. took his family and moved them to Pleasant Valley, located about sixty miles north of Globe, Arizona, when the U.S. Government opened Pleasant Valley and the surrounding Tonto Basin to homesteaders, allowing each family to settle on 160 acres of prime land. J.D. Tewksbury hoped to provide a good home to raise his family and land for each one of his boys so they could also start their own farms and ranches.

John Tewksbury, Jr, J.D.'s oldest son, was the only one of his son's killed in the feud to come. He married Mary Crigger, his stepmother's oldest daughter by her first marriage, and they moved to the first ranch near J.D. where they homesteaded their 160-acre ranch land. His sons James and Edwin teamed up and settled their own 160-acre parcel and worked one ranch thinking that the two of them could grow one ranch faster than each one owning their own ranch, planning to raise a herd of beef cattle.

An introduction to the Graham family:

Samuel Graham was born in Northern Ireland in 1818. Like most immigrants of the time, Samuel wanted to have his own land as it was impossible to own land in Ireland. So he, his wife Jane, along with their oldest son Allen, daughter Margaret, and another daughter Mary, immigrated to America and settled in the town of Boonsboro, Boone County, Iowa in 1841. John and Tom Graham were born in America at the family home in Boonsboro. A younger brother William (Billy) was born in California.

Like most young men in the late 1800's, Tom and John Graham longed for the adventure of the wild west, so they left the family farm in Iowa and headed to California to strike it rich in the gold fields in 1849. Of course, by 1851 the gold strike on the American River near Sacramento was all but over. The Graham's kicked around California working as ranch hands until they heard about a silver strike in Globe, Arizona. Tom and John, thinking where there is silver there must surely be gold, pulled up stakes and arrived in Globe in the summer of 1882. Sadly, for the Graham brothers, they were to learn the two ore's discovered in the mines around Globe were Silver and Copper, so they had to come up with a plan B.

The word around Globe was that there was still land in the Tonto Basin that could be homesteaded under the government Homestead Act. Pleasant Valley was only sixty miles north of Globe, so Tom and John decided to go to there and settled on a plot of land about ten miles up Cherry Creek from J.D. Tewksbury's ranch. They built a log cabin ranch house and corrals on their own 160-acre ranch. They spent the little amount of money they had left after building their ranch to buy a small herd of cattle. At that point, out of money, they went to work for James Stinson, the largest cattle rancher in Pleasant Valley.

Tom and John Graham met Ed and Jim Tewksbury in a saloon in Globe, where they discussed their dreams of raising cattle in Pleasant Valley. They later were reacquainted when they worked as cowboys together for James Stinson driving a large herd of cattle Stinson purchased from Midwest ranchers and arrived at railhead in Holbrook, from where the Grahams and the Tewksbury's drove the herd seventy miles southwest to Pleasant Valley where the Stinson Ranch was located. Over the week long cattle drive the Tewksbury's and Grahams became friends.

Whether it was the Tewksbury brothers or the Graham's idea while on that drive, one thing was obvious: James Stinson was going to need help managing the largest herd in cattle in Pleasant Valley, a herd that numbered 1200 head of white faced cattle. So he went into an agreement with both the Graham's and Tewksbury's to be paid shares after the cattle were sent to market in the form of cattle, that would help them build their own herds. Somewhere during the trip the Grahams decided to approach Stinson with the idea that they would take over running the herd exclusively and so they entered into a contract with Stinson with him to cut all the other cowboys in the valley out of working for Stinson. That would allow Stinson not to have to pay them wages, but instead they agreed and recorded a contract that was best for both the Graham's and Stinson. The official recorded contract between the Graham's and James Stinson gave the Graham's fifty cattle-25 head of cows and 25 calves in lieu of wages for working Stinson's ranch

In The Beginning:

The bad blood between the Tewksbury's and the Graham's is thought by most historians to have begun at that point. The Graham-Tewksbury range war, the only frontier feud of major proportions to occur in Arizona, came to a bloody climax in 1887 in the wild mountain country south of the Mogollon Rim, north and east of the town of Payson. The principals were the half-Indian half Irish Tewksbury brothers and the Iowa-born Graham brothers who were friendly to each other at first, but later became bitter enemies.

The trouble began in early 1883 over misbranding of livestock, but major conflict was avoided for several years. By 1887, however, organized stealing had gone so far in the Pleasant Valley that bloodshed was inevitable. The causes of the trouble and the first outbreaks of violence are discussed below by Clara T. Woody, who lived in Pleasant Valley at the time and whose family had close ties to the families involved in this terrible blemish of Arizona History.

Below is a statement taken by Clara T. Woody, by Pleasant Valley neighbor Bob Voris, whose father was a participant in the feud and was on the Tewksbury family's side as well as statements made by Osmer Flake, LDS historian and business man who dealt with both the Grahams and the Tewksburys from his general store in Heber, Arizona, located that was halfway from Pleasant Valley to Holbrook. Osmer Flake was also a deputy Apache County Sheriff under Sheriff Owens:

> "The Pleasant Valley men traveled in two bunches, says Osmer D. Flake, and did not get in each other's way at all. After reaching the Valley, there was an *understanding*, that the ranges east of the main trail were the Graham's ranges and the ranges west of the divide

belonged to the Tewksbury's. They went heavily armed when they grazed cattle on each other's land for about 18 months before fighting actually started."

The shooting might have been postponed had it not been for the arrival of the Blevins clan to Pleasant Valley.

The Blevins Family:

Early in 1884, Mart 'Old Man' Blevins moved to Pleasant Valley from his Round Mountain ranch on the Guadalupe River near Llano, Texas, with his wife four of his five sons John, Charles, Hampton and Sam Houston, the last barely in his teens along with two daughters and a son-in-law, Mose Roberts. Cooper Blevins, aka; Andy Cooper, the fifth son joined his family later. They purchased a ranch that was owned by a Mormon settler along the upper reaches of Canyon Creek adjoining the flourishing Graham spread and the two families shared some of the same grazing land.

Below is a picture of Canyon Creek that was taken by the author. The Blevins Ranch can be seen in the background

The bad blood between the Grahams and the Tewksbury's made it impossible for any new family that moved into Pleasant Valley to remain neutral.

The Blevins family was Graham supporters because according to Mrs. Blevins, it was too dangerous not to be. Mrs. John Blevins commented on this in a letter to a family member who still lived in Texas:

> "Those who would have been peaceful and would have left the Tewksbury's and the Grahams' to argue out their bloody destinies, were dragged in perforce either by the repeated onslaughts of both sides on their belonging or by suspicion by one faction or another which finally resulted in gun-play and murder. The Blevins family was one of those latter. They didn't actively seek bloodshed."

This may have been true of Old Man Blevins and the four sons who arrived with him and first settled on a ranch, but the fifth son Andy was something else. Andy Cooper, as he called himself, was "wanted" in Oklahoma for selling whiskey to the Indians and in Texas for cattle rustling, horse thievery and murder. One story alleges that he was arrested by Texas officers, was tried and convicted of a serious crime but managed a sensational escape from three Texas Rangers on a train transporting him to prison. Cooper was the name he used in Texas and he kept it when he reached his families new home on Canyon Creek.

Factions Form:

The Graham party received substantial infusions of new blood with the addition of Al Rose, an original valley settler, who had helped Tom choose the site for his ranch. The rest of the Graham men were an assortment of men with questionable backgrounds. They were cowboys who migrated east from working for Aztec Land and Cattle Company, along with prospective ranchers, of whom many openly aligned themselves with the Grahams. Before long they constituted an identifiable Graham *"faction."* They were further reinforced by the arrival of some of Andy Cooper and Hank "Buscadero" Blevans, no relation to the Blevins family along with their friends of questionable character, who had previously worked as cowboys for the Hashknife cattle ranch. The Hashknife was named for the shape of its brand, and was owned by the New York cattle corporation Aztec Land & Cattle Company.

This enormous enterprise came into being in 1883 when a group of Eastern entrepreneurs bought some of the Atlantic & Pacific Railroad's ninety square miles of range land consisting of alternate sections on either side of the railroad tracks. In order to make room for cattle which had previously grazed in New Mexico and Texas, the company went on to make one of the most extensive purchases of land ever made in the United States consisting of a total of 1,125.999 acres.

Aztec was allowed a free choice of sections. As a result, the corporation acquired nearly all the watered sections of grazing land in northeastern Arizona within forty miles of the railroad grant, mostly south of the tracks. The price paid was fifty cents per acre. The western headquarters was located on the Little Colorado River near the Mormon settlement of St Joseph, west of Holbrook. Hashknife cattle, estimated at 60,000 head, grazed on the rich pasture lands above the Mogollon Rim at times ranging far south into Tonto Basin.

Thus there was contact between the Hashknife cowboys and the Pleasant Valley ranchers, and although the huge cattle company took no official part in the feud, some of its hot-headed and irresponsible employees aligned themselves with the Graham faction. Osmer D. Flake recalls them:

> "As wild and lawless a bunch as ever rode for one brand. Always looking for trouble, they simply could not keep out of a good fight."

Odie Faulk, the general manager that worked for Aztec and oversaw the Hashknife outfit for the eastern owned cattle company "was plagued by absentee ownership and rustling." Osmer D. Flake, a local historian went on to say;

> "The Hashknife Cattle Company had some real fine men in their employment; they also had some of the worst men that ever left Texas. Including one of their foreman, John Paine. He feared nothing that walked and loved to fight. He was pretty bad, drank excessively and was always ready to make a six-shooter play."

One of the local ranchers, the Mormon Church historian, Joseph Fish, called John Paine, *"a desperate character"* and adds that his assignment as an Aztec employee was to drive the sheep men off the company holdings.

Osmer D. Flake goes on to report;

> "Paine drove off several herds of sheep and whipped the herders. Not being satisfied with driving off the sheep men, he undertook to drive off the ranchers and everyone else. He whipped several persons who he found upon the range for no other offense than that they were riding on the range looking for their own stock and attending to their own business. Paine's camp soon became the headquarters for horse thieves in the vicinity. Being in

> *sympathy with them, opposed to sheep men, and anxious for a fight, he aligned himself with his friends, the cattle and horse thieves."*

John Paine was one of those Hashknife cowboys who fought on the Graham side. Others, according to Osmer Fish, were Tom Pickett (who had been one of Billy the Kid's men in the Lincoln County War), Buck and George Lancaster, George Smith, Tom Tucker (later involved in the Lee-Fountain troubles in New Mexico), and Robert M. Gillespie;

> *"All of these gunfighters drifted to Northeastern portion Arizona Territory, after the bridge over Canyon Diablo was completed in 1882. Most of them had criminal records in other sections of the country."*

But none of them were as outrageously vicious as Paine. Apache County Deputy Sheriff Will Barnes, who we will discuss in more detail later in this book, remembers Tucker and Gillespie;

> *"Tucker was a big, good-natured chap, and was never looking for trouble of any kind. Gillespie was more stupid than wicked, a Texan of low mentality. He was not a man to be a leader but who was simple minded follower."*

Most of these newcomers were dangerous and unscrupulous as Will Barnes went on to say;

> *"Almost immediately, strange, tough characters began coming into Pleasant Valley who were friends of Andy Cooper. Many of them were Hashknife cowboys, who spent much of their time with Andy Cooper and Hank "Budcadero*

Outlaw," Blevans, who was no relation of the Blevins family, and for unknown reasons became friendly with the Grahams."

In retrospect the "unknown reason" becomes perfectly clear as the reader will see as they continue reading this book. They were all part of an extensive rustling operation with their headquarters in Tonto Basin and operating through and beyond the Arizona Territory.

L.J. Horton, who settled near the town of Payson, Arizona in 1883, and ran a freight business for a living, lost all of his livestock to rustlers over the next three years, and wrote;

> "They were a thoroughly organized band of criminals who, by hook or by crook, planned to take possession of the whole valley including everyone's livestock and land. They used any and all tactics to get the job done including blood curdling acts."

There is plenty of evidence to show that the cattle rustling business was successful and lucrative. Arizona was booming in the 1880's. The Atlantic & Pacific railroad had opened the way to the Eastern cattle markets and packing plants. Cattle ranches exploded in the west. In the Pleasant Valley area, L.J. Horton went on to say;

> "Cattlemen established their ranches from the mouth of Tonto Creek to the Mormon settlement of Gisela. The beautiful basin of the Salt River, above the junction with Tonto Creek, was fully occupied by pioneers."

Obviously the rustlers had plenty of ranches to prey on. Deputy Apache County Sheriff, Will C.

Barnes, who lived there, goes on to tell us how they did their dirty work;

> "For nearly two years an organized band of horse thieves operated in Apache County. The Mormon people, who did considerable heavy freighting between Holbrook, Arizona, Santa Fe, New Mexico and Fort Apache, all had unusually fine horse teams. From them the thieves took a heavy toll. The freighters, as a rule, hobbled their teams out along the road at night, and so many horses were carried off that most of the men used hobbles, which could be locked on the legs of animals. But even those supposedly protected horses turned up missing. The thieves would break the padlocks with a hammer and leave the hobbles on the ground, signifying a challenge to the owners.

Barnes went on to say;

> "The gang that did the work was fairly well known. It operated between Colorado points on the north and Southern Arizona on the south. The Colorado horses would be carried across the Navajo Indian Reservation into Arizona. Over in Tonto Basin, about seventy-five miles south of Holbrook, in one of the roughest, most inaccessible spots imaginable, they had a rendezvous on Canyon Creek, where horses from Southern Arizona and Mexico were brought and exchanged for others from the north. Here in this spot brands were worked over, manes docked, tails thinned out, and all sorts of

schemes used to cover up their tracks. Several men who had gone into Canyon Creek trailing stolen horses were shot on site, or beaten with ropes, set a foot, and warned never to show their faces again in the basin. Two or three failed to return from such trips."

G.W. Shute who lived in the valley corroborates Barnes' story;

"It was not long, until ranchers from the Salt River Valley in Maricopa County began to complain of losing horses and in every instance the trail led toward Pleasant Valley. The same complaints arose in Southern Utah and Colorado. The pursuers from the south always gave up when they reached the Mogollon Rim."

Shute also went on to say;

"It became common talk that Pleasant Valley was being used as a rendezvous for a bunch of organized horse thieves who would steal in Maricopa County and points south and run their take through Pleasant Valley to a market in Northern Arizona, Southern Utah and Southern Colorado. Upon delivery of their stolen stock the operation was reversed. The Tewksbury family owners of the finest herd of horses in the valley did not escape these depredations. From time to time they would miss animals and always the evidence pointed to Andy Cooper, his friends, and association to the Grahams."

The result was *"accusations and recriminations"* and threats on the part of the Grahams to run the Tewksbury's out of Pleasant Valley. Both sides *"armed themselves with Winchesters and side arms and began to ride in groups."* The Graham boys called the dark-skinned Tewksbury's *"Injuns"* and *"blacks"* says Bob Voris who lived in Pleasant Valley from 1880 to 1895, and threatened to *"run the damn blacks out of the country."*

Sooner or later, of course, the thieves were sure to run up against a man who was as tough and determined as they were; he appeared in the person of Jim Roberts, a young settler who had started a ranch under the Rim and was beginning to build up a horse herd with the assistance of a fine blooded stallion. G.W. Shute, a lifelong friend of Jim Roberts repeats the story that Roberts told him years later;

> *"Jim had owned a great work team of horses. One night they disappeared from the pasture in which he had them confined. The following day Roberts, mounted on his fine horse, picked up the tracks of his team and followed them straight to a bunch of Graham supporters but no team was to be found. He inquired about his missing horses and all he could get was a flippant answer that only served to confirm his suspicion that he was actually talking to the thieves. As Roberts turned to go, he heard one of the gang say to his companions, 'That's a damn fine horse he is riding and when he stops tonight we'll get him too.' Well, they didn't get the horse but they made an enemy of a brave determined man who proved to be the coolest, deadliest fighter of them all"*

The thieves were not even above stealing from children. The Colcord boys, Harvey and Bill, were out riding one night and found themselves relieved of their mounts by members of the Graham faction. G.W. Shute sums it up as follows;

> "Strangers entering the Pleasant Valley disappeared without a trace. Horse thieves infested the whole country. A cattleman or farmer, when he turned his horse upon the range to graze, never knew whether or not he would see them again. It must appear by this time that the 'Graham side' had been tabbed far and wide as 'horse thieves.' Therefore, every man's hand was against them. As soon as it became known that a man was on the Graham side, that fact alone dubbed such a man as a horse thief. Therefore, this account's of discrimination there was against the Grahams and not the Tewksbury's, because the finger of justice was always leveled against the horse thieves in those days."

Bob Voris did not want his views or statements made public while some of the Grahams were still alive but finally twenty-five years after the war ended he goes along with G.W. Shute;

> "At the time of the war, the Grahams organized a ring of cattle thieves and what was known as the 'trading ground' was Pleasant Valley. Stolen cattle were driven in at night and then driven out of there the next night. They stole horses and they stole cattle. They would bring cattle in there and they would burn the brands and they would leave them in

> there till they healed up, grew hair back on the burned areas, then they would take them out of Pleasant Valley in the night and they would take them so far and another bunch would take them over and the ones that started out first would be back in Pleasant Valley before sun-up, before it got daylight so they couldn't say they had left the valley."

Jesse Ellison, one of Pleasant Valley's wealthiest and original ranchers, agreed;

> "You could not put a horse in a barn and expect to get him in the morning. You might get him and you might not. They would come and steal them in the night. You might have a herd of cattle today and tomorrow you wouldn't have a sole cow. All that country over in that neck of the woods was mostly a Graham holdout."

Below is a photo of one of the steep canyons in the Sierra Ancha Mountains the Graham's used to hide stock while the brands grew out so they could re-brand the stolen stock. This photo was taken by the author.

Another of the Graham hideouts for livestock in transit was Diamond Butte, a part of the Sierra Ancha Mountains on the way south out of the valley. Its sides were so steep that a horse could not climb them. There was only one trail to the top, so narrow that it could be closed and concealed behind a pile of brush. Here, it is said, stolen horses were rested and grazed while their new brands healed. In two to three weeks the horses were moved out and taken to New Mexico, Southern Arizona or Old Mexico to be sold.

Chapter Three
Introduction of Sheep

By February 1887 the two factions, who had already been ambushing each other, turned to real violence. It was a result of a whole band of sheep slaughtered and the sheep herder being murdered.

The Daggs brothers, with their sheep ranches based in and around Flagstaff, Arizona, owned the largest sheep outfit in northern Arizona. They were finding the Aztec Land & Cattle Company too much for them to deal with. When the Hashknife outfit purchased every other section north and south of the railroad in 1885, it added vast acreage that they owned as well as free grazing rights on the sections they did not own. Life became impossible for the sheep owners who had long grazed their herds on the open pastures north of the Rim. All the water was claimed by the cattle outfit and lawsuits failed to shake their hold.

The Daggs brothers were forced to seek new grazing lands for their sheep. They tried to find room in other areas north of the tracks and again ran into Hashknife opposition. When the sheep men failed to heed the warnings, violence followed. A valuable border collie dog belonging to one sheep herder was killed. Cowboys frequently shot holes through coffee pots and frying pans when the 'intruders' were cooking their meals. John Paine was employed by the Hashknife outfit to see that no sheep watered or grazed on cattle company ranges, and John Paine loved his job. Mormon historian Joseph Fish comments:

> *"The Hashknife outfit hired John Paine because he was a desperate character, for the purpose of keeping all sheep off the range that they claimed,*

which was a strip about forty miles wide and eighty miles long. They had bought every alternate section from the railroad company, and on this ground they claimed it all. From this immense tract it was attempted to drive all the sheep men. Paine drove off herds and whipped herders."

The sheep owners did not give up, but after 1886 they found the Mogollon Rim a difficult and even dangerous place to carry on their business. The range was over stocked with both cattle and sheep. The Hashknife cowboys forced the sheep men into the most barren locations, where the heavy snowfall of the cold winters made it impractical to winter their flocks. Forced to find new winter ranges at a lower altitude, the land they chose was south of the Mogollon Rim in Pleasant Valley, where it had vastly warmer winters. It did snow from time to time in Pleasant Valley. But compared to the long snowy winters of the land on top of the rim, on average 7200 feet in elevation compared to Pleasant Valley with an average elevation of 5000 feet, it was more advantageous in the winter months as well as the rest of the year.

The Daggs brothers needed help to transport sheep and for protection against the cattle ranchers on the way to and while they grazed in Pleasant Valley. So they went into business with the Tewksbury's. A partnership was created based on shares when the sheep were ready to be sheared as well as the sheep that were slaughtered for meat that would be purchased by the U.S. Army.

It was a great partnership on both sides. The Tewksbury's like most of the other Pleasant Valley settlers were tired of rustlers stealing their cattle that grazed on the open ranges. And they thought it would be a way for them to make a living and stop the violence. So they were only too happy to work a deal with the Daggs Brothers. If they kept the sheep on their side of the deadline, they figured they would be ok, and that the Grahams would not bother them or their sheep.

In early February of 1887, Jim and Ed Tewksbury along with their friend Bill Jacobs, who had experience raising sheep, were to guard the band on a trip from Flagstaff to Pleasant Valley. Along with a Basque sheep herder and two Navajo helpers, the Daggs brothers had hired, and four border collies they headed across the high desert of the Mogollon Rim with their destination the Tewksbury ranges in Pleasant Valley. In all they were moving 80,000 sheep.

As the sheep crossed the mesa on the way to the pass which led over the Mogollon Rim, just as they were reaching the trail that lead down from the rim into Pleasant Valley, now SR288, the Tewksbury's thinking all was going smooth, left Jacobs, and the two Navajo sheep herders with the band, and headed to their ranch in the Valley to prepare for the arrival of the sheep.

Back at the Sheep herders camp, the Basque sheepherder, along with his dogs was cleaning up their campsite, getting ready to join the rest of the men to drive the sheep the final stretch of their trip. An intruder came into the sheep camp, murdered the Basque sheep herder and beheaded him, which was one brutal act that is usually a sign left by Apaches.

When Bill Jacobs went back to the campsite to see why the Basque sheep herder was not coming, he found him and the four dogs dead. Jacobs buried the sheep herder's body and marked the grave and then headed back to the band of sheep, to help finish moving them that last leg of the journey. But when he got back he found more carnage.

While Jacobs was at their camp, burying the man's body, the murderer must have been watching Jacobs, because when Jacobs left, he followed his tracks and the tracks of another horseman also heading back to where the band of sheep was located. Jacobs figured that since it was one rider that the Basque was probably killed by him and not raiding Indians. When he got to the place where the two Indians were tending the flock he saw the carnage. The two Indians were alive and came out of hiding and told Jacobs that a gang of cowboys had done the deed and that one man headed south on the trail into Pleasant Valley, who they thought was the leader, while the other men headed east toward Holbrook.

The two Navajo sheepherders told Jacobs that the men showed up about a half hour after he left to go back to their camp. One of them told Bill they took off and hid, while the leader and his friends drove as many sheep as possible over the cliff and then clubbed to death the sheep that would not jump into their death. They told him they were relatively sure the leader was the one who rode away south into Pleasant Valley.

Bill Jacobs and the two surviving Navajo sheepherders drove the balance of the band down the trail and when the leader's tracks split from the trail Jacobs followed the tracks to one of the Graham Corrals and ranch houses, while the two sheepherders took the sheep to Ed and Jim Tewksbury's ranch. They would at least be safe there, while Bill Jacobs made his way back to the Tewksbury ranch. After the Indians described the leader, knowing he was a Graham cowboy, they figured Andy Cooper was the culprit, who later bragged in a local bar in Holbrook, that was overheard by Will Barnes, who just happened to be in that exact bar at the time, that it was he, Andy Cooper who bragged about committing brutal the deed.

Besides the death of the Sheepherder and the dogs, the Daggs brothers reported they lost $90,000 in slaughtered sheep alone. The local papers in Globe, Flagstaff, Holbrook and Prescott all printed the story that the murderer of the Basque sheepherder was trailed to the Graham corrals.

Many writers, novelists and historians alike have assumed that the trouble began and continued as a conflict between cattlemen and sheep men. The real cause of the war is believed to have been this murder of the sheep herder and the band of sheep owned by the Daggs Brothers and guarded by the Tewksbury's, and had been driven over the rim of the Mogollon Mountains plunging to their deaths some five hundred to a thousand feet in some places.

Apache County Deputy Sheriff Will C. Barnes wrote in his book, *"Apaches and Longhorns,"* that the Pleasant Valley War was not one between sheep and cattle men, it was due to the murder of the Basque Sheepherder, coupled with the widespread theft of cattle and horses from ranchers all over Pleasant Valley. The trouble had started long before Mr. Jacobs bought the Daggs sheep into the valley.

Even Tom Horn in his biography claims to have been a mediator but the author will later show that Horn participated in several of the nasty events that took place during the Pleasant Valley War. There is no doubt that he was not neutral, Horn was a Tewksbury Faction member in very good standing. In Horn's own biography *"The life of Tom Horn, Government Scout and Interpreter,"* he would only admit to have been a mediator, but new evidence found by this author indicates he was a lot more than a mediator. Horn took a very active role in the Pleasant Valley War, while he was a Gila County Deputy Sheriff under his boss and friend Sheriff Glen Reynolds. Below is the only statement of admission that Horn made about his involvement in the Pleasant Valley War;

> "Early in April, 1887, some of the boys came to Globe from Pleasant Valley, where there was a big rustler war going on and claimed the rustlers were getting the best of the game."

Bill Brown, Tewksbury Family Historian said; according to his Great grandmother Mary Ann;

> "The trouble came to a head, when Jim and Edwin Tewksbury went to Prescott to answer questions regarding the warrants that were issued for their arrests that were trumped up by the Grahams accusing them of rustling and in fact were thrown out of court for lack of evidence. While they were away their younger brother Frank died of Tuberculosis. Jim and Ed Tewksbury blamed the Grahams for the death of little brother Frank."

Once a fire is lit, however, anyone can get burned, and six months after the brutal murder and mutilation of the Basque sheep herder, 'Old Man' Mart Blevins, the father of five Blevins brothers and a close friend and supporter of the Grahams disappeared. It was late in July one morning in 1887. Mart left his ranch in search of horses that had strayed from their grazing area in an adjacent canyon to the ranch. He did not come back. Hampton Blevins, accompanied by three Hashknife cowboys, who were camped at nearby Pinedale, went in search of him. The three cowboys were Tom Tucker, Bob Gillespie and the notorious John Paine. Robert Carrington joined them later and they made a thorough search of the Valley, finding no sign of the old man. Hampton began to fear that his dad had been ambushed and killed.

The word got around and there was talk of retaliation. On August 2, 1887, Will C. Barnes and the Hashknife foreman Ed Rogers were camped at Big Dry Lake, thirty miles south of Holbrook, on a summer roundup. Tucker and Hampton Blevins rode into camp about sunset. That night Barnes related the following;

> *"All sorts of conferences and medicine talks were going on around our camp. The next morning around the campfire, Ed told me that Tucker, Paine, Gillespie and Blevins were going over to Pleasant Valley to try to find out something about Old Man Blevins, and as they put it to Ed, 'to start a little war of our own.' Roger and I did our very best to talk them out of going but were unable to convince them there was any danger in the trip. After borrowing all the surplus ammunition in camp, they left the next morning but without a pack horse or supplies of any kind, except those used in battle."*

The word spread fast on the frontier in those days and a week later, on August 9, 1887, three men, all heavily armed, rode up to the Newton Ranch, where four members of the Tewksbury faction happened to be. Accounts differ about just what happened but Bill Brown says that according to his great grandmother, Mary Ann Tewksbury, the Blevins brothers and their allies from the Hashknife gang rode boldly up to the main house and, without dismounting, called out, asking to be invited in to eat breakfast. Jim Tewksbury called back from inside the house;

> *"We aren't keeping a boarding house here, especially for the likes of you."*

Angry words followed as Paine wanted to know how many men they had in the loop-holed log cabin. According to Jim Roberts, who was present inside the cabin at that time said;

> *"Jim Tewksbury was standing in the door jamb as he spoke to the riders outside the cabin. As he began to shut the door Hampton Blevins drew his gun and took a shot at Jim, while he was in the process of shutting the front door, secreted behind the door."*

Tom Tucker who was riding with the Graham faction that day, stated the men outside the cabin were fired upon without provocation. Whether or not that's true, a volley of rifle and pistol fire then came from inside the Newton Cabin. Hampton Blevins and John Paine were riddled with bullets, fell from their horses and were dead when they hit the ground. Tucker received a serious gunshot wound in the chest. Bob Gillespie and Carrington sustained flesh wounds.

There were four men inside the Newton cabin, Jim and Ed Tewksbury, Jim Roberts and Joseph Boyer. Newton was not present that day and not one of them was hurt. It was at that point that the two factions realized they could no longer coexist in Pleasant Valley. There was no neutral territory. The battle would be to the finish. And there was not much the law and those who enforced it could do.

Nevertheless, the law, in the person of William Mulvenon, the Sheriff of Yavapai County with its headquarters in Prescott, about one hundred and twenty five miles to the east of Pleasant Valley, tried. Mulvenon was an efficient and respected peace officer whose sensible approach to law enforcement will be discussed later. The news of the Newton Ranch shootout quickly reached Sheriff Mulvenon in his office in Prescott and on August the 10th 1887, On September 10th 1887 the Arizona Champion newspaper, published out of Flagstaff, reported he passed through Flagstaff on August 29, 1887, on his way to Payson. He reportedly deputized every man he came into contact with on his way to Pleasant Valley, to keep them from spreading the word, which at times seemed to be more efficient than a telegram, but most of all Mulvenon wanted to keep the element of surprise.

Below is a photo of Yavapai Sheriff William "Billy" Mulvenon, taken circa late 1880's

It was the first of September when the posse reached the Young in Pleasant Valley. Their first stop was the Perkins Store, in Young, where they just happened to run into Tom Graham, Andy Cooper and several other men of their faction. A few days later Sheriff Mulvenon was interviewed by a reporter from the Arizona Champion newspaper. The following is from the article that was printed by the paper. Sheriff Mulvenon told the reporter;

> *"I did not have any arrest warrants for any of the Graham party. During our conversation, Tom Graham said that if*

> he (Sheriff Mulvenon) did not arrest the Tewksbury's that they, (the Graham's) would take matters into their own hands and fight the Tewksbury's until they were all exterminated."

Sheriff Mulvenon and his posse left the Perkins store and proceeded to the Newton Ranch. When they arrived they found the house and barn burned to the ground. Apache County Deputy Will C. Barnes wrote in his report later the following;

> "After walking around what remained of the ranch house and two newly dug graves and the bodies of two dead saddle horses not far from the graves. Charles E Perkins, the store keeper in Pleasant Valley told us that he and Justice of the Peace, John Meadows from Payson went over and buried the men a few days after the fight. Nobody knows who burned the buildings. The Grahams, according to two different sources declared they did not burn down the buildings." Barnes continued, "Sheriff Mulvenon looked the place over very carefully looking for some evidence that might lead to the detection of the crime but found nothing worthwhile. He realized that his posse of but five men was too small to serve the ten arrest warrants they had for the Tewksbury's and their followers, if they ran into trouble, so they went back to Prescott, with no Tewksbury's with them."

The photo below of the Perkins store was provided to the author by Bill Brown from his Tewksbury family archives

At that point some of the men in the feuding families had had time to contemplate the situation and began to have second thoughts. John Blevins was one of them. After his father's mysterious disappearance and the subsequent killing of his brother Hampton, he decided to relocate most of the family to Holbrook, located seventy-five miles northeast of Pleasant Valley, until peace was restored.

John Blevins, his wife Eva, and their eighteen-month old son Hampton made the move, taking with them his mother Mary Blevins and his younger brother, fourteen-year old Sam Houston Blevins, all decided it would be best to leave their ranch at Canyon Creek and move to Holbrook.

Upon arriving in Holbrook they took up residence in a three room frame cottage on the north side of the railroad tracks not far from downtown with its few stores, half dozen saloons and a post office. Cooper Blevins (aka; Andy Cooper) and his brother Charles, also known by his nickname Albert, remained at the family ranch in Canyon Creek, still hoping to find the body of their father, who just seemed to vanish into thin air. They had no doubt by then that he was dead, and they began working on plans to avenge the death of their father. It was definitely a wise move for Charles to take his family, his mom and brother to

Holbrook so they could try to be out of harm's way.

On the evening of August 17, 1887, just eight days after the Newton Ranch gun battle, Billy Graham was returning home from a dance that took place Globe. As he crossed a creek a few miles north of his home he ran into James D. Houck, the Deputy Sheriff for the newly formed Apache County, under sheriff for the Apache County Sheriff, Commodore Perry Owens, who was also a sheep owner and a Tewksbury partisan.

Houck was the brother in law of the murdered Basque sheep herder. He was apparently after John Graham, whom he held responsible for his brother in law's death. He told Joe T. McKinney, one of the ranchers there in the Holbrook area and also a Deputy Apache County Sheriff when questioned about a warrant for the arrest of John, that;

> "Of course I had a warrant for John's arrest."

Deputy Sheriff Houck gave several accounts of what followed, the first one appearing in the St. Johns Herald on September 29, 1887, over a month after the unfortunate meeting. The reporter that interviewed him reported;

> "We arrived in St. Johns last Monday night fresh from the bloody acts and scenes in Pleasant Valley. On August 17th I was compelled to keep in the brush by some of the Graham men. I saw a man I took for John Graham, riding along the trail. I waited until the horseman was abreast of me. When I called out to him, the man looked up at the same time drawing his pistol. I then discovered it was young Billy Graham, so I told him to ride on, but he chose to stay and fight, taking a shot at me. I

> *returned fire and shot him. I knew he was mortally wounded but he rode away. I found out that he died from his wound a day later."*

Apache Deputy Sheriff James D. Houck, an original immigrant rancher told the story in greater detail to author, William MacLeod Raine, many years later, which was also Houck's official written report. William Raine relayed the story told by Houck as follows;

> *"One day I was coming down from Holbrook and stopped at the Haigler Ranch. I figured I would get supper and stop to rest for a while. Mr. Haigler met me at the front door, he said, 'come on in and get supper but do not stay, the Grahams have been here and I don't want a fight at my ranch.' Haigler went on to say, 'John Graham stops by here every evening and sometimes he comes early in the mornings,' Houck told Haigler, All right. I'll eat supper and take some grub and be on my way. After supper Houck said that he headed out halfway between Pleasant Valley and the trail from the Graham Ranch. I proceeded up a hill. I stopped to rest my horse and slept until daylight. At daylight I headed down on the trail and hid behind a tree. I left my horse on the hill to graze. I knew John Graham would come along and I had a warrant for his arrest and I was going to get him. Instead of John Graham, his younger brother Billy Graham rode up the trail toward me. I didn't have a warrant for him, so when he got close, I stepped out from behind the tree. I startled him. He*

> drew his gun at once. I tried to speak to him but it was no use. Everybody was carrying a gun in those days. He fired a round in my direction. I turned loose of a shot at him. His horse bucked and whirled around, I shot three or four more rounds in his direction. It was the only thing I could do as he was shooting at me as fast as he pulled the trigger. Lucky for me he was a bad shot. I found out later that I did hit him as he rode away and he died from a gunshot wound a day later."

Apache County Deputy Sheriff James Houck's simplest and most accurate statement in his official report filed with Sheriff Owens and given to fellow Deputy William C. Barnes was as follows;

> "We both drew at the sight of each other but I shot first and got him."

Billy Graham's death cemented the alliance amongst the Grahams and their supporters. The tally of the death toll in the Pleasant Valley War stood at four dead men at this point in time, one missing and presumed dead (Mart Blevins), Deputy Sheriff J.D. Houck's brother in law the Basque Sheep herder and Billy Graham, two men from the Graham faction and two men from the Tewksbury faction of the feud. One of the Tewksbury men was Ed and Jim's younger brother, Frank, who passed away from the effects of Tuberculosis, but just as Tom Graham blamed Ed Tewksbury for the death of his younger brother Billy, Ed and Jim Tewksbury blamed the Grahams for the death of their brother Frank. Because Frank passed while Jim, Ed and most of the Tewksbury's were in Prescott answering trumped up rustling charges in 1886 that were thrown out of a court hearing. But Ed and Jim felt as though if they had not been in Prescott answering bogus charges, their brother would probably still be alive, so they blamed Tom Graham for the death of Frank.

On September 2, 1887, just two weeks after the death of young Billy Graham, a lot of the members of the Graham faction along with Andy Cooper and some unidentified allies set out under the cover of darkness and reached their goal at sunrise. John Tewksbury and William Jacobs were busy gathering horses within sight of J.D. Tewksbury's cabin, completely unaware of their dangerous visitors. The horses were about a half a mile away, hobbled for the night and left at the creek so they could obtain water through the night. After getting the horses and herding them back to the ranch, the Graham men advanced cautiously and found cover behind rocks and bushes on the adjacent hillside. Taking careful aim, the bushwhackers unleashed a devastating volley of rifle fire shots into the backs of the two men.

Tewksbury and Jacobs never had a chance. Jacobs died instantly, his back ripped open by three well aimed bullets. John Tewksbury was shot once in the back of the neck. He may not have died immediately, but when help finally arrived, from what was left of the bodies, the help found that John's head had been smashed with a heavy rock.

At the request of the killers of the two men, Hank Blevans and Andy Cooper, they talked Tom Graham into not letting anyone cover the bodies, allowing wild hogs in the area feast on their bodies for up to an hour, before Mary Ann Tewksbury and Mrs. Poloniff, her midwife, got the Graham's to allow them to cover what was left of the bodies. The effect of this atrocity on the Tewksbury's was predictable. Jim Tewksbury said it for all of them;

> *"No damned man can kill a brother of mine and stand guard over him for the*

hogs to eat him, and live within a mile and a half of me."

It took three days before the local Justice of the Peace and Coroner John Meadows came down from Payson with six jurors who performed an inquest on what was left of the body's. The Silver Belt Newspaper, published in Globe, reported on October 1, 1887, that the siege was maintained for eleven days while the dead men lay where they fell-but in fact it was only three days. Storekeeper Charles Perkins arrived shortly after Meadows and four of the men that were with John Meadows dug graves and buried what was left of the bodies, according to the Justice of the Peace along with being the county coroner, John Meadows report wrote in his report;

> *"What was left of the bodies after being badly torn by hogs"*, Meadow went on to say, *the decomposition of the bodies had gone so far that burying them was a most disagreeable task. All we did was to dig two very shallow graves and roll the swollen, mutilated bodies into them with our shovels."*

Chapter Four
Real West Article - 1967

 This chapter is based on a story the author found in the November, 1967 edition of Real West Magazine written by Maurice Kildare, who interviewed a man by the name of James (Jim) Pearce. Pearce was later discovered to be a Tewksbury supporter and was present at this event. In reverse of the true story western writers of his day, he based this story on the accounts of these events solely from his interview with Mr. Pearce.

 In defense of these great past writers, historians today have so much more research available. The more sophisticated readers of today require a true story author to find and present as many sides as possible. It was standard procedure though in those days to take the word of the folks that were being interviewed. I believe it is a very good article and has some weight, so I am presenting it in its entirety, although there are some factual errors that this author has discovered and will present to the reader. For the most part it is a very well written story from one of the men who was in the Tewksbury Cabin during the three-day assault by Tom Graham and his gang of cutthroat outlaws.

 Although, after completing the author's unbiased research used for the completion of this book, along with many talks with the Tewksbury Family Historian Bill Brown, who told the author that his grandmother, Bertha Tewksbury, spoke about this article many times with him over the years. According to Bills great grandmother, Mary Ann Tewksbury Rhodes, who told her daughter many times over the years, and her daughter told Bill's grandmother Bertha, who was very young, but was in the cabin during the assault, that they always had issues with this article. The differences Mary Ann and Bertha had with the story will be presented at the end of this chapter by this author.

After a personal inspection of the property, the burial site of the two men killed, the author and Bill Brown believe, it would have been impossible for a pregnant woman of nine months, who was bedridden to have not only been in two places at once, but even more important, to climb under a fence and then walk three quarters of a mile to the site, where her husband John Tewksbury and his friend Bill Jacobs were brutally murdered, and have the strength to move the bodies and cover them with tarps and quilts to protect them from the wild hogs that roamed in the valley.

Arizona's notorious Graham-Tewksbury feud, also known as the Pleasant Valley or Tonto Basin War began in 1880 just below the Mogollon Rim. The war became a blood vendetta between two major families of settlers: the three Graham brothers from Iowa and the Tewksbury clan who first settled in the valley. Both families raised large herds of cattle.

The two factions and their numerous friends put the bush in bushwhack. They and their supporters killed each other by stealth and gave not as much mercy as a wild carnivore. A large but unknown number of men were killed before the major firefight outlined in the following pages. Estimates by John Meadows, the Justice of the Peace located in Payson as well as L.J. Horton, an original settler, tally the men killed in the PV War at thirty-six, but that does not include the ten to fifteen men who simply disappeared from the valley, never to be heard from again. Most bodies were left lying where they fell. Decades after the feud's end, scattered skeletal bones of these unidentified men were still being found in Pleasant Valley.

The feud reached its bloodiest on the night of September 1, 1887. Two nights previously Ann

Graham was in the kitchen of their home with her husband Tom along with his good friend Charlie Duesha and Louis Parker, Tom Pickett, Billy Wilson and Jamie Stott. Tom Graham was depressed. He had been thinking about the death of his young brother Billy Graham, who came home on the night of August 17, riddled with bullets from, he believed, being ambushed on the Hellgate Trail by Ed Tewksbury, but in fact the deed was done by Apache County Deputy Sheriff James Houck, who claimed he had a warrant for Tom Graham and shot Billy by mistake claiming it was in self defense.

There has never been found any such warrant for arrest of John Graham at that time for horse stealing found in Apache County Records in the courthouse in Holbrook. But a contributing factor in the case of Apache County Sheriff Deputy J.D. Houck's brother-in-law, the Sheepherder, who had been killed and beheaded was supposedly the Deputy Houck's main reason in the killing of Billy Graham, because he openly blamed John Graham, the leader of the Graham faction at that time period, for the murder of his brother-in-law, who was moving the band of sheep from Flagstaff to Pleasant Valley and of course the brutal beheading of the man by one of the Graham cowboys, Andy Cooper. A known killer on the run from the law and a Graham supporter, whose tracks led away from the murder site, and were followed by Bill Jacobs to one of the Graham's ranches, the horse was identified as being owned by Andy Cooper.

It had been two weeks since his younger brother Billy was on his way back home from a dance in Phoenix, when he was shot by J.D. Houck, *(although Billy told his brother Tom, that it was Ed Tewksbury who did the deed)*. Young Billy succumbed from his wounds two days after being mortally wounded from a Houck bullet. Tom Graham was not able to put the death of his brother behind him and his revenge emotions were running strong through his veins.

As the men were discussing the current conditions in and around the valley, all of a sudden the men heard a blood curdling scream from the kitchen. Ann Graham was washing the dishes when a face peered at her through the kitchen window and scared her. Her husband Tom, Charlie Duesha, and the other men grabbed their guns and rushed outside at a dead run, hoping to catch the man who scared Ann, thinking for sure it was a Tewksbury man. They searched the premises that night but were unable to catch the culprit. The next morning, they again searched the grounds around the cabin and found a set of tracks that lead from a horse in a meadow secreted near the cabin, to the kitchen window and then a second set of tracks that lead back to the hidden horse.

Tom Graham spoke with Charlie Duesha throughout that day expressing his gut feeling that the Tewksbury's were probably planning a raid on the Graham ranch. After a full day's discussion, the men came to the realization that the man who peered in the window the previous night was in all probability a scout for the Tewksbury's. Tom Graham decided to send Tom Pickett and Billy (aka; "Jeff") Wilson to scout the Tewksbury Ranch and see if they could find out if a potential raiding party had been formed.

At nine o'clock that evening the door opened and in stepped Pickett followed by Wilson. In the low glow of the kerosene lamp their facial expressions were smug with satisfaction. Tom jumped to his feet with a pretty good idea of what that meant. Pickett spoke with a loud direct voice;

> "We found them all right, there at old man J. D. Tewksbury's place."

From the darkness of the far room corner Charlie Duesha reared to his feet and said;

"How many men did you see?"

Tom Pickett declared;

> *"After going to inspect Jim and Ed Tewksbury's ranch, Pickett said they found it empty. The ranch house contained a dim light but after a close inspection there was no sign of anyone being home.*
>
> *From there we went to J.D. Tewksbury's log home a few miles down the creek. That house also stood silent and lifeless but faint voices could be heard. The quietness and the fact that there were no animals in the corrals appeared, to be a deliberate act to convince snoopers, that no one was at home.*
>
> *We weren't able to go into the house to count the men, but there were twenty-five horses in the corral and we heard a crackle of laughter that echoed from men in a room in cabin. Pickett and Wilson figured they were planning an attack on the Graham ranch."*

Tom Graham had been against violence until his brothers Billy and John were murdered by the Tewksbury's, even though the two men were actually killed by lawmen, both in shootouts. John rather than be arrested and Billy, who was killed by Sheriff Mulvenon in and act of self-defense. After explaining their thoughts and their findings, it looked like the Tewksbury's had gathered a large group of fighting men and were obviously planning a raid on the Graham Ranch. More important was that the men were all safely hidden in J.D. Tewksbury's ranch house, which was the closest of the Tewksbury

Ranches to Tom Graham's ranch. So they were basically trapped with their horses about a half to three quarters of a mile away from J.D.'s cabin. That would make it very hard to reach the horses without being out in the open. Absolutely, they told Tom there was no doubt the Tewksbury's were planning some type of raid.

Tom jumped up from his chair and grabbed his gun belt that was hanging from a peg on the fireplace. He buckled it up and took down his rifle from another set of pegs over the fireplace. He then turned to his friend James "Jamie" Stott, the Bear Springs horse rancher, who had arrived a few days earlier with two new horses that Tom had agreed to purchase. Tom spoke to Stott saying:

"You needn't get into this, Jim."

Stott replied,

"When they run off with my horses, and shoot at me and my friends, I'm in!"

Within minutes Tom Graham and his band cinched up their saddles and were riding. This night Tom hoped the long planned raid would be a final one. Tom had his brother Jim with him along with his cousin Louis Parker and Charlie Duesha, who seldom left his side. The balance of the band consisted of Texas George Graham, another cousin, Andy Cooper (aka Cooper Blevins), and his brother Charlie Blevins, Tom Pickett, Billy (Jeff) Wilson, Jamie Stott and Henry "Hank" Blevins, also known as the "Buscadero Outlaw," again who was no relation to the Blevins family.

This combined force of eleven fighting Graham men was the largest yet to ever ride against the Tewksbury's. It would be the Grahams biggest raid in Pleasant Valley, and the Graham's hoped to wipe out the trapped Tewksbury's with one big battle.

That night a low silver moon covered the cold vast reaches of Pleasant Valley. The Graham fighter's route from the Graham Ranch to J.D. Tewksbury's cabin was over Spy Hill. They all had been over that particular trail so many times, they could follow it blindfolded. Once clear of the creek tributaries, they moved purposefully through the light timber until getting close to J.D. Tewksbury's cabin. Halting, once they got close, the men tied their mounts in a way that would allow them a quick escape. Then they silently converged on the base of a hill overlooking one side of the ranch house below. The men huddled close to Tom Graham, while he whispered brief instructions. Tom said to Tom Pickett,

"Do you want to take five men around back to cover that wash on the far side of the cabin?

Five automatic volunteers followed as Tom Pickett lead them away. Since they had more distance to cover, Tom Graham waited a few minutes before leading the rest of the men with him onto the rocky hill slopes. They spread wide apart into a wide line, keeping within eye distance of one another. Under the crest of the hill each one of the men sought cover, crawling a few feet more before finally lying flat. In that line they were all crack shots, they were men that were experienced in a firefight or a gunfight. Charlie Blevins, Charlie Duesha, Jamie Stott and Hank Blevans, aka; the Buscadero Outlaw.

From their hiding spot they overlooked the dark hole in which the Tewksbury log house stood. No milk cows or calves made noise in the small pens. No horses or dogs were around. All the animals had been deliberately removed to give the premises the false appearance of being deserted and abandoned. For a few minutes the mock reality of the scene caused them to ponder the possibility of a Tewksbury attack at the Graham Ranch at Willow Springs. Then they detected the faint odor of burned wood in the night air and they confidently settled down to await the stirrings of dawn when their enemies would appear.

Meanwhile, in the darkened interior of the two room log cabin, Ed Tewksbury stepped over the extended legs impatiently. While the main group of men rested and slept, he had not quieted down once all night. Being cooped up inside the cabin deeply worried him. He much preferred the forest where a man had room to maneuver.

Like Tom Graham, Ed Tewksbury also had assembled his largest group of fighting men, only Tom Horn failed to show up from Globe as promised. All the men present were to move on the Graham Ranch at Willow Springs at daybreak. If the Grahams were wiped out maybe they could return to peaceful farming and raise cattle again instead of sheep.

In the kitchen John Tewksbury sat whispering to his wife, Mary Ann, who was holding their infant daughter, Bertha Tewksbury (Bill Brown's grandmother).. She was also the Tewksbury brother's stepsister, their father having married her twice-widowed mother in Globe in 1874. On a pallet in the kitchen slept their small daughter, and a half-brother, eight-year old Walter S. Tewksbury. Beside the cold cook stove James Tewksbury engaged in whispered talk with local cattle and horse rancher, James "Jim" Roberts, a veteran of the Civil War and many other gun battles, and last but not least, John Rhodes, another Tewksbury faction member, a crack shot with a rifle and was known in the cowboy competition, because he threw a very long lasso.

Feet protruded towards the center of the floor because there were so many of them lying around in the main room. These included Gil Homes, a Flying V cowboy, who had brought a mule loaded with ammo that day. The ammunition had been furnished by al local Globe jeweler, George Newton, who was a Tewksbury supporting and partisan. The others were Ed, Jim Tewksbury and John Tewksbury's along with his one-time partner William "Bill" Jacobs, John Rhodes, W.H Bishop, Jake Lauffer, George Blaine, William Richards, Joe Boyer, Bob Cody, Eck Coleman, Art Stevens, Bill Varton, James Pearce, George Wagoner and James Pearce's son, Jim Pearce. All together the Tewksbury's had put together nineteen fighting men, who were determined to end the feud with the Graham's. Most were strangers to the valley. Seven additional men had been sent north from Globe by Tom Horn, for the planned raid on the Graham Ranch at Willow Springs and would arrive a little after daybreak. This is the only supposedly written evidence by Horn that he had anything to do with the Pleasant Valley War. But this author will present research indicating Horn had a bigger part in the feud than he was willing to write about in his book, as told to his boss John Coble in Wyoming.

In his own written biography, *"Life of Tom Horn, Government Scout and Interpreter,"* written by Horn while he was on death row and was published after his death, I have included a letter by his girlfriend, Gwendolyn Kimmel to Ed Tewksbury indicating how much respect Horn had for his friend Ed Tewksbury. She was inquiring about Tom's goldmine. I will present this letter and a photo of Horn with all the Tewksbury faction later in this book. Tom did admit to friends in Wyoming later that he was one of the regulators, along with Gila County Sheriff Glenn Reynolds, who were also involved in the hanging of three men who had stolen cattle and horses hidden near their cabin as the ranch was used as a holding place for stolen stock. Horn also admitted to have been involved in the disappearance a crusty old bastard, Mart Blevins, who he knew was also a cattle rustler and horse thief. Horn never publicly admitted these dastardly deeds in writing but did admit them to his friend John Coble (*Tom Horn, Blood on the Moon, written by Chip Carlson.*)

Ed Tewksbury believed the feud would end when the Graham brothers and their friends were all dead. Old man, J.D. Tewksbury and his family were in Prescott and not present at the gun battle, that was about to take place. There would be no aftermath of peace but a lasting hate in all of them that would only end when death closed all of the Grahams' eyes. The Tewksbury's were tired of having their stock rustled, blamed for rustling cattle and horses that they did not do, and of several of their men having been ambushed and killed by the Graham's, who simply wanted the Tewksbury's out of Pleasant Valley, so they had no competitors for grazing rights. With the hour of dawn approaching, Ed Tewksbury was more nervous than ever when his brother John appeared from the kitchen and spoke to Ed;

"Ed, do you want the horses brought back to the corral by the cabin now?"

Ed Tewksbury's voice sighed with relief, but had an uneasy feeling about the quietness that dawn, as he surveyed the area in front of the cabin and spoke:

"We should have done so before now."

While John woke Bill Jacobs, Ed unfastened the door. The moon had set and the sun was breaking through. Scouting the building all the way around by staying in the blackest wall shadow, he surveyed the looming hill, brush and timber. Eternal vigilance was the price of staying alive in Pleasant Valley, which now could aptly be renamed Murder Valley.

Carrying bridles, John Tewksbury and Bill Jacobs walked out of the cabin heading toward the corral.

Reaching the two wire fences, they bent down pushing the lower wire with their feet and squeezed through under the top wire. Since the moonlight was gone, they were not dimly perceptible after gaining a few yards in the knee high weeds and wild grass. Ed waited another five minutes before returning to the house. No shots having been made they both concluded that none of their enemies lurked around.

This is the only instance during the feud that Ed Tewksbury ignored his *"sixth sense"* of surrounding danger and he lived to regret it. Had he been able to see John and Jacobs separate beyond the fence he would have realized instantly why they did so. Heavy dew covered the weeds and grass, but their passage was a clearly defined trail, visible in the dawn light .They should have withdrawn instantly upon discovering the situation.

Over the hill, scurrying morning clouds gave way to thick dull gray as dawn neared. From cover, Charlie Duesha constantly inspected the premises below. Surveying the terrain further out, his eyes moved across the field, suddenly paused and returned to one spot. A moment later he crawled back under the hill crest, and descended for their hiding spot.

Observing the two men move, Tom Graham stood up and searched the ranch surroundings quickly. He also found the trails passing through the weeds and grass, where the dew was knocked off. Two men had walked through there and away, unseen.

Withdrawing from cover, Tom Graham stood up hunkered over and walked over to where Hank "Buscadero Outlaw" Blevans was hiding and spoke to Hank saying;

> *"Hank, go get somebody from the other group to help cover here."*

Hurrying off the hill, Blevans reached the tied horses in a jog-trot and grabbed the bridle reins.

Charlie Duesha approached, already mounted, from beyond the hill.

After circling the fenced field, they reached the creek inside a belt of timber to a shallow ford. Across it the trail forked. No evidence remained of the two men who had left the far house. Which way had they gone? Then Duesha hollered out;

> "Not to old man Tewksbury's cabin.
> They are after their horses, Tommy."

Tom Graham gestured and they started pulling away from trail-side, only to stop abruptly as two riders carelessly splashed through the rushing water, crossing the creek in a hurry. They brought guns to bear before recognizing Andy Cooper and Hank Blevans. The two entered cover their side of the trail.

Events spurred rapidly towards a deadly climax and Tom Graham didn't like their withdrawal from the surroundings a bit. Their absence weakened his force at his father's cabin.

Graham was about to order them back when a sound rippled in the air overhead, stock coming off the mesa. All four men hit the ground, drawing weapons. Cooper sprinted across the trail down which stock must come, to one side of a big tree. The others merely spread apart behind a tree or brush to wait.

Up on the mesa came John Tewksbury and Bill Jacobs, riding bridled horses bareback and on the incline returning back to the cabin, they dismounted as a habitual precautionary measure against sky, silhouetting themselves as easy targets. They descended in a line, leading their mounts behind.

The men with their horses walked past the hiding men as the brassy sun began showing above the distant mountain peaks. The clear morning air suddenly erupted with gunfire. Neither bushwhacked victim ever turned towards the lurking enemy or had even a remote chance of drawing a weapon. Perhaps neither realized he was caught in the same fatal trap.

Bill Jacobs sat on his horse in clear view with his back to Andy Cooper, who proceeded to pump three bullets from his Colt 45 into the back of Jacobs. His body twisted and jerked with each round that tore into his body, finally falling from his Horse, he landed face down, instantly killed, on the ground.

Charlie Duesha never wasted cartridges. He brought John Tewksbury down with one round that went through John's neck and severed his jugular vein and spine. Neither Graham nor Blevins were said to fire a shot. According to Hank Blevans in an interview with writer Maurice Kildare, many years later, he said that he shot John Tewksbury and Andy Cooper shot Bill Jacobs.

Gunshots echoed away in the timber. The running stock cleared the immediate area. Over at 'Old Man,' Tewksbury's house several dogs started barking. The stock must not be allowed to stray into the field where the Tewksbury's might mount an escape, Tom Graham thought to himself.

As the Graham men approached the creek again, a burst of shooting awoke at the distant cabin. A large number of settler's loose hogs, gone feral and dangerous. Andy Cooper laughed loudly at the sight of them and exclaimed:

> "It would be just right if them boogers
> ate up them dead Tewksbury's!"

The firing from the cabin and around it continued as the four rode back well out of range. They hurried into the besieging line in case the Tewksbury's dared to charge out of the cabin. Now, Tom Graham realized the unexpected number trapped in the cabin meant they couldn't all possibly be killed during a break-out. Some were certain of escaping. When his men slowed their fire, the shooting from the cabin died away. The heat of the day wore on into the night.

John Blevins, shifting position, felt the hot breath of death as a rifle bullet singed his left cheek. Such expert shooting could come only from Jim or Ed Tewksbury, Jim Roberts or John Rhodes. All three men never used any weapons other than a Winchester 45-70 caliber rifle. From then forward the gunfight see-sawed into stalemate for three full days.

Having disposed of two of their arch enemies so easily, the attackers moved boldly forward, entrenched themselves into the hillside and besieged the thick-walled and loop, gun holed Tewksbury cabin. Inside the two remaining Tewksbury brothers, Ed and Jim, along with their friends, held their ground for three solid days of fighting.

Near the field where the bodies of the two dead men lay, a herd of half wild hogs rooted for food. Soon after the sun rose, they approached the bodies, where swarms of flies were already gathering, and the hogs began to eat the bodies. One of the Tewksbury's called frantically to their assailants, asking for a truce so they could bury the bodies. Their request was promptly refused by Tom Graham and Charlie Duesha.

A little later Mary Ann Tewksbury, who was staying at the neighbor Henry Polinoff's home, because his wife was a midwife, as Mary Ann was the pregnant, due with John Tewksbury baby. Hearing the gun shots, the two women arrived at the cabin to see what was wrong. They were run off by gunfire at first. The best they could do was to cover the bodies with blankets and tarps with heavy stones to keep the hogs and elements away as there was no fallen brush available. Mary Ann left the dogs on guard, which she hoped would chase away any returning hogs.

After covering the bodies, she walked to the cabin dry eyed and calm and told Ed Tewksbury exactly what happened at the creek, because it was too far for him to know the details. When she was done speaking, Ed vowed;

> *"There is no man going to live that was involved in shooting my brother down and leaving his body lying on the ground for hogs to eat."*

As the afternoon of the third day of the siege wore on Andy Cooper smirking, spoke to John;

> *"We are going to make a bow, and then we are going to shoot a fire arrow on the roof of the cabin and burn the house down like Indians."*

Tom Graham exploded,

> *"Like hell you are! There are women and children inside!"*

The photo below of the J.D. Tewksbury ranch was supplied by Bill Brown, the Tewksbury family historian and archivist. One can see why they had plenty of bacon, pork ribs and hamhocks with so many wild hogs

The ensuing argument ended when Tom Graham vetoed the plan quickly. The fight consumed more time than he had planned on. Tom correctly reasoned that the first shooting would send somebody from Spy

Hill to bring back help for the Tewksbury's." The danger of attack in their rear now existed. However, he stuck it out until night closed down. Re-forming the gang, they rode well away before going their separate ways and into oblivion. Most of them would be slain from ambush within the next month after the three-day gun battle at J.D Tewksbury's ranch cabin.

It was just past midnight of the third night that the Tewksbury's discovered the Grahams had vacated the ranch grounds. The Tewksbury men immediately upon realizing the Graham's were gone made a hasty escape to Cherry Creek. The New Mexico cowboys, who Tom Horn sent as reinforcements rode out immediately and headed back to their homes.

Ed and Jim Tewksbury, Jim Roberts and John Rhodes stayed only long enough to hitch up a wagon for Mary Ann. She drove south to the safety of the Moore ranch on Pinal Creek, taking her children with her. The more seriously wounded men were transported by buckboard for medical help. J.T. Moore sent the wounded men to a doctor in Globe. Subsequently Boyer, Cody and Stevens, crossing into New Mexico, died from blood poisoning.

News of the raid reached the nearby Haigler Ranch and by the end of the day the news had spread through all the ranches in Pleasant Valley. Later that same day the news reached Payson and on the afternoon of September 3, Justice of the Peace John Meadows whose office was in Payson, along with a small posse of six men arrived at the Tewksbury ranch, to perform an inquest on the bodies of John Tewksbury and Bill Jacobs.

Traveling with the posse was a very large man by the name of Tom Wagner, who ran horses at Baker Butte for a rancher. Wagner never forgot the horrible scene where they found bodies torn apart and partly devoured by wild hogs after the Tewksbury's fled. Digging a common grave, all they could do was shovel the scattered body pieces into it.

Below are three photos of John Tewksbury, Mary Ann, in the middle and Edwin Tewksbury on the right were given to the author with permission to use in this book, by the Tewksbury family historian, Bill Brown.

John Tewksbury MaryAnn Tewksbury Edwin Tewksbury

Below is a closer picture of J.D. Tewksbury's cabin, supplied by Tewksbury family Historian Bill Brown. This picture was taken in the 1940's. That is Bill's grandmother Bertha Tewksbury standing next to Jesse Ellison, Jr.

Chapter Five
L.J. Horton, Freighter

In the next several chapters the author will present the history of Pleasant Valley that was recorded by L.J. Horton, who was a freighter in Tonto Basin and was friendly with both Ed Tewksbury and Tom Graham during the Pleasant Valley War. Horton was living in the Arizona Pioneer Home in Prescott during the 1920s, when he recorded memories that would become part of the Arizona Historical Journal. This author has already touched on some of Mr. Horton's experiences as he was located just a few miles north of Payson, Arizona and traveled in and out of Pleasant Valley during the Indian wars which occurred from 1882 to 1884, then the Cattle Rustlers war against the settlers from 1883 through 1888. He explains the when, how and by whom the first sheep entered into the Tonto Basin, which was 1885. Mr. L.J. Horton's account and memory of the facts is vital for the reader to understand what it was like to live in Pleasant Valley and the surrounding Tonto Basin during those tumultuous times.

The author will now present the history of Pleaseant Valley as described by Mr. L.J. Horton a freighter, able to stay neutral during the Graham vs Tewksbury feud. Horton knew Tom Graham, along with Jim and Ed Tewksbury very well having dealt with them during this time period by hauling freight for each family. This author feels his written history of the Pleasant Valley War is very valuable. Again there will be some redundancy but there are a lot of new facts presented in this written history. So here we go!

Horton starts the journey to record his history with a visit with his old friends the Martin brothers, who were also settlers in Pleasant Valley. He starts his history from the day he met the Martin brothers at the Fourth of July celebration in Prescott, 1921, and says he had a long visit with them. One of the brothers, he writes, he had not seen since the feud ended in Pleasant Valley on September 12, 1888, when Tom Graham moved to Tempe, Arizona. Both brothers were married and are highly respected citizens of Prescott. Horton said they talked about the days they were side by side through that long and bitter struggle. And which for the past thirty-five years has left an unjust and untruthful stain against them, and how he is proud that they can go to court and prove the false accusations filed against them.

Below is a copy of the letter from Arizona State Historian James H. McClintock in a letter to L.J. Horton:

> *June 8, 1922*
> *Mr. L.J. Horton,*
> *2011 W. Madison St.*
> *Phoenix, Arizona*
>
> *My Dear Sir,*
> *I would be pleased indeed if you could drop into the office some day and give us the details of the Pleasant Valley War. We are rather short in material concerning that struggle, owing to the fact that most of the men who know anything about it cannot very well talk about it.*
>
> *Very Sincerely,*
> *James H. McClintock*
> *Arizona State Historian*

The above letter from the state historian shows that it has a double meaning. First by admitting that the history of Tonto Basin and the Pleasant Valley War had been lost, and second it did not state how or why the history became lost. After showing the letter to his friends they said;

> "It is our duty that some of us that know the true facts, and a duty to mankind to furnish that history and as you are the only man who furnished the freight to us settlers during that long struggle you should, and we will assist you in every way we can. We want you to write it from day to day as you passed through it."

Mr. Horton went on to say;

> "I will not only write the history of that long and bitter struggle but I will also write the history of what I had found out while I was investigating the best way to enter Tonto Basin."

Below and over the next few pages is the written history of the Tonto Basin and the Pleasant Valley war as experienced and recorded by L.J. Horton

In the year 1864 the first white man, King S. Woolsey, with two hundred citizens fought their way down Tonto Creek and made the famous Pinole Treaty or the Massacre at Bloody Tanks but were able to fight their way out. The true history of how King S. Woolsey came to go into Tonto Basin was told to L. J. Horton, and Marion Derrick. Both were original Tonto Basin pioneers and were neighbors and friends and also fought side by side in the early days, and of course during the Pleasant Valley War.

During the years of 1863 and 1864 Marion Derrick was hauling freight with ox teams from California. He always stopped at Woolsey's station on the Gila River about three miles east of Agua Caliente.

In the spring of 1864 the Apaches raided Derrick's outfit, drove off his teams and destroyed his wagons and all of his freight. Marion Derrick appealed to Colonel Woolsey, who ad been an Indian scout with

General George Crook, who said;

> "That old Apache Chief Nana has always broken all treaties, but I think I can make one with him that will stand."

Marion Derrick writes in his memoirs that it was about the first of August in 1864, when they left with 200 men and followed the trail over what is now known as Reno Pass;

> "*Just as we passed the rim of that mountain that old chief Nana and his braves fought us all the way to where Roosevelt Dam now sits. Then as usual he displayed a white flag and asked for peace. The warriors were held back until after his talk with us before they decided on the next move. I did not know what Woolsey intended to do until I saw both chiefs advance. I also saw Woolsey extend his little sack of Pinole as a token of friendship with his left hand and draw his pistol with his right and fire. Then the chief fell, preventing him from ever breaking the Pinole treaty. Then we had to fight our way out of there.*"

No white man ever entered that sacred warring ground until 1867. Captain Hancock of Phoenix, whose boy Harry is a prominent engineer of the city at the present time, said;

> "*I will tell you how I came to name that creek and valley Greenback Creek and Greenback Valley. You came to interview a man who can give you information as to how to get into the valley because in the year 1867, I had organized a company of Pima Indians to fight the Apaches stealing their ponies,*

> blankets and other goods. They were afraid to venture unless I would go with them as their chief guide."

On the last day of August 1867, Horton and his family left Phoenix, on their way to Pleasant Valley. We followed the trail over what is now Reno Pass, thence down Tonto Creek to the first creek coming in from the north of the Sierra Ancha Mountains, then we headed up the creek about eight miles to a very rough box or gulch. Then we continued through three miles to where it opened out into a valley or meadow land, about two hundred acres. It was the most beautiful place I ever saw with all kinds of wild fruit, where grew wild potatoes and wild tobacco of which I myself enjoyed smoking many a pipe.

The Pima Indians with us had muffled their ponies' feet when we were within a short distance of the Apache camps, before they realized we were approaching. When we came into the camps there were fresh fires burning, small tracks and large, Indian baskets of grass seed and acorns.

At that point, fresh fires commenced to burn a short distance back of the Indian huts; then we heard arrows whiz by us again. Mr. Hancock told the Pima Indians not to expose any of their new improved fire arms.

The Pima Indians with us knew the Apaches intended to make a desperate attack as soon as they got the distance to our location. At the same time the Pima were in the process of locating the Apaches, who were hidden in a bunch of weeds or tufts of grass, where their arrows were coming from. After the first rain of arrows, Hancock ordered the Pima to open fire from their repeating rifles. Ponies pitched forward, dogs yelped as the Indian warriors whooped and scattered in all directions. About three o'clock that afternoon the fight was over.

While the Pima were gathering the ponies and plunder, Hancock, with a long stick was poking in among the rags and scraps of paper. He came across a rolled up nicely tied piece of denim. He unrolled it, and found it and found a bunch of greenback dollars, the money was named the valley Greenback Valley and the creek Greenback Creek, and from then on paper currency has always retained that slang name.

In the year of 1880 Old Fort Reno was re-established. I had read the report of the three Salt River farmers, Jose Greenhall, John Montgomery, and a man that I only knew his last name Robinson, all of whom were dairymen. When they heard about the amazing possibilities that existed in Pleasant Valley, that lay only sixty miles north of Globe, they knew they could make a living churning butter and selling it to the locals for one dollar a pound. They knew they had to attempt to settle, knowing the Apaches would attack them which they did, wounding Robinson with a shot through his lungs with an arrow. But the three men were able to escape to Fort Reno for medical help for their friend. The Apaches considered Pleasant Valley a sacred place and they did not want any white men there.

In 1881 the Middleton family came into Pleasant Valley, entering from the north, and settled close to the Mogollon Rim in the upper part of Pleasant Valley. They came in the fall and in the spring of 1882 they built a log house and a milk cellar.

Indians came about but were apparently friendly and old man Middleton loaned some cooking utensils to a group of them. In July, a neighbor, a young man who was engaged to be married to Middleton's daughter, came over and told the old man that the Indians were on the warpath. The old man could not believe it and said;

"Oh no, those Indians are friendly Indians."

The young man, thinking he had been misinformed sat down on a bench beside the young lady whom he expected to marry. Middleton went to the milk cellar and as soon as he was gone the Indians fired over the gate with bows and arrows killing both the young people and wounding the old man when he came out of the cellar, after he heard the noise.

The story of how the aged man and the surviving members of the family reached Globe two days after the slaughter was something short of amazing. The attacking Apaches were from the band of the famous Chief Victorio.

The Apaches fought with the United States over twenty years before they gave up their cherished hunting ground called Tonto Basin. They clung especially to that part just below the eastern rim of the Mogollon Rim, where existed a series of protected meadows, an amazing place to farm and raise stock, it was called Pleasant Valley. For ages the Apaches used the beautiful area for the retreat, a place where they could hide and enjoy their stolen goods and captives as well as it was effectively easy to defend from approaching enemy.

On July 9, 1882, part of a band of renegade Apaches lead by the White Mountain Apache Chief Natiotish, jumped off the San Carlos Reservation after the melee at Turkey Creek, in which a medicine man was shot by the army for trying to raise the old chiefs from the dead so the Apaches could go back to the old ways. Geronimo also jumped the reservation taking with him forty other renegades and headed south. Chief Natiotish left with about eighty renegades at the same time but he headed north and followed Cherry Creek. When they entered Pleasant Valley the first ranch they attacked was the Sigsby brother's ranch, killing Frank and Charlie, then a few miles upstream they attacked the ranch owned by the Houdon brothers. One brother, Bob Sigsby was shot through the lungs but he escaped to the house and stood them off for four days with no food, and only milk to drink.

On July 15, 1882, after reaching the East Verde River confluence of Cherry Creek, Natiotish led another charge on the Meadows family ranch about fifteen miles away from where the river and creek meet, along the East Verde River heading west to catch the trail that led up to the top of the Mogollon Rim and set up camp at General Springs. The Meadows family ranch was directly in the path of Natiotish and his band of renegades as it lay along the north side of the East Verde River. There was no question about it, Natiotish and his raiding party would stop and try to replenish their supplies at the expense of the Meadows.

Below is the story of the attack as Mrs. Meadows explained it to their friend Mr. L.J. Horton;

> *"It was early in the morning and we heard the dogs barking. My husband said, 'I think the dogs have a bear at bay. I'll take my gun and go over there and kill it,*
>
> *I saw him pass that bare spot in front of the cabin and just as he entered the vines on the other side of the clearing the Indians opened fire. I saw him fall. They kept up a continuous battle, whooping and continually firing bullets on the house. Our boys rushed out with guns to save their pa; the kicking up of the sand around them showed how thick the bullets were falling. I could not see how they got back to the house without being shot all to pieces.*

Harry, our oldest, had always directed all the work; he had us pile up sacks of flour, or any other sacks we could find, in such a way as to furnish protection from any stray bullets. The Indians kept up the battle for about a half hour then they laid off for about the same length of time.

During that time, I was so excited, I did not know what had taken place but I noticed that the boys looked pale. John came to me and said, 'Ma, can you get me some splints?' I said yes then, 'what is the matter?' John said, 'my arm is shot to pieces. I need splints to fix it.'

It was later learned that John had received five wounds but he only mentioned the arm to his mother, it being the wound that had to have immediate attention.

While I was fixing Johns arm Henry was giving orders to Sarah Hazelton saying, 'Our guns are broken, we have none. Take that old single barreled shotgun, put a little powder, crawl up on those sacks and when the Indians are not making any noise shoot it off. It is only a bluff; we want them to believe we have lots of guns.'

A little later my son Henry came to me and said, 'Ma, have you a pair of scissors? Yes, here they are.' He made a quick movement and I saw something fall to the floor. It was part of his entrails. He said afterward that he knew he could not live long and that he wanted to save his mother and the children before he passed on.

The boys had not been able to bring in the body of their father as the bullets got them too soon. The Indians kept up the alternate firing and whooping until about eleven in the morning when John Gray, a nearby rancher, came down the trail. The Indians for some reason ceased firing and allowed him to see what had taken place and also allowed him to continue down to the post where he reported what he had seen.

Five men were all that could be spared from Fort McDonald, Marion Derrick an old Indian fighter who had been with King Woolsey in 1864, Carter Hazelton, and Frank Pethro and son, Abram (Arizona Charley) Meadows, arrived at Fort McDonald from Globe traveling by stagecoach. He had been there competing in a rodeo. There was also a soldier from Fort Reno, on leave for the day, who was stationed there and offered to go along.

The five men saddled and rode to Sidelia, seven miles, then from there another three miles to the fork of Hellgate Trail. Here Derrick halted and said, 'we are only five men coming here to attack the renegade Indians. We are forced to show them something new. We will leave that treacherous Diamond Gap pointing to it, where they have planned to slaughter us.'

He continued to the top of the mountain instead of through the gap, turning to the right until the house could be seen. Here he halted and said, 'I know that all savages that are surprised

> by the sound of repeating fire will take to the tall timber.' Mrs. Meadows told me that when she first heard the strange voices she thought the Indians had surrounded them. Then she listened and distinctly heard them say 'don't shoot, we are friends come to relieve you.
>
> There was great rejoicing but sad rejoicing. My husband was dead. My son Henry was mortally wounded. Son John had been shot five times. We rejoiced because we had been saved from the slow death of torture which would have been our fate if the Apaches had captured us."

The Meadows family had only been out of Fort McDonald one day. The men who helped move them to the ranch had returned to the fort the same day. No doubt the Indians had hidden nearby their cabin and watched them all the while they unloaded and settled into their cabin. Strangely confident and careless, Mr. Meadow had built his house some distance from the spring and his cattle corral off at another distance and also away from the water. More experienced settlers always connected house and corral and made sure of water inside one or the other.

Mrs. Meadows went on to say that when the dogs started barking, she immediately told her husband it was probably the escaped Indians that were on the warpath but the old man insisted it was a bear and that he would go out and kill it. Like dozens of other people who have been surprised by Indians he was strangely unsuspicious of the danger. His body was at first buried in a corner of the cabin but later Horton said, he dug up the body and took it to Payson to be buried next to their son Henry in the Payson cemetery. The soldier who had stopped by to warn them about the Indians, but arrived after the scene of the gun battle, helped them clean up, then he told them at about dusk that he had to go back to Fort Reno and rode away alone on a mule. He got there safely with only one bullet hole in his hat.

The Indians were finally subdued and almost exterminated in the region from both sides of the canyon at General Springs in the Battle of Big Dry Wash, where they were trapped in the pass by cavalry on both ends of the steep mountainous pass.

Below is a photo of the Meadows Ranch that was taken by the author. The old house is long gone. Note the spring in the middle of this picture that is twelve inches in diameter. It is one of the main supply of the East Verde River.

L.J. Horton was in charge of the Meadows estate. Mrs. Meadows lived only about two years after the raid on their ranch, she passed from natural causes. Horton said that he and his wife moved in with Mrs. Meadows at her request, about two weeks before she passed. At the time of her death, Horton found Abram (Arizona Charlie) and his brother Jim Meadows living in Yuma, and her sister Maggie, who was living near Phoenix.

After he arrived in Prescott in 1923, Horton found that a great many people believe the Pleasant Valley Range War was a sheep and cattlemen's war, but Horton knew there was a lot more to the story and he realized someone would have to set it straight.

Horton spent a great amount of time and money to gather up the facts and details that show and prove the Graham's were thieves and robbers before they ever came into Pleasant Valley in June of 1883. They were at the head of an organized band of renegades and criminals, who had been waiting for the settlers to clean out the Apache, then by hook or by crook were planning on taking back possession of Pleasant Valley, that they considered a sacred place.

L. J. Horton continues; both Tom and John Graham were originally from Iowa and were working at the Bloody Tank Gold Mine near Globe in 1882. In late June of 1883, they met Ed Tewksbury in a saloon, who talked them into coming up to Pleasant Valley. Warrants for their arrest for cattle rustling had been issued and were found by Horton issued in May of 1883, and were signed and notarized by Judge Hicks. This is further proof that the Grahams were a band of criminals long before they ever entered the Tonto Basin. When they arrived in Pleasant Valley there were three officers of the law, that served as constable, who were also tasked with keeping law and order, they were Dud Noland, Marion Derrick and Bill McDonald. They were given the task to serve the warrants and arrest Tom and John Graham.

The Grahams refused to surrender when they were served and armed to the hilt. They drove the officers carrying the warrants from the valley. The above criminal record of the Grahams was taken from the courts of Prescott, the Yavapai County Seat at that time. This happened three years before the sheep ever entered the Tonto Basin or Pleasant Valley, which provides evidence that it was not originally a sheep and cattlemen's war. It also provides compelling evidence that the Grahams were an organized band of criminals before they ever entered the valley.

The entry given by Judge Hicks is as follows: Territorial Annual Calendar; The Territory of Arizona vs John Graham and Thomas Graham; Warrants signed by Rush and Herndon, F.R. Dann, November 10, 1884. Both cases were indefinitely postponed. There is no statement as to what the crime was or where the warrants were issued.

Arizona Charlie Meadows wrote in a letter to Horton that the Yavapai County court recorder will have the trial records as to when James Stinson, with the Grahams as witnesses, was trying to prosecute the Tewksbury's for alleged cattle rustling. Arizona Charlie's letter relates to the death of his father in the Indian attack;

> *June 15, 1922*
> *Yuma, Arizona*
> *Mr. L. J. Horton, Phoenix, Arizona*
>
> *Dear Friend,*
>
> *My brother John has been dead three years now, so also are Jake and Mobbly our younger two brothers. I am still kicking along. The Indians raided our home in Diamond Valley, July 15, 1882, killing my father and mortally wounding my oldest brother Henry and also wounded John in five places. The boys got back to the house and with the women stood the Indians off. They had just raided the Sigsby ranch and killed Mr. Houdon and Charlie Sigsby and wounded Frank Sigsby. John as Justice of the Peace and coroner buried John Tewksbury and Frank Jacobs. I do not*

think that any of the Grahams prevented them from doing it but the men did not want to take the chances which would have been suicide. The women covered the bodies with blankets. I was there the day after the inquest serving bench warrants for witnesses for Sheriff William Mulvenon.

Best Wishes,
Arizona Charlie Meadows

    Horton also found another written report, that is actually a little off the subject, but does show how prime Pleasant Valley was for raising stock. Three Salt River farmers by the names of John Montgomery (who later was elected as the sheriff of Maricopa County), Jose Greenhall, and Bill Robinson talked about the wonderful dairy farm possibilities in the Tonto Basin. At this time butter was selling for one dollar a pound, only fifty miles from Pleasant Valley and the region was covered with bear grass and succulent plants as cattle feed. This was a place where milk cows and beef cattle would thrive. These men went into the valley in 1881 and were immediately attacked by Apaches with Robinson seriously receiving an arrow that was shot through his lungs. His wound did not entirely disable him and the three men were able to escape to Old Fort Reno, where Robinson received medical treatment and survived. Fort Reno had been re-established in 1880.

    Horton knew the government had been fighting the last wild savages, the Apaches of the Southwest United States for fifteen years and finally in 1880 had re-established Old Fort Reno, to provide protection for the residents. The same fort originally used by King Woolsey when he fought his way down Tonto Creek in 1864 and then fought his way out of the valley.

Horton, his family and three other families, knowing the unsuccessful attempts being made at entering into Pleasant Valley from the north, decided to come in from the south over Reno Pass. On a bright, sunny day of November the 4th of 1883, they left Phoenix and on November 7, they arrived at Round Valley, located eleven miles south of Tonto Basin.

That first night one of his horses was stolen and the next morning, as Horton was following the tracks, two soldiers from Fort Reno came up to him and said:

"Have you lost something?"

Horton said, as he pointed to the shod tracks;

"Yes, those tracks show that a horse thief has stolen my horse because no Apache ever puts shoes on his horse's feet. I came out here expecting to have Indians to fight but instead thieving rustlers have stolen one of my horses before I even get to the rim of the Tonto Basin."

The two soldiers spoke;

"We are soldiers and don't know much about the valley but the two men coming yonder are Pleasant Valley stockman and have been to the fort to report that rustlers are stealing their stock and they needed assistance from the army post to help run them in."

When the two riders rode up to Horton they introduced themselves as John and Edwin Tewksbury. It was the first time Horton met them. They asked Horton;

> "Give us a description of the stolen horse, because we are pretty sure we know where they took your horse. We are hot on the trail of those rustlers. This valley is a holding spot where they keep their stolen stock until they can sell them in Phoenix. When you get to the valley below we will be there with your horse."

When Horton arrived at the valley the two men were waiting or him. Horton asked;

> "How much do I owe you for returning my horse?"

They said;

> "Nothing at all,"

It was the friendly principle, which they showed the true men that endeared each of the Tewksbury's toward settlers. The men went on to say;

> "We have gotten those rustlers in a bad fix. We have recovered sixty-nine head of horses they have stolen and sold in Phoenix. There is a current warrant for their arrest in the hands of the authorities in Payson."

Early on the morning of November 1883 as Horton was on his way to Payson, Arizona, and passed by a beautiful high plateau a few miles north of the town. The plateau was several miles wide and there were a lot of wild patches of melons and other wild vegetable plants and it lay at a perfect farming level of the 4000 feet elevation. The plateau was composed of a series of a lot of little grassy good valleys that you could drive from one to another; often with the bottoms were covered with white clover and always fringed with timber where you never tired of wandering, especially when you occasionally would see a herd of deer or wild turkeys.

One day a neighbor settler, Marion Derrick and his wrangler Jack Siedell were showing Horton some of the places where Horton could locate a ranch. They pointed out a cow and a calf. Mr. Derrick said;

> "That calf must be nearly two years old. It has neither mark nor brand on it but as long as it stands by its mother's side with a brand, the rightful owner of the calf is never disputed. When rustlers steal the cow and put their brand on it, we call that mavericking. Unless the rustler is smart enough to get the calf out of the territory, at the time of our round up the calf will find its way back to its mother. We have only one law and that is justice."

Below is another photo taken by the author of part of the ranch land that was once owned by L.J. Horton.

Chapter Six
John Meadows and Tom Horn

L. J. Horton writes that his first experience with a rustler proved a great success. In other words, never trust them. Always demand the money in advance and keep all goods until you get the money in your hand. With that philosophy, Horton never had any trouble with them. Settlers never kept books but with Horton's way of doing business, he never lost a single cent. Whenever he sold a herd of steers, it might be one, two, or three years in a row, they always came forward with a broad smile and said:

> "How much do I owe you? They would extend their hand in friendship. Their last handshake was as warm as the handshake the first time we met."

In early 1883, Horton built a log home in the west end of the property that is pictured in the last chapter and located a few miles north of Payson. It is on a one hundred and sixty-acre parcel, that the government allowed each settler to own simply by registering his land claim. After building his home he proceeded to install fencing all around the ranch.

In the spring of 1884, Horton writes that L.J. planted his own patch of watermelons on the upper east end of the ranch that paralleled State Route 87, the Payson to Strawberry road near the wild melon patch. After the melons ripened a man by the name of Landing who claimed he was a cattle rustler, along with his wife and two children, pitched a tent on the other side of the melon patch. That land was not on Horton's land and was in fact land that was also available to be settled, so Horton never had a second thought about his presence. Each morning Horton would walk around the ranch to make sure wild horses did not damage his fences that kept his cattle inside his ranch pastures. Horton writes that he always carried a shotgun that he used to keep rabbits away from my farm land.

Several evenings after he first met Landing he came along and he greeted me in a friendly manner saying;

> "Would you like a piece of watermelon? Horton said yes, Landing immediately climbed over my fence, went into the melon patch and picked up a melon and handed it to Horton."

Then Landing pointed to his rifle saying;

> "From now on I will keep away all of the rabbits from this place."

Horton writes that he thanked Landing for his assistance. While they sat eating the melon Landing told Horton about the good shooting qualities of his gun and how he had just won a turkey at a shooting contest in Payson. As Horton turned to walk away Landing told Horton;

> "I have jumped this ranch because you have too much land on your property. Then he said I will not charge you for that melon this time but the next time you will have to pay fifty cents for a melon."

Horton turned around and walked back up close to him and said;

> "Will you please repeat what you just said to me? I think I did not understand you or may have heard you incorrectly?"

Landing stood up tall and said in a loud voice;

> "You have settled on too much land in your ranch and I have jumped this

> part of your ranch. The next melon you get from this watermelon patch you will pay me fifty cents for it. My name is Landing, and I am also a rustler and a black-smith. I am also the best shot in the Tonto Basin."
>
> "Mr. Landing, rustler, crack shot of the Tonto Basin," Horton said, "I have been on the frontier all of my life. I have seen or met all kinds of bad men. We old Californians have always looked on a rustler, sluice robber or claim jumper as the most degenerate type of criminal known to man. Usually we let them hang to the limb of a tree or threw them into the brush because they were not worth digging a hole to bury them in. Now Mr. claim-jumper, I will tell you what I will do to you. You can camp here as long as you like, but if I find a melon rind in front of your camp, I will hold you responsible for it and I will attend to you in the proper manner, do you understand?"

Horton turned his back on Landing and had walked about sixty yards when he distinctly heard the cocking of a rifle;

> "Horton turned around just in time to see Landing taking deadly aim at his back. Horton rushed toward Landing at full speed with his shotgun in hand aimed in Landing's direction. Horton said he knew he had to close the distance between he and Landing in order to kill him with the double barreled shotgun and he only had five shells with him as he made his evening rounds of his property. But to Horton's surprise

when Landing saw him coming toward him at full speed with both barrels cocked, he trembled and shook so badly that he could not hold his gun up. He banged away and kicked up dust close to his feet then he jumped behind his wife. She held up her petticoats to shield him, Horton said he thrust his shotgun around her hunting for a vital place to discharge the gun because it was a case of kill or be killed. Horton saw Landing's wife tremble and stated loudly; 'Please don't shoot, please don't shoot my husband."

Just then a little boy about eight years old came running up and said;

"Mister, mister, please don't shoot my pa! Horton said he stopped, looked at him and said, 'I won't have to shoot your pa if he will give me that rifle.' As soon as Horton uttered those words the stock of the gun was shoved out from under his wife's petticoats and Horton said he grabbed it, saying 'give me the ammunition belt as well.' This was also shoved out to him. Horton took the rifle and struck it on a nearby rock bending it like a hoop. The lady asked again: "You will not kill my husband? No, Horton said, 'I will not' he answered."

The woman then stepped to the side, exposing Landing standing there trembling, quivering and too badly scared to stand up. He said to the lady;

"I won't kill the dirty lowlife claim jumper. He isn't worth the powder to blow his worthless ass outta this valley.

Now my lady, since you have the sand to save that dirty dude, I will talk to you. If that treacherous dude ever leaves one melon rind in front of this camp, I will settle the matter with him."

Horton also writes about some of the blood-curdling crimes committed over the next three years by what he calls an organized band of Graham rustlers and murderers, before a sheep ever entered the Tonto Basin, by providing the day and date of each crime committed, along with how many men were killed. There are conflicting reports but by Horton's count there are the bones of over sixty dead rustlers laying bleached by the sun on the ground in that little place ironically called Pleasant Valley. Henry Martin, who took the place of the Spanish herder, who was killed on his way to the valley from Flagstaff transporting the Daggs brothers' sheep, figured by his count in 1885 that there were thirty-six killed during the range war to that date.

John Meadows, the Justice of the Peace and County Coroner in Payson at the time of the Pleasant Valley War records indicate the body count on both sides to be thirty-four men murdered, including their names, dates of death and where they were killed. L.J. Horton's count of the dead is also thirty-four men, the same as John Meadows.

Some folks ask why Horton decided to come forward after so much time had passed since these events took place to share his experiences. To this there is a very simple explanation. The fear of dark alley assassins sealed our lips and prevented them all from talking about the range war for the last thirty-four years. Horton goes on to write that we knew that there were some left alive, who were just as full of revenge as those men who are dead and gone.

Knowing of the above possibilities, Horton writes that he hired a well-known official, Judge Charles

Payne Hicks (1858-1895), a Superior Court Judge, whose office was in the Territorial Capital, Prescott, Arizona Territory. Together Horton and Hicks were able to gather the facts and dates of each crime and death in from records in Prescott, Payson, Phoenix, McDowell, Tempe and other sources. The facts show that from 1883 to 1886 the Grahams and their followers were the most revenge driven and thoroughly organized band of criminals. They were prepared to commit any and all kinds of crimes and each one carried large rewards for their capture.

The Grahams actually went to the extent of hiring a noted criminal letter writer by the name of Llewellyn, who sometimes lived in Prescott but most of the time lived in Phoenix. It was his job to write letters showing the good character of the Grahams and the bad character of the Tewksbury's. These letters were written to deceive the public by constantly keeping before them such statements as the following;

> *"Tom Graham, one of Tempe's most prosperous farmers, who married a minister's daughter, has returned from one of his large stock ranches in Pleasant Valley and reports that the thieving half-breed Indians, the Tewksbury's, were stealing his stock and that he is now prosecuting them in a Prescott court."*

James Stinson, the largest cowman in Pleasant Valley did have Tom Graham arrested for perjury, because he gave false testimony to the court on a cow stealing charge against the Tewksbury's. Graham acknowledged his guilt by giving and paying a bond rather than face the charge in open court.

Tom Graham did in fact marry a minister's daughter but it was at the point of a gun, so to say, because he was behind bars, *(considered today as a shotgun wedding)*. The Grahams had a dark alley partner by the name of Charlie Duesha, who pointed with pride to the many bullet and knife scars on his body but no one ever saw his opponent because he always silenced his struggling victims before he left them.

One night Charlie Duesha was sent by Tom Graham across Pleasant Valley some fifteen miles to Horton's friend Henry Martin's ranch. He asked Martin if he could speak to a cowboy that worked for him by the name of Chris Jerkensen. Henry told Charlie that the young man works as a cowboy for him but was out on one of his ranges, tending to my cattle. Duesha told Martin to tell Jerkensen that he would be back here tomorrow and wanted to see him on business. Henry Martin told L.J. Horton, that when Chris came in that night he informed Chris what had happened, that Charlie Duesha had come by to see him and left him the message he was coming back to see him on business the next day.

Henry Martin told Chris that if Duesha was looking for him that it was not a good thing and Martin advised Chris to leave the territory, immediately. As Chris rode away he told Henry;

> *"I do not know what the Graham's have against me, because I don't know them and I have never spoke an ill word or done anything wrong against them."*

According to Martin, the next day Tom and John Graham along with Charlie Duesha, came to Martin's ranch looking for Chris and rode all around the property before they left. My friend Henry Martin saw them but they didn't see him. From what Horton was told by Martin, Chris was able to escape the wrath of Tom Graham and his men. The reason was never discovered as to why Tom Graham, his brother John and Charlie Duesha were so set on finding Chris Jerkensen, but they definitely were looking for him and it was not on normal business. It was obvious they had something bad in store for Jerkensen.

In the spring of 1885 the Tewksbury's and William Jacobs went into the sheep business hoping that the Grahams would leave them alone if they were not raising cattle. They leased a large herd of sheep from the Daggs brothers, the territory's major sheep raisers whose headquarters and grazing land was just outside of Flagstaff. Before the herd of sheep even entered the Tonto Basin the Spanish herder was shot by Graham rustlers. By the fall of 1885 the Tewksbury's were heavy in the sheep business.

At about the same time a cattle rustler by the name of Gladden also arrived in Payson in late 1885. He was looking for a half-breed sheep herder who was spending money lavishly. He insisted upon meeting the head officials of Payson. Upon being introduced to Emory Chilton, the Yavapai County Deputy Sheriff, whose office was located in Payson along with John Meadows, Justice of Peace and Coroner, Gladden said:

> "I have killed two men, I had to do it. I will not be arrested by you or anyone else."

While he talked, he patted his gun in a significant manner. Then he insisted on treating the crowd in a saloon called Basic's Beer Saloon. After everyone had been poured their drink, including Horton, who was present that day in that very saloon, Gladden, leaned forward and looked down the line to Ed Tewksbury and said loudly:

> "Here's where I draw the line. I will not buy or drink with a black man."

The mother of the Tewksbury boys was a California Indian squaw and his father was Irish, so Ed was quite dark. The family was among the earliest settlers in Pleasant Valley and always stood for justice. Ed was always well dressed, usually wearing gloves. As Gladden spoke, Ed quietly removed his gloves and placed them in his pocket. Then he walked down the line and confronted Gladden, slapping him soundly on both sides of his face, paused a moment, and repeated the punishment again, saying loudly so every man in the bar could hear;

> "If you can't use both of your guns then just draw either of them."

Gladden made no attempt to draw either of the guns in his belt but once on his feet, he ran out of the saloon with his hands extended up and hollering as he ran:

> "Give me my rifle, give me my rifle!"

After Horton left the saloon a fellow guest at the Pioneer Home, George Goliard, told Horton that he was also present at that saloon the day Gladden came in.

Ed Tewksbury saw Gladden and told him to walk down the road to the right distance and then turn and we will shoot it out but Gladden kept going neither stopping nor looking around. Horton went on to say;

> "That was the last of Gladden who had come into Payson to run a bluff and try to scare us".

There were only three really rough trails entering Pleasant Valley. The upper trail, just below the Mogollon Rim at his father W.B. Horton's ranch, which lay on the creek named after his father, Horton Creek. L.J. Horton, the writer of this dissertation writes that a few miles to the south was the dead line between the two factions; then five miles below down the gulch was a trail known as the Hellgate Trail. And in the southwest part of the valley, coming from Lower Tonto was the Jerked Beef Butte or the Houdon trail. This was an ideal retreat for the Graham band as soon as they could drive the original settlers out of Pleasant Valley.

A man by the name of Converse helped me build my cabin and the corral. After we finished the construction he left and headed back to his home in Flagstaff. He traveled on the upper trail under the Mogollon Rim to where the trail connected with the road at Strawberry, now State Route 87, from there to the top of the Rim. At that point he fell in with a stranger, who said he was on his way to Flagstaff and asked Converse if he could ride along with him.

> *"Converse told Horton that the stranger and he traveled along together. Along the ride they came to a sheep camp. The stranger with whom he traveled swapped horses with the sheep man getting ten dollars to boot. The sheep man took forty dollars out and gave the stranger ten and replaced the balance in his pocket. Horton said they resumed their journey. A little while later the stranger said he had lost his note book and suggested that Horton ride on a while he would go back to see if he could find the notebook. About forty-five minutes later the stranger came back shortly and said he had found it. We jogged along for a while; presently the stranger said; there is water down there. I think we had better camp. It was a tank where lots of stock watered which completely covered our tracks."*

In the morning the stranger took from a sack on the back of his saddle a horseshoeing outfit. He then took off his horse's shoes and turned them around so the tracks of the animal showed that he was going south to Payson instead of north to Flagstaff. We had not traveled more than a mile when he said;

> "Well, here is where I say goodbye and then he headed westward."

Converse told Horton that he continued on the road north for about three hours. Then two officers came up and placed him under arrest. They told him they had been following his tracks. One of the officers elaborated by telling Converse they actually followed his tracks from where a sheep man had been murdered and robbed the day before. Converse told Horton later;

> *"They took me back to where the sheep man was murdered and found out they were after the wrong man. Converse told me when he returned to my ranch. He said they turned him loose and told him to go back to his friend L.J. Horton, and wait there as they might need to use me as a witness when they caught up to the stranger. After Converse described the stranger, the deputies told him that the stranger was Andy Cooper, whose real name was Cooper Blevins"*

In a day or two a man armed to the hilt came to the door of a log cabin owned by one of Horton's neighbors in Pleasant Valley. There was no one at home but the woman of the house. The man entered the cabin and explained to the woman that he was being pursued by officers.

> "I am tired so I'll fight it out here. You can go out into the timber where you will be safe. He sat down, placed his guns across his knees, and partly closed the door, awaiting the coming of the officers. Within minutes the officers rode up to the front of the cabin, dismounted then they knocked at the door.
>
> Come in, said the same stranger who had been riding with Converse. They pushed the door open. 'I am Cooper Blevins, said the stranger, the man you officers have been looking for. Can I do anything for you?' The officers told him they would see him later and they rode away."

The woman in the cabin told Horton later that one of the deputies was Apache County Deputy Sheriff Will Barnes. A few months later on August 28, 1887, Cooper Blevins, aka Andy Cooper, attempted the same strategy with Apache County Sheriff Commodore Perry Owens in Holbrook. From the written report of his deputy Will Barnes, the sheriff knew they were going to ambush him so he kicked open the door and when the three men went for their guns, he fired killing Cooper Blevins and two of his younger brothers along with wounding the third brother that was present. I will go into this gunfight in great detail later in this book.

This notorious horse and cattle thief, Cooper Blevins, who came so near getting my friend Converse convicted of the murder of the sheep man, which he himself had committed, thought he could commit any crime and escape, then go down to the Graham stronghold, where with the protection of the Graham faction, he would be safe from all law. He made only one mistake, going to Holbrook, which was not part of the Graham Stronghold.

Converse came back to Horton's house as requested by the officers. Finally, after a couple of days he resumed his journey to his home in Flagstaff. Fresh horse tracks indicated our place was being watched while he was staying at our (Horton) ranch. When Converse left he agreed to drop me a line so I would know if anything happened to him on the way out of Pleasant Valley. I never heard from him again or from the officers who had sent him back to wait the summons as a witness in the killing of the sheep man. Horton believes that the cold blooded murderer, Cooper Blevins, probably waylaid and killed the two officers and then watched around Horton's house and killed Converse when he left the second time for Flagstaff, to cover up the last trace of evidence of the murder of the sheep man for a lousy thirty dollars. Horton said he really has no proof but he did find out that Converse was shot to death and the two officers never made it back to Payson. They may have simply run out of the territory and Horton said he can't blame them for getting out of the territory, if in fact they really did leave.

The case for the murder of all three though can be made from the fact that as soon as Andy Cooper arrived back in Pleasant Valley, the Grahams sent him around with that infamous contract that read as follows:

> "We, the stockmen of Pleasant Valley, who have signed our names below, agree to pay Andy Cooper fifty dollars for each and every one of the Tewksbury scalps."

The Grahams knew that they were safe in carrying out the above contract because anyone who lived there at that time knew that it would mean sure death for any man, unless he belonged to the Graham rustlers, to enter the Valley. And it is an historical fact that can be verified by a dozen or more men of that date who saw and read the notice.

We have further proof of when the above contract was presented to all of our neighbors. One neighbor signed it through fear and under duress, and he left Pleasant Valley the next day. Another neighbor George Haigler, of which Haigler Creek is named after, would not sign the contract and was forced to leave his home. J.D. Tewksbury, the patriarch of the Tewksbury brothers fled to the Salt River Valley and became one of the largest sheep man in the Arizona Territory. Deputy Sheriff McFadden, also living in Tonto Basin, whose business it was to assist in arresting criminals was forced out of Pleasant Valley by overwhelming odds and driven from his home. He and his family stopped by my home on their way to the Salt River Valley.

There were only four old-time settlers left in Pleasant Valley, who were in the way of the Graham rustlers, who had not yet been forced into the fight or forced to be on the Graham's side of the feud but they were all served the same famous notice:

"You will be killed on sight."

They were, L.J. Horton, Al Tompkins, Marion Derrick and James Piatt. Derrick and Piatt both lived at the entrance to Pleasant Valley on the Hellgate Trail. Tompkins lived with three miles of my home on the upper trail of the middle prong of Tonto Creek. Horton writes:

The four of us along with the Tewksbury's had all met a notorious rustler by the name of John Booth. Booth had previously tried to buy my ranch, and prevented me from jumping the place of an absent neighbor. We met him on the trail as he was coming in with his cattle, twenty or thirty head of odds and ends with all sorts of brands, and throwing our guns on him we turned him back and told him to keep going. We found out that a large reward had been placed on his head and we believe one of his fellow rustlers turned him in for the reward. Honor among thieves? In any event he was hung before he ever went to trial.

About the beginning of the first of August in the year 1887, my neighbors James Piatt, Marion Derrick and Jim Roberts, who later became a Yavapai County Deputy Sheriff stationed at Jerome and I were notified that the Graham's were coming after our horses. At that point all four of us ranchers were located on the west side of the dead line of the war zone on Horton's Creek, we managed to avoid being drawn into the war.

The four of us knew that if the Graham faction succeeded in stealing our stock, and if we attempted to recover it, the rustlers would show us no mercy. They had stolen over a hundred head of cattle from me. I could not afford to lose my horses, being the main asset in my freighting business that I now depended entirely on to make a living, because almost all of my cattle had been stolen.

Horton drove his horses into the corral that was built out of huge pine logs to protect the stock from Indians. His house and the creek water were at the back part of the corral because nearly all of the other settlers built their homes so the water and house were in separate places but men had been killed going from one to the other.

Horton placed his guns so that the barrels protruded out between the logs and then hid in a dark, shadowy part of the corral to await the coming of the robbers. In the morning he found a lot of ropes, picket pins, and hobbles lying on the ground within twenty feet of the big pole bars. Tracks about the spot showed that the robbers had laid them down at that point they tiptoed over the logs to a point from which they could not have failed to see the gun barrels protruding from the corral fences. It must have looked pretty spooky to them for they did not even stop to pick up their ropes, but tiptoed back to a big pine tree and then down to where they had left their horses. They continued from there over to Jim Roberts' ranch three miles west and stole his horses. The next day he trailed them to the rustler's headquarters. When he arrived they told him that if he came back he would be killed on sight.

During the day all four ranchers were on constant guard when meeting strangers in order to know whether we were talking to friendly settlers or rustlers. Also around the end of the first week in August again in 1887, Horton received a warning that the rustlers again were coming to take his horses. A well armed stranger riding a fine horse stopped at his ranch in the middle of the afternoon. He dismounted and said to Horton;

> "Where can I stake my horse? If it is ok I have been riding all day and would it be ok if I stay here tonight?"

Again it was a way of life on the frontier to be hospitable to others by providing a meal or two and a place to rest. Horton immediately said;

> "'All right, you can find a good staking down there next to the corral in the little barn that holds my hay."

After a while Horton rang the dinner bell and told the man that supper was ready. The stranger came in but went out again as soon as he had finished his meal. By this time Horton was sure the stranger was one of the Graham rustlers, because only the rustlers rode the range prepared for action and this man was definitely armed and ready for action.

The next morning when the stranger came in for breakfast, he sat down on the opposite side of the fireplace from Horton and watched him closely as he asked the following questions;

"Do you know the Grahams?"

Horton said yes. Then the stranger asked Horton,

"Do you know the Tewksbury's?"

Horton told him that had met them. Then the stranger asked Horton,

"Do you know the Drew's?"

Horton told the stranger, yes. Then the stranger asked Horton,

"When was the last time you saw them?"

Horton answered,

"Oh, it's been some time ago. I really don't remember the last time I saw him."

Then Horton writes that his wife was washing dishes and spoke in a surprised voice,

"What's the matter with you, L.J. she asked? They were both here last Sunday and made a long visit."

I thought the jig was up, but instead, the stranger came over and shook hands with me and spoke,

"Mrs. Drew is my sister and I will tell you what brings me here. I am a deputy sheriff from Apache County and I am looking for stolen horses and the rustlers who took them."

Horton was relieved and asked the man if he would take a friend's advice? The stranger answered,

> "Yes, I was just hoping you might be able to give me some information that might help me locate these rustlers."

Horton spoke to the stranger telling him that if he went across the dead line, that he would never come back. Then he told the man that it doesn't matter how fast you draw or straight you shoot or how brave you are. If you are a deputy sheriff looking for horse thieves, you will never live to reach your sister's house which is just over that ridge.

> "I will tell you what I will do. There are two stray horses around here. I don't want them about, as I am sure they are stolen stock and I do not want to be drawn into this war if I can help it. I will show you the stock. Maybe they are some of the ones you're looking for."

Horton said they both rode up the gulch and he pointed out the strays to the deputy. Sure enough, they were part of the bunch he was hunting. Horton advised him to go back to Strawberry that night, some twenty miles to the west, and he should not come back to Pleasant Valley until the war ended as his life was not safe. I told him sixty-nine head of horses had been stolen and had been traced through the Graham stronghold to Phoenix by deputies and reclaimed, if his errand had been suspected by the rustlers he would not have left the valley alive.

There was a speedy revenge planned for the brutal murders of Bill Jacobs and John Tewksbury by twelve settlers in Pleasant Valley after the report of the brutal murders had been handed to all of us by Justice of the Peace, John Meadows on his way out of the brutal death scene at the Tewksbury Ranch two days after the shootout took place. His report stated as follows;

> "I was held up twice coming in here and I do not know what may happen before I get back to Payson. I am handing you a copy of this report because I want to let the people know of the unbelievable conditions revealed to me by those two brothers, Tom and John Graham. After they had committed the most brutal murders known to man, they planned to shift their revenge from the men they had ambushed to the noble and feeble woman with a three-day old baby at her breast and for four days and nights, she was forced to take sheets from her bed and weigh them down with rocks to keep the hogs from eating them up. While those brutes rode the valley terrorizing the people, saying they would kill any man who helped the woman bury the murdered men."

Mary Anne Tewksbury then sent their friend, Jim Roberts, over to the Justice of the Peace and County Coroner, John Meadows, in Payson, twenty miles away to come and perform his duty and bury what was left of the bodies. She also instructed Jim, after delivering the message to Meadows, to continue over the mountains to Prescott and notify Yavapai County Sheriff William "Billy" Mulvenon that we, and all of the other settlers, would have to surrender to the rustlers, who were our mortal enemies unless we obtained help from Yavapai County or the United States Government.

When John Meadows reached Old Man J.D. Tewksbury's place, where John and his family were living and saw the situation. He set out to try to get some men to help him bury the bodies. According to the report he filed, the bodies were in terrible condition, for the men had been shot from behind as they were coming toward the house after gathering their horses from where they had been left the night before, near Cherry Creek and on their way back to the cabin with the horses. After being shot, their heads had been crushed with stones, to make it seem like Indians had done the killing.

John and Tom Graham rode all over the valley, warning the people against helping bury the dead men. There were a number of hogs in the region who had gone half wild and they tore the mangled bodies. Mrs. Tewksbury covered them as best as she could with sheets or blankets held down with stones.

The first man whom John Meadows tried to get to help him was a man he had known in Payson. This man was terribly afraid and begged John not to force him to go. He said;

> "I know you are the Justice of the Peace but my life is in danger. I have been warned by the Grahams that I would be killed on sight if I helped to bury the dead men."

Afterwards Justice Meadows and Mary Ann Tewksbury, John Tewksbury's widow, gathered up all the bones of the two men that they could find, and buried them. Having completed his work, Justice Meadows left Pleasant Valley thinking he would travel over the Hellgate Trail back to his office in Payson.

Before he arrived at the head of Hellgate Trail, he decided to cut across to the upper trail and stay at Horton's ranch for the night. This sudden change of mind saved his life and the life of L.J. Horton, because the gang had planned to waylay and murder Justice Meadows at the beginning of Hellgate Trail, so the report of the brutal murder would never reach the people. Ironically the news of his death was already printed in the Holbrook paper.

The next morning after Justice John Meadows left our ranch home. At this point in their lives LJ and his wife were living at his dads ranch north of Pleasant Valley. Horton said he rode down the creek to the place where the Hellgate began to look after his missing stock. Horton writes that he came back through the pine forest by way of the Platt ranch trail, when all of a sudden three heavily armed men drew their guns on him and told him to halt. All of us settlers were very guarded as to how we answered any questions put to us. The one who appeared to be the boss asked;

> "Do you know anything about John Meadows, the Justice of the Peace?" I said, "What is the matter with John Meadows? "He was murdered last night on Hellgate Trail. We have been down there and could not find any trace of him and you are just coming out. You are the man we want."

This was a very serious situation for Horton to be in. If he fell into the hands of the Grahams, Horton knew what to expect. If these were Sheriff Mulvenon's men, and thought Horton might be one of the Graham cowboys, and might be involved in the murder of Justice Meadows, there is no telling what they might do to him. When we met up with the other party who were coming toward us, the captain said,

> "Have you got him? Yes! I think we have the right man."

The leader of the party that had surrounded Horton answered. Then turning to Horton he commanded,

> "Tell the captain the same story you told me."

I told the captain of the group of men, that John Meadows was not dead. In fact he stayed at our ranch last night. Horton told these men he would tell them what ever he could to help them. He told them his name was L.J. Horton, and he lived just over the ridge. If they were willing to come with him to the top of the hill, they could see the chimney of his ranch house. Then he instructed the Captain to leave him on the ridge with a guard, and go down and ask to speak to his wife, Mrs. Horton about John Meadows. She will tell you that Justice Meadows did spent the night with them and left earlier that morning, at about nine o'clock and headed toward the upper Hellgate Trail that goes back to Payson.

The commander considered my suggestion for a moment and decided to follow my suggestion. Some of the men remained with me on the ridge, while the rest accompanied their captain down to our ranch house. They seemed satisfied with the result of their investigation for presently the captain beckoned us to come down to our cabin. Mrs. Horton looked up and waved her white apron and I could see she was not alarmed by this sudden visit of strange armed men.

When we reached the cabin, we learned that my wife invited the captain and his men to dinner and that he had accepted for the crowd. The captain told us that they were deputies under Yavapai County Sheriff Mulvenon and that he was on his way from Prescott over the southern trail to investigate the news report stating that John Meadows was killed, and it was his job to find the body of Justice of the Peace Meadows and bring those whom were guilty to justice.

The newspaper exposure, coming from John Meadows, the Justice of the Peace in Payson, the way it did, was the worst blow that could have happened to the rustlers because it showed the true facts, which had been kept from the people through terrorized fear so that those who did not live close to

Pleasant Valley had no idea the true conditions that existed in the valley. All that read the report by the sheriff said;

> "We will repeat what we did to the Indians at the Battle of Big Dry Wash. There were fifteen ringleaders who knowing the hangman's rope was waiting for them."

Here is what our neighbor Henry Martin reported to the sheriff after watching who came in and out of the Graham Stronghold the day before he arrived in Pleasant Valley. All day from two to six rustlers of lesser crimes left on the dog trot, winking and blinking at every bush they passed. The sheriff and his posse arrived at the stronghold at Pleasant Valley on September 13, 1887.

An official tally of the number of the men killed that day shows, that none of the rustlers lived long enough to get a hundred miles from the valley. This suggests that the settlers together with the law officers completely annihilated the last rustler as follows;

> "John Graham and another desperado who refused to surrender to the arrest warrants, when they were presented, decided to shoot it out and were riddled with bullets at the Graham stronghold. Rustlers Scott, Stott and Wilson were hung close to the stronghold. Rustler Tom Tucker and another desperado with him were both riddled with bullets near the old Tewksbury ranch in Pleasant Valley when they decided to shoot it out rather than surrender. Another Graham rustler Jack Booth was hung in Globe as I reported earlier in this report.

> *Andy Cooper, aka Cooper Blevins and three of his brothers who were present with the Grahams the eleven days of the standoff at the Tewksbury ranch were killed in Holbrook also as Horton mentioned in an earlier chapter. Charlie Duesha died in Phoenix in the late 1929 at a sanatorium from the gunshot wounds he received over the years to his lungs. Tom Graham was killed at Tempe. Ed Tewksbury was arrested for his murder but there was not enough evidence to indict him so he was released from custody."*

Yavapai County Sheriff William Mulvenon combed the countryside for three weeks looking for witnesses to help him sort out who killed thirty-four men. There was not one witness to ever testify in court, who ever saw a settler or a Tewksbury man draw a gun or shoot one single rustler, whose bones lay bleaching on the ground of that little place, ironically called Pleasant Valley. Judge Charles Hicks, a Yavapai County Probate Judge at that time, and several other men, who are now residents of the Pioneer Home were at the trial held in Prescott in 1888. They have all stated that every single one of the Tewksbury men, were turned loose and free of any crime committed in the Pleasant Valley War.

After they returned to their homes about the first week of August 1888, a seven-day cowboy tournament was staged in honor of those loyal and struggling settlers who had twice succeeded in saving the country, first by annihilating the last Apache renegade savages in the United States at the Battle of Big Dry Wash, where the settlers said that none but a dead Indian is a good Indian. Then on September 12, 1888 after five years of the most treacherous and most brutal warfare known to the southwest those same twelve settlers who knew no fear said only a dead rustler is a good rustler. It was a great gathering and will long be remembered, coming as it did at the close of that five year struggle.

Buckey O'Neill, publisher of the "The Hoof and Horn," a monthly newspaper, dedicated to the sale of cattle brands and other livestock, published in Prescott, Arizona, was present to report this event. Below is the article, presented from a copy that this author has in his research material, that was published in his paper of the roping contest and horserace to celebrate the exit of the rustlers in Pleasant Valley.

A Week's Sport at Payson

Payson, Arizona, November 5, 1888, by Buckey O'Neill, Editor of the Hoof and Horn- The following are the particulars of the grand time people have been having at Payson up to the present time.

The principle feature of the four day's sport was the horse race between Crowder and Hungry John. The race was won by Crowder and by a 45- foot margin. In the evening ball and supper was participated in by a number of ladies and gentleman.

The second day was spent in different sports, such as foot races, scrub races, (generally lambs, sheep, piglet or calves). In the afternoon a turkey and chicken shooting match took place; the fowls being furnished by Mr. Tackett.

The third day's sport began with roping and tying steers. The first prize of $50 was won by "Arizona Charlie"

Meadows; his time was 1 minute 24 and a half seconds. John Rhodes of Pleasant Valley was next, but had the misfortune to make a complete failure.

Next came Tom Horn, also of Pleasant Valley, winning the second prize of $25; his time was one minute and 47 seconds, doing very nice work. George Felton and his brother Ben of Rye, both brothers of O. C. Felton, the Deputy Yavapai County Sheriff in Payson, Arizona and Bob Samuels, of Rimrock, failed to tie their steers. The last man to enter the contest was John Gillen, of Payson who won the third prize, which was a fine pair of spurs; his time was two minutes and 23 seconds. The spurs were made and donated by Mr. C. Hackers of Prescott.

There were three contestants for the best lady rider. Miss Mollie Berchett winning the first prize of $25; Mrs. Bordman, winning the second place prize of $2.50 and Mrs. Gillen of Payson winning the third place prize of $1.50.

A contest of bronco riding was the last even on the program for the third day and was hotly contested by Gordon Felton and "Arizona" Charlie Meadows. Gordon Felton won first place and $25, Meadows winning second place and $15.

The fourth and last day's fun was concluded with a roping match between "Arizona" Charlie Meadows of Payson and Tom Horn, of Pleasant Valley. Each man to rope and tie three steers for $50 a side. Meadows won the event *in four minutes and 28 seconds to Horn's six minutes and 24 seconds. This final event sent the Pleasant Valley boy's home satisfied the Paysonites are still their superiors in roping, tying and riding.*

The picture on the next page of the contestants of the rodeo that took place in 1888 and not 1886, was taken by Buckey O'Neill, who was there to report for his paper the Hoof and Horn, while in Payson to celebrate the exit of the last of the rustlers from Pleasant Valley. Buckey in all probability was there for political purposes, to promote himself, since he was running for the position of Sheriff of Yavapai County.

This picture appeared in his Hoof and Horn newspaper along with the article above. It is a picture of the Tewksbury faction of the Pleasant Valley War, who competed in the celebration rodeo, and horse race event to celebrate the fact that the rustlers were gone from Tonto Basin and Pleasant Valley.

The photo below was supplied by Bill Brown, again the great grandson of John Tewksbury and step grandfather John Rhodes, who married Bill's great grandmother Mary Ann Tewksbury after John was brutally murdered by the Graham Faction.

Below is the letter from Gwendolyn Kimmel, also provided by Bill Brown, of the school teacher, who befriended Tom Horn in Wyoming when he first arrived there and who remained his good friend until his death. This letter is further proof that Tom Horn was in fact part of the Tewksbury faction of the Pleasant Valley War. With instructions from Tom Horn, she sent this letter to Ed Tewksbury inquiring as to Tom's involvement in the Pleasant Valley War (feud). A copy of this original letter, was given to the author by Bill Brown, again the great grandson of John Tewksbury. Sadly, his great uncle Edwin passed away April 4, 1904 from Tuberculosis and according to Bill, his great uncle never saw the letter before he passed.

Denver, Colorado
March 1st, 1904

Mr. Ed Tewksbury,
Globe, Arizona

My Dear Friend;
I feel that I must address you as such, for you and Tom Horn were close friends, and I was the best friend Tom ever had. You have doubtless heard of the school mam who taught the Miller-Nickell school. Well I am she. John Coble, also Tom's friend and I are together compiling a book about Tom, which will be published soon. This book is to consist of Tom's autobiography which he wrote while in jail, and of articles, John Coble, Judge Lacey, Attorney Burke and me. Next to Tom, I shall probably write the most. I wish you to give me a full account of your association with Tom, where, when and

how you met him, what your relations were together and all about the Tewksbury-Steward (Graham) feud. In his autobiography, Tom barely touches on the feud, because he brings this in near the end of his book, and he was hurried while writing the closing pages.

This however, was an important event in Tom's life, and I wish to give it its due attention in my narrative. Now remember, that I know next to nothing about the feud, so tell me explicitly all of its history. Perhaps you have some pictures that would be appropriate for the history of your and Tom's association. If so, I shall be very glad to get them. I think your picture ought to be in the book.

Perhaps you know of some friends of Tom's who could tell me interesting things about Tom. If so, do by all mean. Can you tell me where I can reach Mickey Free by letter? Tell me everything you can about Tom that will show him as what he was, a nervy, big hearted man. We want to set Tom right before the world, and by doing so we will punish his enemies, as I said the book is to be published in a few weeks, so give me the desired information as soon as possible. We are keeping the matter of the book as much a secret as possible, for we wish to spring it as a surprise on the public.

John Coble was in Denver today. He is to be married on March ninth. I am very glad he is going to have the happiness of "owning" a nice girl all by *himself, but my happiness is mixed with pain, for his marriage reminds me so vividly of my loss of Tom.*

Are you married? If so, how long have you been married? Have you any children? What is your occupation? This is curiosity I know, but I am interested in you because of the friendship between you and Tom. The lives of nearly all of Tom's friends in Wyoming have turned out so happily. Tom and I have been the ones to Suffer.

Tom once owned two small ranches in Arizona. Did he sell them? If so where? Where were they located? Did you ever hear of Tom's fighting a moonlight duel in Arizona or some neighboring place? If so, tell me about it. Tom once owned a mine in Arizona which he sold. Do you know what he did with the money? My only reason for wishing to know this is to get a better idea of his life.

Now I hope that because of your friendship for Tom you will answer all of my questions fully. This is perhaps the best thing you can ever do for poor Tom. I hope you have nothing to do with then newspaper reporters. With the best of wishes for you and your dear ones, I am your friend,

*(Miss) Gwendolyn Myrtle Kimmell,
No. 1644 Lincoln Avenue,
Denver, Colorado, March 1st, 1904.*

On the next page are photos of Gwendolyn Kimmel and Tom Horn taken in 1902, while Tom was waiting for his date with the hangman, having been convicted for the murder of Willie Nickell. Although Horn had a reputation as a killer, this author believes he was innocent of the murder of the fourteen-year old boy, but for sure he took a lot of lives over his career, the number of which has never been established. These two pictures were found in our National Archives.

L. J. Horton continues the story;

Folks came from all parts of the territory to see those twelve settlers and their families from that little place called Pleasant Valley, where a man's life was snuffed out at the wink of an eye. But this gathering was different from all other frontier life he ever saw because usually with gambling and drinking there would be bloody noses, a dead man or two. This gathering of men who knew no fear come into the saloons, pulled off their arms, hung them on a peg or hook, sat down at a gambling table, lost or won a hundred dollars, not a cross word or an unkind expression ever came from them.

The cause of the peaceable conditions that existed is easily explained. On September 11, 1888, after Horton had shown Justice John Meadows' report to the settlers, they all said again;

> "We will repeat to the rustlers just what we did to the Indians at the Battle of Dry Wash. All day long four to six at a time who had committed lesser crimes with a swinging trot, winking and blinking at every bush they passed by and before the sun went down all had skipped the country except fifteen that were shot or hung which completely annihilated to the last rustler."

Anytime during that seven-day contest if a rustler had come to town with all his arms it would have been impossible for him to live and cross the street, but when the settlers were free of that element, their home was every honest man's home, wild country of wild men at a wild time in Tonto Basin.

In the fall of 1887, Horton took an inventory of the stock he had left, including his present and future possibilities. Then as usual, every fall, he left to spend the winter in Phoenix. He was well pleased with his potential future. His records showed at that time he was milking 31 head of cows. He had not sold a steer or a cow. He had been able to keep all of his five year's increase. His freighting business more than paid all of the expenses. He had at different times added a few head from that source to the 133 head of his original stock.

The rustlers had stolen a good amount of cattle from him over the previous five years, but his current inventory showed that he should have 211 head of beef cattle with which he was very pleased. He knew he had selected the best range possible. This included the upper Tonto Basin, the northern forty miles of the Mogollon Rim, which towered over his property 2111 feet above his land which was a little over 5000 feet in elevation. His land was protected from blizzards where the breezes are continually shifting the clinging vines and flowers. And where seven underground rivers ranging from five to forty feet wide gush out from under that wonderful rim, and at different places disappear in a cavern where the sound of falling water is all that is left to indicate to anyone that water existed nearby.

Horton returned to his father's ranch in Tonto Basin on April 5, 1888, loaded with supplies. Along with his trail wagon he was also loaded with fruit trees and shrubbery to beautify his place. Everything looked the same as when he left in the fall of 1887, except for the fact that he could not find one single animal, nor were there any signs of cattle around the salt lick, a place he had prepared so the cattle could help themselves. He rode and searched the range for three months and failed to discover any cattle or any evidence of where they had been taken. In July Horton gave his shrubbery to his neighbor Charles Martin.

Once more in his life, like the blowing of a leaf, he was cast back with only the blind future to guide him. He never in all his wanderings had found a place that he had learned to love as well as he did Tonto Basin but some powers had willed that it should be his lot in life to go from one new county to another, subdue Indians and other rough elements and those that follow should be blessed with wealth and prosperity, largely from his own efforts.

Horton knew from the events that had taken place in the last four months would force him to seek some new endeavor, but what that would be and what kind of toil it would generate, he did not know. He had already spent one half of his life wandering and
searching the frontiers for new opportunities or new industries.

On the last day of October in 1888, Horton turned his cattle and range over to Mr. Ellison the father in law of Arizona Territorial Governor Hunt, who lived seven miles from Horton's ranch and now is living in

Phoenix stating;

> "I guess the rustlers have stolen all of my cattle. Do the best you can with my range and my cattle."

In 1891, Horton got a letter from Mr. Ellison saying;

> "Mr. Horton, I do not believe you have any cattle here. I herewith enclose eight dollars for one old cow. That was all I got out of that five years struggle with the rustlers."

L.J. Horton was an amazing historian. He was able to stay neutral along with his neighbor William Colcord and the Houdan Brothers. They along with Jim Roberts, lived just below the Mogollon Rim in the Tonto Basin just north and east of the town of Payson, Arizona. Horton Creek is named after his family. L.J. Horton from the request of James McClintock, our first Arizona historian sent a letter to Horton asking him to record his recollections of the Pleasant Valley War. A copy of the letter is part of this author's research along with a full documentary of his life that was also sent to McClintock.

Chapter Seven
Back Alley Assassin

Old timers call it Duesha Canyon. It is located a couple of miles West of the town of Aguila, Arizona along Arizona State Highway 60, a favorite route of folks traveling from Phoenix to Las Vegas, Nevada. The Canyon is named after Charlie Duesha, who came into the Arizona Territory in the 1880's. Charlie Duesha was a man who was hard to kill, but did his share of killing.

He is said to have killed thirty-two men in his illustrious career as a gunman. He claimed that number in conversations at various times and at other times he claimed that he could not remember the exact number of men he killed. Most of the killings were not recorded. There is no paper trail of the dead men Duesha claimed to have left in California, Texas, Nevada, Kansas or in Pleasant Valley.

Duesha was an Old West enigma for sure. Those close to Pleasant Valley, and its main town of Young, Arizona along with historians have said the more they find out about Duesha, the less they know about him. Duesha knew the Tewksbury clan from meeting them in California during the gold rush years. They offered him a job tending their sheep in the mid 1880's as the famed feud between the Tewksburys and the Grahams was heating up. Duesha came from California to take the job.

Once Charlie Duesha arrived in Pleasant Valley, the first man he met was Tom Graham at the Perkins Store, having stopped to ask directions to the Tewksbury ranch. Tom convinced Duesha to come to work for him instead of the Tewksbury's. It was not really hard to sway old Duesha, because he was a cowman and not a sheep man. Tom and Charlie immediately took a liking to each other and a lifelong friendship ensued.

Duesha told the Tewksbury's he had decided not to take the job they offered. He told them that he was not cutout for herding sheep. So, he went to work for Tom Graham. The reader needs to understand at this time period the Grahams and the Tewksbury's were still on a friendly basis. They met in Globe a couple of days after the Grahams arrived in Globe, probably at a saloon. It was Ed that convinced Tom Graham to come up to Pleasant Valley to start his family cattle ranch. Charlie Duesha stayed at Graham's side until Tom was murdered from ambush in Tempe, Arizona on August 2, 1892.

Duesha was known widely for his deadly skill with a six gun and was Tom Graham's bodyguard for more than ten years. When an unarmed Graham, who had taken up farming in Tempe after leaving Pleasant Valley, was cut down at seven o'clock in the morning while taking a load of barley to market, Duesha was not with him. He was tending to chores on the farm.

Tom Graham lived most of the day of August 2, despite his fatal wounds. One slug had severed his spinal cord. He was coherent until about two hours before his death, and time and time again named Ed Tewksbury and John Rhodes as the men who ambushed.

Sometime after Graham's death, Charlie Duesha found his way to the huge ranch West of Aguila that runs along the South side of Highway 60 nearly the entire distance from Aguila to Wenden, Arizona. Duesha holed up in a remote canyon on this ranch, which is now made up of four hundred twenty-seven sections, now owned by Charles Robson of Robson's Mining World on Highway 71 a few miles East of Aguila. Duesha had long been prospecting and mining. He occupied himself in that trade in the canyon that now bears his name. At one time, John Moore, the father of Kearney Moore and grandfather of Roy Moore, both well-known ranchers in the Aguila and Congress area, held some gold mine claims with Duesha back in the Harquahalla Mountains around the canyon. Duesha and Moore also had claims in the Wickenburg and Congress Junction areas.

The first picture is of the canyon where Charlie Duesha's mine was located. The second picture is of the entrance to the mine. These two pictures were found at the Arizona Mining Museum

Charlie Duesha was badly crippled, from a hard life, by this time also suffering pain from the many wounds he received fighting throughout his life. The pain from all of the injuries from the many fights finally had taken their toll. With so much pain from injuries and his old age, Duesha relied heavily on his skill with a pistol and rifle. Duesha was born in Kentucky in 1838 and fled his home and the whip of an abusive brother when he was twelve years old. He stole his brother's pistol and left Kentucky to strike out on his own.

Heading West Duesha took up with a band of renegades and soon found himself in a pitched battle with Indians. Charlie caught hell after the fight for not keeping up his end of the battle. He figured the renegades were either going to kill him or leave him in the plains to die. That night he stole the leader's saddle and horse and made his escape ending up in Visalia, California after making his escape. He found work at a nearby cattle ranch as a drover. While working at the ranch he fell in love with a young beautiful Mexican girl. The trouble was that the senorita had a boyfriend who was a matador.

The matador caught Charlie with his woman in her adobe home. The matador locked the front door of the windowless cabin. The two men could hear the senorita outside, cheering for her boyfriend urging him to kill Duesha. Inside the dark room the two men struggled with knives to the death. Finally, a knock was heard from the inside of the door. When the door was opened Duesha staggered out of the hut and collapsed on the ground, bleeding profusely.

Inside the blood spattered adobe hut, the matador was sprawled on the floor, dead. Duesha was still alive, but badly cut up. As he was recovering from his severe wounds, the senorita took off with another man. Duesha eventually recovered from his wounds, but he had been crippled for life from the severing of many nerves in one of his legs. He was limited forever in the use of his left arm and the nerves in his right arm were severely damaged. His left arm being the better of the two, Duesha worked on his left arm and learned to deal out death with a pistol from his good arm and hand. The fierceness of the duel earned Duesha the name, "El Diablo" among the Mexican Community.

Duesha killed two more Mexicans in California over a mining claim dispute. While in custody, he escaped from a nearby San Francisco jail and killed a sheriff's deputy during the escape. By the time he was involved in this incident, Duesha had already killed several Indians and a white man in a gunfight in a saloon at Fort Benton on the Missouri River in the middle 1850's. A mob formed after that killing, so Duesha exited in a dead run.

At one point, Duesha went to Santa Fe, New Mexico where he became angry, when he lost all of his money at a local gambling house. Angry Mexicans pursued him into the night. A short distance down the dark trail, Duesha got into position behind a large rock. As the band of Mexicans came down the trail, Duesha blasted the first one with a sawed off shotgun. Then he killed two more with his pistol. The rest of the men fled.

Duesha then found his way to Sonora, California where he and another miner struck a rich gold claim. Organized claim jumpers came down on him and his partner one day. His partner was killed. Duesha cut down two of the claim jumpers and the rest escaped. Duesha was arrested for murder and was locked in a one room cabin by the sheriff. While jailed, Duesha was tipped off that the sheriff was in cahoots with the claim jumpers. That night a couple of deputies came to take him to be lynched. Duesha grabbed a gun from one of them, then shot and killed both lawmen and escaped.

The photo below of Charlie Duesha was supplied to the author by Bill Brown. Charlie is the man on the right in the photo. They man on the left was his doctor, circa 1920's

Chapter Eight
Buscadero Outlaw

The Author's father always told me that you are known by the company you keep. He said many times to the Author growing up as a boy;

> *"Birds of a feather flock together. You are known by the company you keep."*

With this in mind it is necessary to cover the background of Hank Blevans, aka the Buscadero Outlaw, who was part of the Graham faction in the Pleasant Valley War. Blevans was born in Texas in 1858 and on the run from Texas when he arrived in Arizona. Tom Graham certainly attracted some low life individuals and it does not bode well for him with regard to the people he and his brothers surrounded himself with during the Pleasant Valley War.

In 1932 Hank Blevans took John Winslowe, the author of a magazine article called, The "Buscadero" Outlaw," during an interview Winstowe had with Blevans to the Tewksbury ranch and showed him the graves of William Jacobs and John Tewksbury, then he led Winslowe over to the spot, where he and Andy Cooper hid concealed behind bushes and waited for Tewksbury and Jacobs to come down the trail near them at which time they bush wacked both Tewksbury and Jacobs in the back killing them instantly. Blevans went on to tell Winslowe;

> *"I would have gotten Ed Tewksbury too except as he told Winslowe, he was the victim of an unfortunate thing."*

That unfortunate thing that Blevans speaks about is the fact that he was arrested, tried and sentenced to a second, long prison sentence for armed robbery of a stagecoach lifting several bars of silver bullion and some jewelry in the coach strong box. Luckily, there were no passengers on board. The details of this robbery will be discussed later in this chapter.

In order to back track and cover the outlaw life of Hank Blevans and how he arrived at the side of the Graham's in the Pleasant Valley War, we need to go back to his first armed robbery in the New Mexico/Arizona Territory. It was a cold December night in 1881 along the Southern Pacific Railroad line between Lordsburg and Deming New Mexico. Approaching the train station at Separ, New Mexico Territory the engineer noticed the signal arm was down, which indicated he needed to stop the train and move it himself. He was curious as to why the arm was down. While braking he passed the lighted station and noticed that there was no telegraph agent on duty.

The engineer wanted to know the reason why the rail was closed but no agent appeared for him to question. Instead of the railroad telegraph agent, a man in boots with a bandana pulled up over his nose under the hat brim jumped up into the locomotive cab with a gun leveled at both the engineer and the fireman. The man spoke to the engineer.

> *"You just take it easy and nothing will happen to you and your fireman, hog head."*

The outlaw held the gun on the fireman and engineer for about fifteen minutes and nobody spoke a word, then they heard a loud explosion that woke the passengers. Some of the passengers and railroad employees stuck their heads out of windows to see what was happening. The outlaws fired several shots in the air, at which time all that were looking out the windows pulled their heads back into the train. Another fifteen minutes or so passed, according to the engineer's report when they heard a voice call out in the dark;

"Okay, let's ramble!"

At which time the man holding the gun on the fireman and engineer simply said just before jumping out of the train on a horse that was waiting there for him:

"So long pards!"

The engineer's report went on to say, that people came out of the passenger cars along with the engineer, the conductor and the fireman. They all joined in the search for the telegraph agent, who they found tied up in the station. Once untied, he sent a telegram immediately to the office in Lourdsburg and Deming, New Mexico Territory telling the details of the robbery. But at that point nobody knew how much money the outlaws took. They soon found after the express manager was untied, that the loud noise they heard was the dynamite the outlaws used to blow up the safe, and escape with $54,000 being stored in the Wells Fargo Express car safe. The fact that the robbers knew enough to raid the Wells Fargo car and leave the passengers alone, indicated they had inside information with regard to the amount that was on that particular train.

New Mexico County Sheriff Harvey Whitehall and a posse were formed immediately and along with two Wells Fargo Railroad detectives, the officers were all on the trail of the outlaws within an hour after the robbery took place. They followed the trail of the five riders, that appeared to be streaking toward the Arizona Territory. But Whitehall lost the trail about thirty miles south of Lourdsburg, New Mexico in a long sandy stretch of ground.

Law officers from Southern Arizona Territory were also notified by way of telegram with a description of the outlaws and that the outlaws were headed to their area. Working with Wells Fargo agents in and around Deming, New Mexico the officers tracked five men that fitted the description of the outlaws to a ranch near Willcox, Arizona. The owner of the ranch was arrested on suspicion of harboring the outlaws. The officers knew the man had nothing to do with the robbery but they were sure he knew something about the gang. After being questioned at great lengths, the man admitted;

> "They were around my place back in the hills for a few days. They bought horse feed, butter and eggs from me. The only name I ever heard mentioned was that one of them was called Buscadero."

The officers knew that Buscadero was no man's given name, so they figured he was called that name from him wearing a unique looking gun belt that was called a Buscadero.

From the description of the outlaw being called Buscadero by his friends, and the rancher in custody for harboring outlaws, the officers deducted that the man was none other than Henry "Hank" Blevans was an outlaw from Texas, who was wanted for murder and was a known gunman and killer.

From the ranch the officers followed the trail of the five outlaws to Tucson. Knowing or sensing that they were being chased, once the outlaws reached the outskirts of Tucson, they split the loot and went their separate ways to make it more difficult for the posse to follow them.

At that point, Hank Blevans pointed his horse north with Prescott, Arizona Territory as his destination. Along the way he stopped at the railroad station at Maricopa Wells. To his liking, while he was there a stagecoach came through on its way to Globe. What a convenient stroke of luck for Blevans! He followed the stagecoach a couple miles north east of the station, pulled it over, holding the driver at gunpoint while the passengers unloaded, he emptied their pockets. The take was right around $2500, which was all he needed to keep him going. From there he headed northwest toward the farming town of Phoenix, Maricopa County, Arizona, where he could easily hide as folks were coming and going on a regular basis.

Sadly, no matter how quiet he was, people like Blevans seem to attract trouble even if they are not looking for it. Blevans was only in Phoenix for a couple of days when trouble found him. He related the story to author John Winslowe;

> *"I was sitting at a bar minding my own business when a drunk standing next to me started to hassle me, the man finally simply said, isn't the world big enough for you, why do you have to be here in this saloon? I said maybe a few bullet holes in your hide will teach you some decent manners. At that point the man went for his gun and that was his last move. I pulled my gun and put two slugs in his chest."*

The sound of the gun shots brought the town marshal, Henry Garfias into the saloon. When questioned by Garfias, Blevans told the marshal that he was minding his own business when the man lying on the floor started the trouble and drew down on him. He told the marshal that he had no choice but to defend himself.

Garfias questioned a dozen or so men in the saloon at the time of the shooting and they confirmed Blevans story of self- defense. Ordering the body of the dead man taken away to the morgue, Garfias turned to Blevans and spoke;

> *"It looks like it's a clear case of self-defense, so youre in the clear but don't*

leave town for a few days."

Blevans dropped his head down in despair as the marshal spoke, nodding in agreement with the decision and Garfias terms, but in his mind he knew the marshal was going to look to see if there were any papers circulated about a man who fit his description. And that after the incident hoping that he might be there in Phoenix, and most important, if he fit the description of any wanted outlaws. Although Blevans used a different name, his description could be found through the many different sources lawmen used in those days.

Blevans decided it would be best if he moved on toward his original destination, Prescott, Arizona, that lay about ninety miles north and west of Phoenix. For all he knew there could be reward posters out for him from crimes he committed in Texas and New Mexico, for sure Marshal Garfias would obtain the information. Wells Fargo certainly had reward posters posted all along their lines for the holdup he pulled at the train station in Separ. It was lucky for Blevans, the descriptions Garfias found of the outlaws that pulled the recent robbery at Separ did not resemble him.

When Blevans arrived in Prescott that fall he found the town rough and tough, just the kind of place he could call home. Later that winter Blevans met and befriended two local cowboys, Ike Grooms and Hugh Zinfield. Grooms and Zinfield told Blevans that they had spent the past year rustling cattle in Apache County. Grooms told Hank there were some great deep canyons that made nice holdover places, where new brands were applied as the hair grew over the old brands. Grooms went on to tell Hank that they had two buyers for stolen stock, one in New Mexico and another buyer in the Sulphur Springs Valley near Tombstone.

After talking it over with Grooms, Blevans knew he was a wanted man there were not many places for him to hide, Blevans decided that with the absence of lawmen in Apache County and the readily available stock to be stolen, it sounded like a good place for him to hide and make a living.

Two weeks later, after purchasing supplies and ammunition, the three men crossed the Tonto Basin and into Apache County. In the first month working the area, they collected eight hundred head of cattle owned by the Hashknife cattle company, located near Holbrook, Arizona. Part of the herd was sold to the buyer in New Mexico and the balance was sold to the buyer in the Sulphur Springs Valley.

Since stealing cattle from the Hashknife spread was so easy the three outlaws decided to go back for more stock. But this time they were only able to steal two hundred head, because the Hashknife general manager placed riders as guards all along its outer range borders to prevent rustling. Looking for more stock to steal, they stole two hundred head from the Greer Cattle Company, whose herd was located grazing around the town of Concho, Arizona Territory. Some of the stock was sold to their buyer in New Mexico. The balance of the herd was driven to nearby U.S. Army forts where hungry soldiers and Indian agencies waited with open arms.

Two of the Greer brothers, Nat and Dick, along with eight of their best gunmen and riders caught up with Blevans, Grooms and Zinfield along the Salt River. A running gun battle occurred when none of the outlaws were willing to give up. Grooms was killed and Zinfield was wounded in the running firefight, but always looking over his shoulder being suspicious of every movement in the brush, when the shooting started, Blevans hid in the brush and rode out the other side with bullets zinging by his head and body. Grooms was shot and killed in the gun battle. Zinfield was wounded in the firefight, but managed to make his escape right behind Blevans. The two outlaws hid out in the White Mountains for a couple of weeks while Zinfield recovered from his wounds.

From their hiding place in the White Mountains the two outlaws headed for Alma, New Mexico. While on the trail to Alma the two men went on a holy tear, robbing stagecoaches along the way. They were joined by five other outlaws. So the seven outlaws got totally drunk together and when they sobered up they decided to rob a train then split up.

Riding toward Grant, New Mexico, they stopped at the Atlantic and Pacific Railroad tracks, and piled up cross ties on the tracks. When the train stopped they took over and blew the express car safe around ten o'clock that evening. By pure luck, having no prior knowledge or information, the safe contained shipments of money in excess of $80,000, upon discovering this large amount of money, Blevans knew the whole law world would be on their trail, so he directed their flight south into the sixty-mile long lava beds, which would be harder for the lawmen to track. They decided to split up at that point and decided to bury most of the loot in a cave. They all took spending money and buried the rest of the 80,000 dollars from the robbery.

Somehow or another Blevans and his sidekicks were reported by the Greer brothers as the Kit Joy Gang, who were a bunch of ruthless train robbers and killers. Zinfield and the other outlaw with him were arrested and held for questioning, when a local citizen was murdered. Blevans went looking for Zinfield and in the process was surrounded, arrested and incarcerated with his friends. That night word reached the jail that a lynch mob was headed their way to hang the Kit Joy Gang, including Blevans and his companion Hugh Zinfield.

The mob broke into one of the doors in the jail where the three men were being held. Upon entering the jail cell the mob spotted Zinfield and the other outlaw and went for them, not seeing Blevans, who was sitting in the dark against the wall opposite to the other two men. Seeing his chance for escape, Blevans slipped in with the mob and when his friends were led out of the jail, Blevans slipped away in the darkness. Within minutes he stole a horse and was on his way. His friends fought the crowd for as long as possible but in the end they were hanged.

Blevans rode like a maniac toward the Tonto Basin where he thought he could hide from the law. Along the way he pulled three stagecoach robberies that netted him peanuts, but enough to get him to his destination, replenish his grub and ammo. He saw a wanted poster hanging outside a store indicating the law was looking for the *"Buscadero Outlaw,"* with a pretty accurate description of him. He decided the Buscadero gun belt he wore was a dead giveaway so he abandoned it and wore a regular gun belt,

A photo below of a typical Buscadero gun belt (on the left) was found on the Western Action Gun-Belt and Holster website. The difference from normal gun holsters (on the right) is that the cartridge loop part of the belt is typically six inches wide.

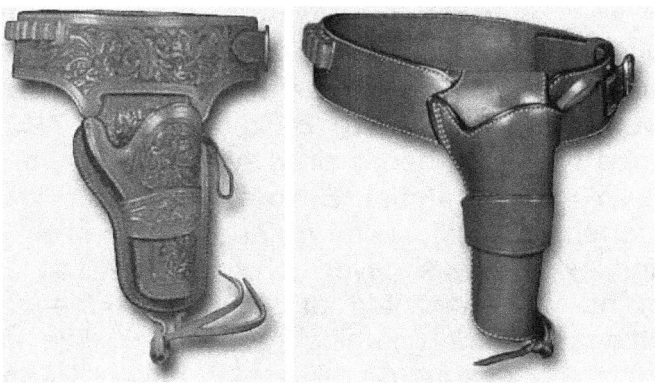

Blevans reached the Perkins Store in Pleasant Valley, none the less for wear. His horse needed feed, water and rest. He stopped to take care of his mount and then went into the store to get supplies. The author of the magazine article, John Winslowe, according to Blevans, it was there that Blevans met and befriended Tom Graham and Charley Duesha. Blevans indicated this to Winslowe in 1932, when he took the author to the site where John Tewksbury and William Jacobs were killed.

Hank Blevans was no relation to the Blevins family and their outlaw son Andy Cooper. There is no doubt that Charlie Duesha knew right off that Blevans was an outlaw and would fit right in with their gang of thugs. Winslowe said when he interviewed Charlie Duesha, many years later, that when he asked him about Blevans, Duesha just smiled and nodded his head, indicating that he knew Hank Blevans. Just how much Blevans was involved in the Graham-Tewksbury feud is really not known but by his own admittance in 1932 to John Winslowe, he participated in the ambush of John Tewksbury and William Jacobs.

Blevans also told the author John Winslowe that the siege on the Tewksbury ranch lasted three days. He said after the deed was done, he and another outlaw left Pleasant Valley, the Graham faction of the war and went to Globe. From there Blevans got involved in even more dastardly deeds. While in Globe his illegal deeds drew him a long sentence in the Yuma Territorial Prison this again was the unfortunate incident he referred to earlier in the interview. He was never convicted of killing anyone but he was convicted of stagecoach robbery and cattle rustling. Emerging from prison a little after the turn of the century, a broken man physically and way too old to follow outlaw trails, Blevans went to Young, in Pleasant Valley. Just where Blevans obtained the money to buy a ranch and remain there until his death in 1943 at the age of 85, will never be known. One thing for sure though, he had money hid out all over the frigging country from all the robberies he committed over the years. Again, it seems like the Graham faction of the Pleasant Valley War had attracted another slime ball that fit right into their gang of dark alley asassins, they were bad men that fit right in with Andy Cooper, Charley Duesha and John Paine! And of course they were a perfect fit for the leaders of the Graham Faction of the Pleasant Valley War, Tom & John Graham.

This photo of Hank Blevans, in 1932, was taken by John Winslow and appeared in his magazine article.

At this juncture, the author would like to present a short biography of the writer Maurice Kildare, who also wrote under the name John Winslowe. Kildare was one of the first true story writers of the 20th Century. He interviewed many folks and wrote their stories. He interviewed James Pearce, who was a Tewksbury man and Hank Blevans, who was with the Graham faction of the Pleasant Valley War, long after the feud ended in 1892. With his live interview from these folks he was able to write the two articles that this author is presenting in this book.

Maurice Kildare aka; John Winslow

Maurice Kildare wrote and sold so many true stories for all of the True West stories, selling them to Wild West, True West, American West, and many other western magazines in the 1950's, 1960's and the 1970's. Some were purchased at the same time for the same magazine, so in order to sell his articles he wrote the stories under several pen names. Two of those articles are references in this book, one written under his name, Maurice Kildare and the other written under the pen name, John Winslowe.

He had a couple of full length books published, one of them is a real classic that I have read several times called "Navajo Trader." It is his biography. Kildare grew up on the Navajo Reservation and his father owned a trading post. Maurice went to work for his father when he was a boy and took over the trading post after his father passed. It is important for the reader to understand the difference In those days it was acceptable to interview one person involved in an event, write the story and that was all that was necessary to sell an article. That process will not work today. But we historians today are very lucky to have these stories available.

Chapter Nine
Uncle Jim Roberts

The next two chapters will be dedicated to the memory of James Roberts, aka Uncle Jim or simply Jim Roberts, who was a member of the Tewksbury faction. If Charlie Duesha, Andy Cooper, Hank Blevans and John Paine were the toughest lawbreaking bad men who ever entered Pleasant Valley, who aligned themselves with the Graham faction, then there is no doubt that Jim Roberts aligning himself with Ed & Jim Tewksbury along with John Rhodes, put four of the best marksmen with a pistol or rifle on both sides of the war and all were Tewksbury men. These four men were enough to make the difference for the Tewksbury's in their plight against the Graham's, because not only did they have great skills with a pistol or rifle, they were hardnosed men who most importantly, had right on their side. Jim Roberts was right in the middle of the Pleasant Valley War from the beginning to the end. Roberts was a fair, honest, tough man, and the best gun hand with a pistol on either the Tewksbury or the Graham's side of the feud.

James F. Roberts was born in Beaver, Macon County, Missouri on March 27, 1858. It has been said with a lot of truth that Missouri, Kentucky and Texas supplied more pioneers for the settlement of the West than any other states. During the 19th Century, the young men of those states were born with wanderlust and a love for adventure strong in their blood. Their fathers and mothers before them were the pioneers who had claimed the Civil War torn country from the Indians. It was little wonder that the sons of such parents should turn their faces westward in search of a new land that would satisfy their adventurous youth.

This was Jim Roberts' dream, a heritage that he could not deny. And so, at the age of eighteen

Roberts turned his face to the wild Southwest territories of New Mexico and Arizona in search of excitement and to make a life for himself in the last frontier in our great country.

The Sioux of the northern plains were still on the warpath, but of the most of the Sioux under Chief Sitting Bull had fled to Canada after Custer's defeat at Little Big Horn, for the most part, because of the abundance of game in Canada, along with the fact that they could roam in peace. By this time much of the fighting spirit of these people had disappeared. They simply wanted to live in peace and keep their way of life, living off the land. They really had no choice but to look for new land, because the buffalo hunters had just about wiped out the buffalo their main source of food and clothing in the plains, along with the fact that they did not like the reservation system that was being imposed on them by the U.S. Government. But most of all if they did not cause any trouble the Canadian Government allowed them to live in peace.

It is little wonder that this young man, with a heritage of pioneering forefathers, should drift westward until he found a land to his liking, a land raw and rough enough for any adventurous lad of the 1879's. And he found it in Arizona, the last frontier.

After wandering about the Arizona territory for a year or two, Roberts finally unsaddled his horse at a beautiful spot along the head water of Tonto Creek and staked his claim to his 160-acre parcel of land. The area would later be known as the Tonto Basin. Pleasant Valley lay a thousand feet below Robert's property but only about twenty miles south. The land had been designated by the United States Department of Interior as land that could be settled allowing each settler to stake claim to their own 160 acres of land, obtain a deed for their property and start their own ranch or farm.

In this lonely, remote and wild but beautiful spot known as the Tonto Basin, Jim Roberts built a cabin and corral near a creek, so that he had a constant supply of water. From his ancestors, Jim Roberts inherited a love of fine horses, and he quickly saw the possibilities of producing a hardy strain of horse flesh, crossing the tough wiry range mares with a spirited Midwestern prize blooded stallion. With patience he saved his money until he had enough funds to purchase a purebred stallion. It was a beautiful animal with a deep broad chest and a long flowing mane and tail. It is little wonder that every cowboy, rustler, and stockman in central Arizona longed to drop a rope over its head.

Jim Roberts became known for his accuracy with his Colt 45 pistol and his 30/30 Winchester lever action rifle, both of which he practiced with over three hours every day. He also became famous for his great horses, but like most of his original settlers in the area, the Colcord and Houdan families, who were his neighbors, his stock began to disappear, for it must be remembered, Tonto Basin was far removed from the forces of the law and order. The nearest law officer being Yavapai County Sheriff William Mulvenon, whose office was in Prescott, Arizona, the Territorial Capital, located over a hundred fifty miles west of the Tonto Basin. Jim paid little attention to the few head of horses that disappeared now and then, for that was to be expected in the stock business, but when his prized stud went missing, he *"saw red."* That stud was an entirely different matter, and he was going to find the stud and bring it back to his ranch.

Jim Roberts would never talk about his experiences during the Pleasant Valley War but his good friend Al Peach was willing to state the following for the record;

> *"Jim Roberts was one of the original settler's in Pleasant Valley arriving in*

> *1878. He built my cabin, barn and dug my well as soon as he arrived. He became good friends with Ed and Jim Tewksbury, who were always available when he needed help. They told him that their family raised sheep in the valley even before the cattlemen settled there, and that at the time the shooting started, they were preparing to increase their cattle herd and dispose of the sheep. The Tewksbury's, along with Peach, Colcord, Houdan, Middleton and Roberts declared the Grahams were a testy and troublesome group, who started the feud over a comparatively minor incident."*

Ed Tewksbury told Al Peach that Roberts trailed the thieves who stole his prize stallion to their camp at the edge of Mogollon Rim and found his stallion and two of his mares in the possession of three men he had seen before with the Grahams. When he confronted the men, pointed to his brand on the stock and said he would be taking back his stock, the men drew their pistols. Jim quickly outdrew them, proceeded to shoot all three men before they could get their pistols out of their holsters, killing all three men.

A little while after this incident the minor incident Al Peach speaks about that little incident that took place in the bar in Payson with Ed Tewksbury and the rustler Gladden, the open rupture between the Graham and Tewksbury factions had crystallized. Jim Roberts tried to stay out of the feud but with the death of the three rustlers, accusations flew thick and fast over the range. But still Jim took no part in the feud that was gathering in the dark, threatening clouds on the horizon of this peaceful land, not until he returned one evening to find his cabin a pile of smoldering ashes.

Jim spent the next few hours riding the range and slaughtering as many Graham cattle that he could shoot, quitting only when he ran out of bullets. The following day he showed up at Jim and Ed Tewksbury's ranch and offered his services. Jim Roberts' rage knew no bounds. He openly declared war against the Grahams, and thus the Tewksbury's gained their most valuable fighting man, along with John Rhodes, a local Pleasant Valley cowboy, who made a name for himself as a great shot with a rifle and who also was a great roper. They were the two men who made the difference in how the Tewksbury's were able to survive the Pleasant Valley War.

Jim Roberts was involved in almost every major gun battle that occurred during the Pleasant Valley War. In the fight at the Middleton ranch, that was bought by George Newton, the Tewksbury's jeweler friend who lived in Globe, Arizona. For instance, Roberts shot Hampton Blevins out of his saddle, while Blevins' horse was running at a full gallop. The forty-five slug from Roberts' pistol blew away the top of Blevins head, then without stopping to take a breath, Jim turned and put a bullet through the lungs of Tom Tucker, although Tucker lived from the wound, which was very unusual with Roberts amazing accuracy. Tucker rode away from the battle but immediately cleared out of Pleasant Valley. At the same time during the firefight, Ed Tewksbury shot John Payne, who died before his body hit the ground as well as then turning his rifle on Gillespie and putting a slug in him as he rode away. It was a good fight, and it made the headlines in the St. Johns Arizona Herald on August 18, 1887.

Then on August 30, 1887 the feud reached its bloodiest event. Suspecting that the Graham's would retaliate for the shooting of Blevins and Tucker at the Newton's Ranch, Jim Roberts talked Ed Tewksbury into getting help from their friend, Deputy Gila County

Sheriff Tom Horn and some of his friends from Globe as Roberts suspected the Graham's would retaliate for the gun battle that took place at the Newton place, and probably planning an attack one or more of the Tewksbury Ranches.

With an eminent attack from the Grahams in the planning stages, Jim Roberts set a coyote trap, *(bring the enemy to you on your terms and not on their terms)*, for the Grahams early in the afternoon on that same day. He used himself as bait, by making camp in a hollow by a spring on the Graham's range. To make sure they knew he was there, he let himself be seen by one of the Graham cowboys working that particular range. Just as he had hoped the word of his presence got back to Tom Graham, who took the bait and went into action.

Roberts stationed Ed and Jim Tewksbury along with several of the Tewksbury's friends, strategically behind a number of big boulders that dotted the area around the hollow. The brush was so thick an open field of fire was impossible. The Grahams would have to ride into the hollow, right into Jim's camp, and as he pointed out to Jim and Ed Tewksbury, a man lying prone can always outshoot a man on a horse, which is exactly what happened. The shooting lasted less than a minute and left one of the Graham men dead and several wounded with the others running for their lives. Jim and Ed, along with the rest of the Tewksbury men went back to John Tewksbury's home for the night, with a pretty good idea that this would not be the last time they saw the Graham's, probably really steaming from hatred, they were surely planning another raid on the Tewksbury's.

The next morning September 1, 1887 was the famous battle at J.D. Tewksbury's cabin in which John and William Jacobs were shot in the back and killed, an incident that has already been discussed earlier in this book, as they were coming back from getting their horses. Their bodies left where they were shot and, lay there for two days, while being partially eaten by wild hogs. That gun battle, according to some historians, lasted eleven days but actually it lasted three days, until the Grahams were informed that Sheriff Billy Mulvenon was on his way from Prescott. There were no other casualties on either faction during the rest of that three-day gunfight. Jim Roberts was one of the nineteen men in the fortified, J.D. Tewksbury cabin at the time of the gunfight.

Jim Roberts' life in Pleasant Valley wasn't all shooting and fighting. He often took time to ride over to one of the nearby railroad camps of the Atlantic & Pacific, the Santa Fe and the Prescott Railroads, to buy, as he said, the hottest tamales this side of Hades. Jim was well versed in border Spanish and was well liked among the local Hispanic folks, who worked at the cantinas and restaurants. He was an open minded man and was known to squander a month's earnings on one wild spree.

Tonto Basin rancher Robert Sigsby, who had a cabin that was a couple of miles from the Middleton cabin where the gun battle took place, reported that Tom Tucker, after showing up at his ranch in bad shape from his wounds, told Robert that as his horse slowed down from running he slipped into an unconsciousness state and fell to the ground. He told Sigsby that it rained and hailed that night and he woke up from his unconscious state. His horse was gone, so he dragged himself several miles to Sigsby's cabin. According to Robert Sigsby:

> "Tucker was in terrible shape when he arrived at his cabin. In the hot afternoon sun, flies had swarmed his wound. Maggots already were crawling around the torn tissue."

Sigsby applied frontier remedies that he knew and somehow, the rugged Tucker survived. But as soon as he was able to ride he left Pleasant Valley and its war, never to return.

Bob Gillespie, who had also been wounded in the hip at the Middleton Cabin shootout, having been shot by Ed Tewsbury, went into hiding, and then joined Tucker at Sigby's ranch cabin and they both rode out of the valley. They told Sigsby they were going back to New Mexico, where to all amazement Tucker became deputy sheriff at Santa Fe and then moved to Texas, where he died at a very old age. Gillespie retired in Santa Fe.

The Tewksbury men who were in the Middleton cabin on August 10, 1887 is not fully known, other than years later Jim Roberts said that he and a neighbor Joe Boyer along with Jim and Ed Tewksbury were the occupants but, Roberts would not name any others that were present.

Yavapai County Sheriff William Mulvenon did not waste any time when he heard about the shootout at the Middleton Ranch. He immediately formed a posse and headed for Payson. He secured criminal complaints and warrants for the arrest of John Tewksbury, Ed Tewksbury, William Jacobs and Joseph Boyer for the murder of Hampton Blevins and John Paine earlier at the Middleton Ranch along with Payson Justice of the Peace John Meadows, who joined them on the trail.

Mulvenon then led his posse into Pleasant Valley after being joined by John Meadows and several other deputies from Payson on August 23, 1887, along with several deputies and a constable from Flagstaff, who also met them in Payson, that was at that time was still in Yavapai County. Among the Flagstaff men joining Mulvenon was Deputy John Francis, who later became one of the largest sheep owners in Northern Arizona and John Weatherford, who at the turn of the century, built the Weatherford Hotel in Flagstaff, and was its owner for more than thirty years.

Sheriff Mulvenon and his posse were the first of any law officers to intervene in the Pleasant Valley War, which had been going on for several years in one form or another before the shootout at the Old Middleton Ranch. When the posse arrived at the scene of the shootout, not much was left as it had been burned to the ground. Jim Roberts related later that the Tewksbury men inside the cabin went out after what was left of their assailants to check on those who had been killed. At the same time they looked up and saw or more forty horsemen that appeared on a hill in the distance.

According to Roberts, they were too far away to identify, but the men fled back into the cabin to safety. A horseman rode up in front of the cabin. It was then Roberts noticed they were Indians. The Indians looked over the scene, thinking everyone was dead, they rode away. Right after they left the Tewksbury men got on their horses and rode off as well, going back to their own ranches.

When Sheriff Mulvenon and his men arrived at the Middleton Ranch they found the place not only abandoned but burned to the ground. Speculation has it that the Apaches returned to attack the men in the cabin but found it deserted so they torched it, which was a typical Apache strategy. Sheriff Mulvenon after a thorough search did not find the bodies of the men who were killed at the cabin. The Tewksbury's had already buried the dead Graham cowboys.

When Sheriff Mulvenon arrived at the Tewksbury's, the posse found the ranch deserted. From there Mulvenon and his posse went to the nearby Perkins Store which was not more than a mile from the Graham Ranch. There they met Andy Cooper and a group of the Graham cowboys. The sheriff's posse accompanied by Cooper and his cowboys then went in search of the Tewksbury's, who Mulvenon was carrying arrest warrants. They followed the trail from the burned Middleton cabin to an area so rugged with ravines and canyons that Mulvenon finally gave up the chase, fearing they might be walking into an ambush.

Sheriff Mulvenon and his posse decided to return to Prescott still carrying his arrest warrants that he was unable to serve. Andy Cooper and the Graham faction cowboys pledged to do what the law could not accomplish, as Mulvenon rode back to Prescott. Meanwhile back at the Territorial Capital, a grand jury was convened and returned indictments that broadened the warrants issued in Payson. The indictments were issued on December 3, 1887, nearly four months after the Middleton Ranch shootout, and were apparently brought about at the urging of the Graham's.

The men indicted for the murder of Hampton Blevins were Ed and James Tewksbury, Joseph Boyer, Jim Roberts, Jacob Lauffer and George Wagner. For some unknown reason, the name of John Paine was not given with Blevins as a victim in this indictment. While the Grand Jury was in session, in November, the Graham and Tewksbury factions were summoned to Prescott to testify. They rode into town one early November day in 1887 and were quartered at camps placed side by side.

Sheriff Mulvenon expecting violence to erupt any time put extra deputies on duty. The citizens also fearing violence armed themselves everywhere they went in town. Fear gripped every fall day that November. These men were locked in a deadly, bloody feud that could explode at any time, engulfing downtown Prescott. It didn't happen though, Tom Graham and old man J. D. Tewksbury ordered their men to ignore each other, and hold the peace while out of the valley. Both sides obeyed their leader's orders.

On the following pages is an article that was published in the June, 1991 issue of the Traveler monthly newspaper periodical, published in Prescott, Arizona. It was a republished article that originally appeared in the Prescott Courier when the Tewksbury's and the Grahams were in the Territorial Capital to answer questions on their indictments. The article delves further into the gunfight at the Middleton Ranch.

When the Pleasant Valley War Panicked Prescott

Even though Pleasant Valley is located north and east of Payson just below the Mogollon rim repercussions of its range war reached Prescott, which was the Capital of the Arizona Territory in December of 1887. Legal action brought against both sides brought the two factions to Prescott under subpoena. The bitter enemies were housed together at the corrals of the OK Store on West Gurley Street.

Prescott citizens, sure that a bloody clash was eminent, armed themselves when they went on the street. Townsfolk lived in terror of the moment they felt surely was at hand, the moment the Tewksbury and Graham factions would clash in a bloody gun duel on their downtown streets. Below a published account in the Prescott Journal Miner Newspaper of what was thought in the firefight that was said to have started the open fighting of the Pleasant Valley War.

"On August 10, 1887, seven cowboys, three from the Graham ranch and four from the Hashknife ranch, set out with Hampton Blevins to search for old man Mart Blevins, who had disappeared and had been missing for more than a week.

It was a beautiful summer day in the valley when about noon the group rode up to the cabin of the Middleton Ranch. Some say the Graham faction boys planned on stopping for dinner, even though the Middleton Ranch was known to be owned by George Newton at that time, a cattleman who had sided with the Tewksbury family. The usual custom of the range at that time was to feed all folks that stopped at any ranch in the valley for breakfast, lunch or dinner.

Tom Tucker seemed to be the leader of the Graham cowboys that day. He was a Hash Knife cowboy. So were John Paine, Bob Gillespie, Bob Carrington and Hampton Blevins along with two other cowboys whose names have been lost in time. Once the men reached the front door of the ranch house Tucker called out asking;"

"Is Mr. Belnap here? We have business with him." Jim Tewksbury appeared at the cabin door and replied; "Nope, he just rode off." According to Tucker, the cowboys then turned to ride away. According to Jim Tewksbury though, Hampton Blevins started to pull his pistol. Inside the cabin, a number of Tewksbury factions had gathered for *dinner. Among them was Jim Roberts.*

When Blevins went for his gun the fight began. In the next instant, John Paine drew and fired a round in the direction of Jim Tewksbury who jumped back through the cabin door just in the neck of time."

At the same instant, a bullet from the pistol of Jim Roberts crashed into Hampton Blevins brain. He teetered in his saddle for a second then his dead body crashed to the ground. It was thought then that he was the first white man to die in the feud. Following the first casualty of the conflict, a Basque sheep herder, but in fact Jim Roberts killed the three Graham cowboys that stole his prized stallion and two of his brood mares just a week earlier and there were several other folks who went missing and were never found or heard of again. According to Roberts;

"In the next moment all hell broke loose. Once the shooting started, it was rapid and unrelenting. The horses of the Graham men swirled in panic and crashed into each other as they turned to escape. John Paine's horse was shot from under him, crashing to the ground and pinning Paine under it. As the cowboy struggled to free himself, Jim Robert's aimed his rifle at Paine's head and shot. Paine was struggling violently to free himself from under the dead horse. Instead of smashing through his head, the bullet took off his ear. It was one of the few times in Robert's life he failed to put a bullet where he intended.

> At that moment Paine freed himself and took off running, blood streaming down his head from where his ear had been. He made only about six or seven steps when Jim Tewksbury's rifle barked and Paine was dead.
>
> Immediately after shooting Hampton Blevins, Roberts turned and put a round in the lungs of Tom Tucker almost knocking him out of his saddle. His horse broke into a wild gallop as the shot hit the rider who hung on as the horse ran wildly from the scene."

The District Attorney was forced to ask for dismissals of all indictments on the grounds that neither side, the Graham's or the Tewksbury's would testify against each other. With that in mind, the Graham and Tewksbury factions returned to Pleasant Valley, and the war resumed with renewed intensity.

Below is a photo of the Old Territorial Capital in Prescott the way it looked when the Tewksbury's and Grahams were in town to answer their indictments. This photo was found in an Arizona Vacation Guide.

During the five years prior to the Middleton Ranch clash, charges of cattle rustling had been brought by each family against the other. In the mean-time the Daggs brothers of Flagstaff, one of the largest sheep ranchers in Northern Arizona were contacted by the Tewksbury brothers. Sick and tired of fighting the Graham faction over cattle that had been rustled, they decided to work the Daggs brothers transporting their band of sheep to Pleasant Valley for wages, and guarding them until they were ready to be sheered and the wool was sold at market, that way they could offset some of their losses from rustlers.

The deal worked out for both parties because the Daggs were looking for a range below the Mogollon Rim to graze during the winter months, to get their sheep out of the snow filled ranges above the rim, so a deal was consummated by the Tewksbury's and the Daggs brothers.

Doing all they thought they could do to eliminate cattle from the Pleasant Valley range and make it possible for the two factions to co-exist, the Tewksbury's and their followers tried to make life work for all of the ranchers in the valley because there was no way they were going to allow the Graham's to run them out of the valley they originally settled. When confronted by John Blevins, Paine and Tucker that fateful morning at the Middleton Ranch and were told by the gang in no uncertain terms to leave the valley, as Jim Roberts said later;

> "We told them point blank we were not leaving the valley, that's when Blevins, Paine and Tucker went for their guns."

In December of 1887 indictments for the Middleton Ranch shootout, and the death of twenty-two-year-old, Billy Graham, the youngest of the Graham brothers, who was shot and killed by Apache County Deputy Sheriff James Houck, while Graham was on his way back to Pleasant Valley from a dance in

Phoenix were issued in Prescott. Deputy Houck reported that he had a warrant for the arrest of John Graham and thought Billy Graham was John Graham when he came upon him on the Hellgate trail. He reported that when he called to Graham, that Billy drew his gun and Deputy Houck said he fired back at Billy Graham in self-defense killing the young man with one shot to his chest. There has never been a warrant found for the arrest of John Graham but it must be noted that Houck's brother in law was the Spaniard sheep herder hired by the Daggs to transport their band of sheep to Pleasant Valley and that one of the two Apache braves, who were working for the Daggs as drovers and somehow escaped, reported to Houck that he saw Andy Cooper in the area. Andy Cooper or Cooper Blevins his real name, later admitted that he had killed the herder and beheaded him to make it look like Indians had done the deed.

It must also be further noted that, per Billy Graham's dying statement, Ed Tewksbury must be questioned, since in Deputy James Houck's official report, he explained in great detail the circumstances surrounding the death of Billy Graham. The reader should also consider that the Grahams hated Ed Tewksbury and used every excuse known to man to blame him for crimes that he had nothing to do with and who could prove he was nowhere near the scene of dozens of crimes he supposedly committed. Ed was no choirboy but there is no way he could have possibly been in all the places where he was suppose to have committed crimes.

The death of Billy Graham weighed heavily on the mind of Tom Graham. A few weeks after the death of his younger brother, Graham vowed to drive the Tewksbury clan and their sympathizers from Pleasant Valley any way possible.

Chapter Ten
Jim Roberts - Lawman

The long Pleasant Valley Range War and rustlers took a financial toll on most of the rancher's in Pleasant Valley and the adjacent Tonto Basin, who were involved in war, and Jim Roberts was no exception. But it also made Jim Roberts a great lawman. After the major hostilities were over in 1888 many of the survivors had to ride toward farther frontiers. Jim worked for a time in the copper camps around Jerome, but not for long. His reputation as a first class fighting man had spread through the territory, and when William Owen Buckey O'Neill was elected the Sheriff of Yavapai County on November 8, 1889 the first Deputy Sheriff he chose was Jim Roberts on December 18, 1889. This is the telegram that Sheriff O'Neil sent to Jim Roberts;

> *Your reputation as a fair and honest man, who has always been on the right side of the law, they don't always elect the best man, so Jim, I am asking you to be my special deputy sheriff. I want the best gun in the Pleasant Valley War on my side.*

Taking the job as a Yavapai County Deputy Sheriff was the start of a forty-four career as a lawman for "Uncle" Jim Roberts as he was called, ending upon his death, when Jim was seventy-five years old and still toting his twin Colt Peacemakers protecting the people of the town of Clarkdale. He served so well under Sheriff O'Neill, that the next man to take the office, Sheriff Lowery, also asked for his services as top deputy. Then on December 8, 1892, Jim himself was elected to a lawman office, and for the next eleven years he wore a Yavapai County Constable's badge.

Right after Jim took office as the Yavapai Deputy Sheriff he met Permelia Kirkland at a fundraiser dance in Prescott that he attended with Sheriff Buckey O'Neill. Her parents had been the first white couple married in the Arizona Territory. At that time the twenty-year old, *"Melia"* was the belle of the town. Roberts asked her for a dance; and he also gave her a lump of candy. Two days later, in a black bow tie and a high-buttoned suit, Mr. Roberts came to call. Miss Kirkland was engaged to another man at the time but she ended that relationship. Jim Roberts and Permelia Kirkland started dating and were married on November 17, 1891.

On April 4, 1904, at the end of his third term as Yavapai County Constable, Jim took the job of town marshal of nearby Jerome, the last of old Arizona wild mining camps. There were so many gunfighters in Jerome that every man was a law unto himself. Armed robberies were committed on the town's main street at high noon and drunks ravaged the town every night. Finally, the peaceful citizens realized they needed a town marshal. At a secret meeting they hired Jim Roberts. This job required a man of barbed wire nerves, and such men were getting scarce in the Arizona Territory.

Jim was forty-six years of age when he took the job as town marshal of the roaring mining town of Jerome. His first act as town marshal was to give public notice that any man carrying or wearing a gun while in town would be arrested on sight, and he gave the citizens twenty-four hours to check their weapons before coming into town. Marshal Roberts appointed a special deputy whose job was strictly to check guns in and out when visitors entered or left town.

After the first twenty-four hours in the office of town marshal, Jim stepped out of his office and into the street, looking for violators. He figured any man who was still carrying a gun meant to draw on him. Three men drew on him the first day he took office. Nobody tried it the second day.

> *"The hand is quicker than the gun," was a statement Jim was fond of saying. While a man reached down for his gun, Jim would be reaching for the man's face, a thumb in the eye, a fist in his windpipe or a square shot on his nose, but if his opponent was out of reach, then Jim would simply fire from the hip and at close range the opponent did not survive."*

At that time Jerome was a town of single men and saloons. The men for the most part worked underground ten hours a day, six days a week; the saloons worked twenty-four hours a day, seven days a week, behind thick stone shutters designed for keeping outside shooting out and inside shootings in. Paydays were every thirty days; the night after a payday, no one was safe in the streets.

Below is a picture that appeared in the Jerome Times newspaper in 1930, as it would have looked when Jim Roberts was the town marshal.

There are those who recall Roberts taking off up the mountain after a Mexican Desperado, the Marshal mounted on his favorite mule, "Jack," and leading a little white burro to carry back a desperado's corpse straddled over the pack animal. In the years before the town had a jail, on the night after a payday Roberts had what looked like half the population was handcuffed to posts, wagon wheels and wagons around the town's main street.

After cleaning up Jerome, Jim was asked by the town's citizens to take the job as town marshal in the nearby town of Clarkdale, Arizona, which was also a mining town. Clarkdale looked like a green pasture to an old stud, past his prime, so Jim answered Clarkdale's call and spent the rest of his life there as the town marshal.

The Old West stereotype of bad men on horseback had already become a myth. These were modern times. The town residents suspected that Marshal Roberts might not be able to handle an up to date robbery, if planned by big city crooks with automatic weapons and the new fast automobiles, but then it was highly improbable that he would ever be called on to do so.

One of Roberts deputies, went on record as stating that he will never forget how he was broken in by Marshal Roberts his first day on the job. Three men started a gambling feud in one of the saloons, resulting in the murder of a fourth man who was a professional gambler. The saloon owner said they called him a cheat, even though he was not cheating and the three of them shot him on the spot.

After killing the man and taking all of his winnings they fled town effectively sending a challenge to Marshal Roberts and his deputy to come get them. Marshal Roberts told the deputy;

> *"Go get three pack mules and we will go after them." After the deputy arrived back at Roberts' office he told the deputy," when we catch up to the men*

and approach them," Roberts told the deputy, "you take the middle fellow and I will take the man in front and the other guy." When they confronted the outlaws the young deputy said his gun hand began to shake. Roberts noticing this said, "get out of the way sonny, I will get them all." A few minutes later all three men lay dead. The deputy said it all happened in the blink of an eye. Then they loaded the three bodies on the three pack mules and went back to Jerome. "Just another day on the job is what Roberts told the young deputy." The deputy went on to say that Jim never talked about his experiences in Jerome or during the Pleasant Valley War. He was an unassuming mild mannered man who simply did his job and did it well I might add."

Below and over the next few pages the author would like to present a story that took place while Clarkdale Marshal Jim Roberts was still on the job at the age of 70. This story is meant to reinforce the tenacity of the original settlers in Pleasant Valley and why they would not surrender to the outlaw Graham faction. It shows that Jim Roberts was a testimony to true grit.

On June 21, 1928, Clarkdale Marshal Roberts was still on the job at 70 years old, when Central Arizona suffered its first bank robbery. The bank robbers were Willard Forester and Earl Nelson, both men hailed from Oklahoma and had criminal records. The local bank manager David Saunders backed Marshal Jim Robert's account as to the facts of the robbery and the end result, when the inquest was held on the bodies of the two dead robbers, along with the circumstances leading up to their deaths.

The main business establishments of Clarkdale were located in a two-block area in the center of town. Main Street divides these blocks that are bound on the east by Ninth Street and on the west by Tenth. On the corner of Main and Ninth was the T.F. Miller Company's large department store. The first establishment to the west was the bank, and the second door from that was a combined tobacco shop, soft drink dispensary, a newspaper stand and a billiards parlor. The town's folks knew it as the *"Cigar Store."* It was used as a base by officials in gathering information about the robbery. It was owned by William Conner whose wife Margaret was a part-time employee of the bank.

Across Ninth Street from the Miller Store were the high school buildings. Diagonally across were twin buildings separated by an arcade, with round concrete pillars supporting a tile roof. These buildings housed the post office and the town manager's quarters.

> *"I, David Saunders, arrived at the scene of the robbery within a few minutes of being told of it. A crowd had assembled in the street between the Miller Store and the high school and at the rear of the school's manual training building was an open touring car rested against the guide wire of a power pole. The dead body of a young man was slumped against the steering wheel. I could see a bullet hole in the back of his neck.*
>
> *Up at the Cigar Store I found the local justice of the peace assembling a jury of six men at the request of the county coroner in Prescott. I was asked to serve on this jury, so I was made acquainted in detail with the*

circumstances surrounding the bank robbery and its aftermath events. "

Below is a photo of Clarkdale, Arizona circa 1930, looking from north to south. This photo was found on the Clarkdale Historical Society website.

The inquest jury's first order of business was to obtain the testimony of Marshal Jim Roberts, who told them that he was on his regular foot patrol that morning, making his rounds at about nine o'clock. He said he saw a Chrysler touring car with the top down, parked in front of the Miller Store and close to the bank. He said it had Oklahoma license plates on it, then he went on to say that it was no surprise to have tourists in town so he didn't give it a second thought.

Jim told the jury that he continued his patrol, but as the thought of the empty Chrysler kept recurring, he cut short his regular rounds and doubled back, passing to the rear of the Miller Store building and paused at the corner of the store at Ninth and Main Streets. From there he could look around the corner of the building and see the bank. The car was parked in the same spot and was unoccupied. He placed his back against the brick wall, and took up a favorite post, standing on one leg, his other leg bent with the sole of his foot against the wall. By moving his head a few inches he was able to see around the corner of the building.

Just after one such inspection Roberts saw a man who had come from the post office and had started toward the Miller Store suddenly stop and start a retreat. Thus alerted, Jim looked up the street to see two men, both carrying pistols and one was carrying a sack, running from the bank toward the parked Chrysler. They jumped into it and started to move just as bank manager, Dave Saunders, also with a pistol in his hand came rushing out of the bank and began shooting toward the two fleeing men.

Saunders' firing was so wild that Roberts stepped back to the safety of the building's corner, with his Colt .45 drawn and ready. As the driver swung the car around Roberts' corner traveling south, the passenger saw Jim and took a shot at him, but the careening of the car made the shot go wild. Roberts returned fire holding his pistol with both hands. He took careful quick aim and fired two rounds.

At the entrance to the alley in the middle of the block the car suddenly swerved left, and taking a curving course crossed the street and turned toward the high school manual training building. There it was brought to a halt by a guide cable supporting a power line pole.

The driver of the car remained in his seat, but his companion leaped from the car and began to race away. He didn't run very far. Fred Fogel, who had been digging a trench to install a new water line to the school house, was alerted by the sound of shooting. Being a member of the territorial militia Fogel had been trained to think and act quickly. Almost before Roberts shouted command to stop, the fugitive had reached him. Fred brought the man down with a flying tackle. A few moments later Jim Roberts was leading the handcuffed fugitive away while listening to his ravings and threats against bank manager Saunders who, he claimed had betrayed him. With others Saunders said he inspected the body in the car. The cause of death was plain, a bullet hole in the back of the neck. One of the folks on the jury proclaimed;

> "Old Jim's eye and shooting ability is as good as ever."

The same thought was echoed throughout the morning. Though it was known Dave Saunders had been firing, Jim Roberts goes on to say, I never heard any suggestion, then or in the next fifty years, that Dave might have fired the fatal shot. At the Cigar Store, we the jury members first inspected the body of the immobilized robber, and unanimously agreed that he was dead. Papers found on the body showed his name to be Willard Forrester. The captured man, Jim Roberts informed us was Earl Nelson. Dave Saunders, in an extremely nervous condition, testified only that the two men held up the bank, took all the cash they could locate, then departed. He had fired some shots, but the bullet that killed Forrester was fired from Jim Robert's pistol.

Jim Roberts testified that he had fired twice at the fleeing criminals, but did not know whether it was he or Saunders that had killed Forrester. Saunders, apparently on the verge of a nervous collapse, was excused. Bob Southard, the banks cashier and assistant manager, gave the jury the details of what happened inside the bank.

Besides Saunders and Southard, attending to the bank's business that morning was Marian Marston, who alternated with Margaret Connor as the teller. The cash drawers had been filled and a few customers had come in when Forrester and Nelson entered the bank and announced their purpose. While Nelson stood at the door with a drawn pistol, Forrester cleaned out the cash drawers and the vault, placing in a sack the loot which included a $35,000 cash to be used to cash the local miner's payroll checks.

As customers came in, Nelson herded them with the others into a corner of the lobby near the vault. Then Forrester ordered the half dozen customers into the vault. Then as he started to swing the heavy door shut, Saunders declared;

"You can't lock us up in here!

Forrester immediately exclaimed;
"I can and I will!"

Saunders pleaded;

"Nobody else in the bank has the combination but us that you want to lock in the safe, with so many of us locked in the vault we will all suffocate in thirty minutes. So you want to add mass murder to your crimes?"

Saunders statement made Forrester pondered for a minute before making his decision, and then he said;
"I'll not lock you up in the safe if you'll give me your word that you won't leave the vault for five minutes after I leave."

Dave Saunders said Forrester closed and latched the grillwork door in front of the vault, Forrester and Nelson ran out of the bank into the street. To Saunders a promise made under duress had no value. The moment the robbers were out of the bank he was able to reach the latch in the grill door, which he flung open. He then rushed to his window, and seized the loaded revolver which he kept covered up on a shelf beneath the counter. He then rushed to the street and opened fire on the robbers, who were by then on a dead run escaping, Southard witnessed Saunders wild shooting, but then or later saw no evidence that Dave had scored the shot that killed the fugitive who was driving the car. It was decided by the jury that the robber met his death at the hand of Marshal James Roberts.

Margaret Connor, the other bank teller that was on her way to work that exciting morning, and was interviewed by a local reporter and said;

> "I had been to the Cigar Store to get my daily newspaper. I was standing in front of the bank when Dave Saunders burst through the front door with a pistol in his hand. Seeing me, he shouted, 'Get inside, Margaret!' then he started firing at a moving car with two occupants. From Dave's hasty firing, which started in the general direction of the post office. I was just hoping there were no casualties. My son, Herbert Junior was with a friend in the arcade when the shooting started.
>
> One of Saunders' rounds struck one of the supporting columns, causing both boys to hit the deck. They saw Lee Snider, an employee at the railroad depot, suddenly jump into the air and clasp his hand to his body near his hip. A pistol round had struck his watch, smashing it, but with no more damage to Snider than a bruise."

When the robbers' car disappeared behind the high school the two boys joined others who were rushing to the scene. They saw Forrester slumped behind the steering wheel, but he was not quite dead, Herbert said his lips were moving and he was heard to say;

> "Where's my hat?"

That was Forrester's last statement before he expired. Earl Nelson, the other bank robber was tried and sentenced to serve twenty years in the Arizona State Penitentiary in Florence. He fulfilled his sentence and was released. He went back to Oklahoma and was never heard from again.

Dave Saunders after gathering his composure and with his newfound reputation was appointed the state bank examiner where he served in that capacity until his death some twenty years later.

James F. Roberts, one of the *"last men standing"* from the Pleasant Valley War, a man ready to uphold the law by quiet means if possible but by violence if necessary, died from a massive heart attack, while making his rounds, still on the job as Clarkdale Marshal, at eleven o'clock the night of January 8, 1934.

Below is a picture of Jim Roberts taken circa 1920, found in our National Archives.

Chapter Eleven
Will Barnes -Lawman

In this chapter the author will present a biography of Will Barnes, who owned a local ranch near Holbrook, Arizona, who also served a Deputy Apache County Sheriff under Sheriff Commodore Perry Owens at the time of the Pleasant Valley War. Barnes played a major role as a lawman in and during the Pleasant Valley War. He published his memoirs in a book called, *"Apaches and Longhorns."* In his book, Barnes recorded many incidents that he investigated or was involved with both of the Tewksbury's and the Graham's.

Will Croft Barnes, was born in San Francisco, California on June 21st, 1858. Barnes spent his childhood years in Gold Hill, Nevada. His father died when Will was only seven years old. During his teens, Barnes and his mother lived in LaPorte, Indiana. The family moved to Lake Calhoun, Minnesota, when Barnes was in his early twenties and they finally settled in Indianapolis, Indiana.

On July 1, 1879, a twenty-one year old Will Barnes enlisted in the U.S. Army in Washington, D.C., for a five-year enlistment. After Boot Camp, the Army assigned Barnes to the Signal Corps with a rank of private second-class. He was sent to signal school at Fort Whipple, in Arlington Heights, Virginia, that was located across the Delaware River from Washington, D.C. While training at Fort Whipple, Barnes learned military signaling, including the use of both wigwag *(Morse code using flashing lights that was used by our U.S. Navy and Coast Guard through WWI and WWII)* and he also took a course the electric telegraph, along with a crash course in meteorology. Barnes qualified as a telegraph operator and assistant weather observer by early January 1880. Private Will Barnes' first assignment took him across the continent, to San Diego, California, to the divisional headquarters of the military telegraph corps.

Traveling to San Diego the trail went through the telegraph office at Pioche, Nevada. Barnes delivered two instruments to the Signal Corp in Pioche. One instrument was called a rotator, a weather instrument that Barnes described as a four-foot mercurial instrument, that was held in an upright position to work. On January 13, 1880, Barnes arrived at the Signal Corp office at San Diego to finish his training and was promoted to the rank of private first-class. Will Barnes was there just a little over a month, then on February 19, 1880, Barnes received orders to report to Fort Apache in the Arizona Territory. Barnes was charged with two responsibilities, post telegrapher and weather observer.

Barnes' arrival at Fort Apache, brought the Signal Corp into the weather reporting service on June 28, 1878. Less than a year after the arrival of the telegraph machine and Barnes, Fort Apache was online and charged with completing regular weather reports. The station there was considered by the Army to be a *"first-class"* station, which meant that it was supposed to take *"six complete meteorological observations daily,"* three of which included a sunset prediction, that were to be telegraphed to the Office of the Chief Signal Officer in Washington, D.C. The principal observations had to be made according to Eastern Standard time, because they were taken simultaneously with those at other reporting stations, so the Fort Apache operator had to make his first daily report long before the crack of dawn;

> *"There could be no fudging on this business, Barnes recalled, because, the instruments had to be read at 3:39 AM, the report made out and put into code and ready for the call signals, which came over the wire from El Paso,*

Texas, at exactly 4 a.m. If you weren't there to answer, you had a painful few moments of wire conference with the Chief Operator, who was a commissioned officer. Yuma was the western most telegraph station and it sent the first report. Then, each man, listening to his fellows, picked up the report, in his turn, ticked off his ten or fifteen cipher words, signed his initials, got the "O.K." from El Paso and went back to bed. This happened four times every blessed day, rain or shine, peace or war, Indians or no Indians, unless the line was down; which it often was. Even then, we had to record the weather and make our report by mail. The last word in our code message at 9 p.m. was our prognostication, "fair," or "foul," as to the ruling weather for the next twenty-four hours. Prescott was at one end of a branch wire from the main line with Fort Apache at the other end. It was some five hundred miles around long and about one hundred and fifty across at its upper end. I soon discovered that during an average period if it was clear and lovely at Fort Apache, and Prescott predicted "foul" for the next twenty-four hours at that place, it was safe to predict "fair" for Fort Apache that time, but to make it "foul" for the next day's prophecy. Nearly all storms came from the west, and the rule generally held good during the seasons when storms were frequent.

From the beginning, Barnes took his telegraphic and meteorological duties seriously, for Second

Lieutenant William A. Glassford, who had been a year ahead of Barnes in the Signal School at Fort Whipple, inspected the Fort Apache station in December 1880 and wrote in his report that he found the books and records in excellent condition, very neatly and accurately kept. Lt. Glassford's official report stated Private Barnes had done a very highly respected job.

In August of 1881, while most of the Fort Apache troops were on their way back from the defeat by Apaches at Cibecue Creek, a few remaining soldiers stationed at Fort Apache were told that a group of Indians was on its way to attack Fort Apache. The nearest help would be from Fort Thomas, some ninety miles away. The telegraph wires had been cut between Camp Thomas and Fort Apache by the Apaches the day before. Two soldiers went out along ten miles of the telegraph lines but they could not find the breaks.

Private Barnes and another Private named Owens volunteered to travel different trails to see if they could find the breaks in the telegraph lines. That evening, when Private Owens rode to a spring near an Apache camp to water his horse, he was killed. As Barnes approached another Apache camp, he tied each hoof of his horse with a piece of saddle blanket to muffle the sound of his horseshoes on the rocks.

Barnes made it across the creek so quietly that the Apaches didn't realize he was there until after he had crossed. By then Barnes was out of their rifle range so he was able to escape the Apaches wrath. Fortunately, Barnes met a company from Camp Thomas on his way back to Fort Apache. The next day Barnes found the break in the telegraph line and was able to repair the break. Communication was re-established and the Army sent reinforcements from Camp Thomas to Fort Apache. The Apaches wisely exited with great haste.

For these and other actions Barnes was awarded the Medal of Honor. The official record in Barnes' personal file shows two recommendations, one by Major Cochran *(commander at Fort Apache)* and the other a formal recommendation by Colonel Eugene A. Carr, the commander of the 6th United States Army Cavalry Regiment, who was in charge of the U.S. Army in the Southern Arizona Territory, which was headquartered at Fort Apache. Major Cochran wrote in Barnes recommendation the following;

> *"In the highest terms during all the trouble at Fort Apache, Barnes was prompt and unhesitating in the discharge of all duties assigned him, more than once being exposed to great danger."*

Colonel Carr wrote in his recommendation letter for the Congressional Medal of Honor the following;

> *"Private Barnes gallantry in action, in the attack by Indians on the post on September 1st, 1881, for his gallant act in this particular event, Private Barnes is entitled to great credit for good conduct & attention to duty during the trying period, from Aug 29th to Sept 10th, as well as at all times while on duty here, and particularly for going out with one man to repair the line, when it was suppose that Indians were lurking near the road."*

On November 8, 1882, General William T. Sherman himself approved it as both the Commanding General of the Army and the Acting Secretary of War, authorized, the inscription on Barnes' medal to read:

> *"The Congress to 1st Class Private Will C. Barnes, Signal Corps, for bravery in action, September 1st 1881, at Fort Apache, Arizona Territory."*

Private Will C. Barnes received the Congressional Medal of Honor in a retreat ceremony at Fort Apache in the spring of 1883 by General William T. Sherman.

On June 1, 1882, the Signal Corps promoted Will Barnes from a first-class private to the rank of sergeant. Then on July 19, 1883, Doctor C.H. Allen, the acting assistant surgeon at Fort Apache completed his annual physical of the soldiers at the fort. Sadly, after performing an annual physical on Sergeant Will Barnes, Dr. Allen informed Barnes that he was no longer fit for military duty and signed a certificate of disability for Will Barnes' discharge from active duty stating;

> *Sergeant Will Barnes is incapable of performing the duties of a soldier because of Hyperemia of the Retina, and that he considered the "degree of disability to be about one-half."*

After his disability retirement form the U.S. Army, Will Barnes purchased a ranch near Holbrook, Arizona, and went in to the cattle business. He also took a job as a Deputy Sheriff of Apache County under Sheriff Commodore Perry Owens, to make ends meet as the cattle business was not going so well, with the rustler element and the dropping of price of beef from the Eastern Stock buyers, Barnes was also elected to Arizona's 18th Territorial Legislative Assembly. Will Barnes wrote a number of books, including his memoirs *("Apaches and Longhorns: The Reminiscences of Will C. Barnes")* and *("Arizona Place Names,")* a book that is still the standard reference book used today by the weather service. With the cattle business dying after the turn of the century, Barnes took a position in 1907 with the U.S. Forest Service to develop and preserve grazing lands. In 1928 he worked for the U.S. Geographic Service and retired from the government service in 1930.

Below are two photos of Will Barnes, that were found in our National Archives. The one on the left was taken in the 1880's and the one on the right was taken a few years before he passed.

Will Barnes, died from complications of a sudden illness at the Veterans Hospital in Phoenix, Arizona on December 17, 1936. In 1937 Barnes' ashes were interred in Arlington National Cemetery, where the simple marker over his grave bears the inscription: Will Croft Barnes/ Sergeant Signal Corps/ United States Army/ 1858-1936, Medal of Honor from his involvement in the Apache Wars.

Military authorities in Arizona memorialized Barnes on January 11, 1958, by unveiling a plaque in memory of Barnes at the dedication of the Will C. Barnes Memorial Field House at Fort Huachuca, Arizona. The Army again honored Barnes on May 16, 1964, when it named the Army Reserve Center in Phoenix after him.

Chapter Twelve
Barnes Involvement in the Feud

It should be obvious from reading Will Croft Barnes autobiography that he was a very credible resource. He lived in Northeast Arizona, experienced the cattle rustling problem himself, was a lawman to boot, and had a first hand knowledge of what happened in the Pleasant Valley Range War. In the following two chapters the author will present Will Barnes experiences during the period of the Pleasant Valley war, from 1883 to 1892 that is taken directly from his memoirs, because it is important that the reader experience as many views as possible from credible witnesses.

With this in mind, in this chapter the author will present Will Barnes written experiences regarding several major incidents that took place in the Pleasant Valley War, as well as incidents that took place in and around Holbrook and Winslow, that were also indirectly or directly involved with the Graham vs Tewksbury Feud, a more accurate name for the Pleasant Valley War. There is always going to be some differences in Barnes own words as compared to those that have been reported by others but as stated, Will Barnes was a credible source.

One of the most exciting incidents in Will Barnes' Arizona life occurred at Holbrook in September, 1887. For nearly two years an organized band of horse-thieves and cattle rustlers had been operation in Apache County. The Mormon people, who were involved in the freighting industry between Holbrook on the Santa Fe and also Holbrook to Fort Apache, all had fine horse, mule and oxen teams. From them the thieves took a heavy toll. The freighters, as a rule, hobbled their teams out along the road at night to eliminate them from being stolen, even doing so, there were still a lot of horses carried off, so the freighters resorted to using lockable hobbles, similar to shackles, on the horses' ankles. But even those horses would sometimes turn up missing. The thieves would break the padlocks with a hammer and leave the hobbles on the ground.

> *A hobble is a device that prevents or limits the locomotion of an animal, by tethering one or more legs. Hobbles are most commonly used on a horse. They are typically made from leather, rope, or synthetic materials such as nylon. Western hobbles are normally used to secure a horse when no tie device, tree or other object is available to secure a horse. When traveling across open lands, if a rider has to dismount for various reasons, the horse can be secured. Hobbles also allow a horse to graze and move short and slow distances, but prevent the horse from running off too far. This process is handy at night if the rider has to get some sleep so in the morning he can find his horse, not too far away.*

The gang that was guilty of these deeds was well known throughout the area. They operated between Colorado on the north and Southern Arizona on the south. The stolen Colorado horses would be driven across the Navajo Indian Reservation into Arizona. Then from there they were driven into Apache County about seventy-five miles southwest of Holbrook, upon their arrival at several stock holding ranches. One of these ranches used to store stock in transit was thought to be Jamie Stotts ranch but there was no proof at this point in time. The stolen stock was stored in some of the roughest, most inaccessible canyons imaginable, in the steep and rugged Sierra Ancha Mountains and also the heavily wooded National

Forests. The thieves had a rendezvous point on Canyon Creek, where horses from Southern Arizona and Mexico were bought and exchanged for others from the north. *(The Blevins Ranch)*

In this spot brands were worked over to change the old brands, the manes docked, tails thinned out, and all sorts of schemes used to cover up their tracks. Several men who had gone into Canyon Creek trailing stolen horses were shot, or beaten with ropes, set on foot, and warned never to show their faces again in the area. Two or three failed to return from such trips. At Holbrook Sheriff Commodore Perry received a telegram indicating the gang would be bringing through a band of stolen horses from the north on a specific night.

Determined to satisfy himself about some questions about the transportation of stolen stock, he sent Deputy Barnes at noon one afternoon, telling several men he was going out antelope hunting, so the outlaws would not be warned that he was coming after them. By dark the next day Barnes was hidden away in a little cave that overlooked the trail coming up Black Canyon and on over the mountain to Canyon Creek. About two o'clock in the morning, Barnes heard the ring of shod feet on the rocks. With his glasses, he watched a bunch of some twenty horses move past, not more than twenty-five feet away. Ahead of the herd rode one of the suspected horse thieves and three rode behind the horses. Barnes reported that he recognized all four men. Deputy Barnes official report of the incident was that the men were Andy Cooper in front and three of his brothers were the men trailing the herd. Barnes was so close to the men and the herd of stolen horses that he recognized these men at night.

About noon the next day a party of six Mormon settlers trailing the tracks of their stolen horses passed Barnes who was hiding in the cave. Barnes told the Deputy Sheriff with them, what he had witnessed during that night. They wanted Barnes to join them in their pursuit, but feeling sure they would all be either killed or held up, Barnes declined.

It turned out just as Barnes expected. Riding down the trail to the Canyon Creek ranch, they were held up by three armed men and advised to turn back on pain of death. Thinking discretion to be the better part of valor, they turned back. The men who stopped them were not masked, and Barnes recognized them as the four men who rode by him with the stolen stock that previous night, as Andy Cooper, along with three of his brothers.

According to John Blevins the only surviving Blevins, Barnes was with that posse, that came to their cabin where they were staying that day and rode up to the front of the cabin. He said, one of the posse hollered out that they had a warrant for the arrest of Andy Cooper, aka Cooper Blevins, who John said was in the cabin with him and two of his brothers. Andy told them to come in and get him that he would not be going to jail. John said Cooper put two pistols on the table and hollered to the posse;

> "I have two pistols sitting on the table and I am right here, I will not be taken alive so come on in and get me."

John Blevins went on to say that he heard the posse members talking and the next thing he knew was that they rode away with one of them stating;

> "Not today Andy none of us are ready to die."

It is thought by this author that Barnes probably mentioned this incident to Apache County Sheriff Commodore Perry Owens, in passing conversation after Barnes went back an filed his report. With this in mind the author believes that this knowledge was very valuable to Sheriff Owens when he went to make his arrest and heard the same threat. He knew Andy Cooper having worked with him in the past when they were employed as cowboys for the Hashknife spread. So he was familiar with all of Andy's schemes and habits. So Owens knew exactly what to expect if and when he ever had to serve an arrest warrant on Andy Cooper.

The Blevins family had a home in Holbrook, and ironically they never had a ranch house or any building at their Canyon Creek ranch. This is very suspect. Supposedly the family lived on the ranch including Mart Blevins, his wife, two daughters, four sons, a son in law and one daughter in law. So where did these people live if there was not one building on the Canyon Creek Ranch at that time. This was a little weird to say the least. Andy Cooper or Cooper Blevins was their stepson.

Below is a picture of Holbrook, Arizona, (circa 1930's). But it would have looked almost the same in the late 1880's just no cars and the street would not have been paved. This photo was found in our National Archives.

The family also spent time in their little three-room frame cottage, in Holbrook, that was located on the north side of the railroad tracks in Holbrook, and from time to time Andy Cooper, whether on the run or just passing through town, would spend the night at their cottage in Holbrook or at the old man's ranch at

Canyon Creek. On the opposite side of the tracks in downtown Holbrook were the half-dozen saloons, restaurants, the post-office and two or three stores that made up downtown Holbrook. For two months the Apache County Sheriff Commodore Perry Owens carried a warrant for the arrest of Andy Cooper for the crime of cattle rustling and horse stealing. It was sworn to by Board of Trustees of the Apache County Cattle Growers' Association of which Barnes was secretary and treasurer. The reader must understand, cattle rustling was not a capital offense in those days, but for sure horse stealing was punishable by death if convicted or simply lynched when they were caught.

At that time Will Barnes writes, that he was a member of the County Commissioners Office of Apache County, and was also on the Territorial Commissioners Board that held regular sessions at nearby St. Johns, Arizona Territory, that he served as the Apache County Capital. The Board members knew of the un-served warrant, and were determined to learn why the sheriff was reluctant to make the arrest of Andy Cooper.

Summoning Sheriff Owens before the board, they inquired as to the reason he had not served the arrest warrant for horse stealing on the fugitive, Andy Cooper. His reply was that he had not been able to locate Cooper. Barnes had seen Andy Cooper ride into Holbrook not two days before the meeting, and told the sheriff after his meeting with the board, that Cooper was holed up in the family cottage across the street from the railroad depot in town. After a rather lively session with the board, the sheriff was advised that unless Cooper was arrested immediately the board would start proceedings and oust him from office for failure to do his duty.

After the meeting with the Board, Sheriff Owens went back to his office in Holbrook, upon his arrival he loaded his rifle and his pistols, and when Deputy

Sheriff Barnes offered to go with him to serve the arrest warrant on Cooper, the sheriff said;

> "Thanks Will, but this is my job and I know the culprit and thanks to you and my previous experience working with the suspect, I am fully aware of what to expect, so I will be prepared for the worst, hoping for the best."

Sheriff Commodore Owens stationed Barnes across the street at the train depot just in case he needed backup. Owens took off his hat and fixed his long hair, smiled at Barnes and said let's get it done. Fully armed with his rifle and two pistols, the sheriff walked down the middle of the street toward the Blevins cottage. There was no doubt about the personal bravery of Sheriff Commodore Perry Owens, knowing there would be a fight the towns people headed for shelter, because they knew what was about to happen. Sheriff Owens was born on the anniversary of Commodore Perry's fight on Lake Erie and was named after Perry. He knew Andy Cooper well, but it was common belief that he was avoiding the arrest, feeling sure one or the other would be killed. Perhaps both, for each man would be shot dead. This author believes from previous knowledge of what happened to Barnes when he tried to arrest Andy Cooper at the cabin they trailed him, he knew there would be a shootout with Cooper when he tried to make an arrest.

Sheriff Perry Owens nearly always carried two revolvers, and could draw either with his right hand or his left with amazing speed and he was deadly accurate with either hand. Several times on the round-ups Barnes wrote that he had personally seen Owens stand twenty feet from an empty tomato-can and keep it rolling and jumping with alternate shots from his two guns until it was torn to pieces.

Andy Cooper was a single-handed pistol shooter, but was very accurate, and was a master of the quick draw. A few days after Owens had been called before the Board of Commissioners, Barnes writes that Sheriff Owens was with a round-up wagon about ten miles above Holbrook, when he rode into Holbrook and had barely got back to his office. While Barnes and Sheriff Owens shared a cup of coffee, Barnes told Owens that where he could find Andy Cooper. Barnes said for some reason the sheriff went to the drugstore, kept by the local town marshal, Frank Wattron, who was one of the bravest and nerviest of men Barnes says he ever met, then he left the drugstore, walked down to the livery stable for some reason and then came out and walked down the street to the Blevins cottage. Barnes situated himself at the railroad station, on the back of the building on the platform from which he commanded a clear view of the Blevins house where Sheriff Cooper was going. Barnes sat down on a bench and waited for action in a perfect place to provide immediate backup if needed and readied himself, because he had a feeling his service would probably be needed. Barnes wrote in his book and also in the report that he filed with Sheriff Owens the following;

> *"I saw Sheriff Owens leave the drugstore alone, carrying his Winchester in the crook of his left arm. He walked straight across the track to the livery stable, went in for a moment or two, then came out and strode boldly up the road toward the Blevins house. He afterwards told us he had stopped to have a last look at his 'shooting irons.' When Owens left the drugstore Wattron and several others came over to the depot and joined me. Frank Wattron said the sheriff refused all help."*

Owens looked over at Wattron and Barnes and continued talking;

> "I am the sheriff," he said, "and don't want anyone hurt. I can take him alone."

A bay horse with a saddle on his back was tied to a big cottonwood tree about twenty-five feet from the front door of the Blevins house. Barnes memories of the affair, which has been the best recording of the events that has ever been found goes as follows: The Blevins house was a frame, L-shaped one, with a little porch in front from which two doors opened. Reaching the house, his Winchester on his arm, Owens stepped boldly onto the porch. We could hear every step he took, and his knock on the door at his right. Owens with a six-shooter in his hand, opened this door about six inches and yelled to the folks inside;

> "Andy, this is Sheriff Owens, I have a warrant for your arrest for horse stealing, let's have no trouble."

Andy Cooper's response was;

> "Give me a few minutes. I'm not ready yet,"

At the same time attempting to close the door, Owens, however, slipped his foot into the opening, which prevented it from closing completely. He didn't hesitate a second. He heard the rustling of guns and realized it was shoot, or be shot. It was no time to parley. A bullet from his Winchester crashed through the wooden door, struck Cooper in the pit of the stomach, and passed clear through his body.

Owens jumped back off the porch, throwing a cartridge into his Winchester barrel as he did so, he knew there were people in the room in front of him at his left, who had no particular love for him. The door of this room opened a few inches, and John Blevins,

Cooper's half-brother, a young man about twenty-two years old, shoved a six shooter through the opening and fired at Owens, not over five or six feet away. The bullet missed him, but hit the horse tied to the tree in front, squarely between the eyes. The horse pulled back, broke the reins with which he was tied, ran about a hundred feet and dropped dead.

The animal had been tied there, possibly, for a quick get-away. Blevins, after his one shot, slammed the door. Owens fired through it, the ball crashing into young Blevins' shoulder, putting him out of the fight. This was Owens' second shot, both effective. Owens heard someone moving in the room at his right. He ran to the front window, and saw Cooper with a revolver in his hand peering through the window, evidently trying to locate him. He fired a third shot, which tore through the boards and struck Cooper in the hip.

Throwing another cartridge into his rifle, Owens whirled toward the door of the room just as another brother, Hamp Blevins, not over fourteen years old, stepped boldly out with Andy Cooper's well-known ivory-handled six-shooter in his hand. His mother was screaming at the top of her voice, trying to hold him back. The boy seemed absolutely fearless with the intent to kill Sheriff Owens.

> *"Where is the son of a bitch, so and so, the young Blevins hollered, and went on saying, I'll get him."*

All of the witnesses standing on the depot platform across the street heard Owens plainly. The words were hardly out of his mouth as Owens' fourth shot struck young Sam Houston Blevins in the breast. He dropped dead across the doorstep. Owens, every sense alert, stood boldly out in front of the porch. He knew not how many more men might be in the house. He knew there were at least two women, a wife and a mother, either of whom was capable of handling a six-shooter as well as any man. His ears caught a noise, as if a window was being raised. He ran to the corner of the house.

The son-in-law, Mose Roberts, was climbing cautiously out of a window of the back room with a six shooter in his hand. It was evidently his intention to make a surprise attack on the sheriff from that side. Owens' fifth shot passed through his chest. Owens then calmly started for the livery stable to get his horse. Several men started across the tracks towards him, A. F. Banta, local Justice of the Peace, in the lead.

"Have you finished the job?" Banta asked. "I think I have," was Owens curt reply.

The two photos below of Andy Cooper and the Blevins Cottage were found in our National Archives

**Andy Cooper   The Blevins cottage in
Circa 1880   Holbrook, AZ. Circa 1930**

Owens led his horse out of the livery-stable, mounted, and rode rapidly out of town. He told Barnes later that he felt he would be safer away from there until the excitement had died down. The interior of that cottage was a dreadful and sickening sight. There was one dead boy, and three men desperately wounded, lying on the floors. Human blood was over everything. Two hysterical women, one the mother of two of the men, the other John Blevins' young wife, and their dresses drenched with blood, were trying to do something for the wounded. Cooper died that night. Roberts lived about ten days. John Blevins recovered from his wound. Within a week, word reached Holbrook that Mart Blevins, the head of the Blevins family, and another son, Charlie, had been killed over in the Tonto Basin, being victims of the Pleasant Valley War in that region. The warrant for Andy Cooper's arrest was afterwards turned in by the sheriff to the clerk of the county court. Across its face Owens had written;

> *"The party against whom this warrant was issued was killed while resisting arrest."*

A grim and gory page in the history of Apache County was closed. Those of us who stood on the depot platform and watched with staring eyes, the entire proceedings felt as if we had witnessed a gladiatorial combat of the old Roman days. In all the wild events of Arizona's wildest days there is nothing to surpass this affair for reckless bravery on the part of a Peace officer. Looking back over it all, Barnes writes that he felt that day, that Sheriff Commodore Perry Owens was justified for not making a hasty arrest. As near as any of us could estimate, the shooting was all over and Owens on his way back to the livery-stable to get his horse inside of five minutes from the moment he left the stable to make the arrest. The event occurred between three and four o'clock in the afternoon on September 4, 1887.

The diagram below was completed a by Deputy Sheriff Will Barnes and attached to his report to the Apache County Commissioners Board. This diagram shows Barnes amazing pride in recording facts. This diagram was found in his book Apaches and Longhorns and is public domain.

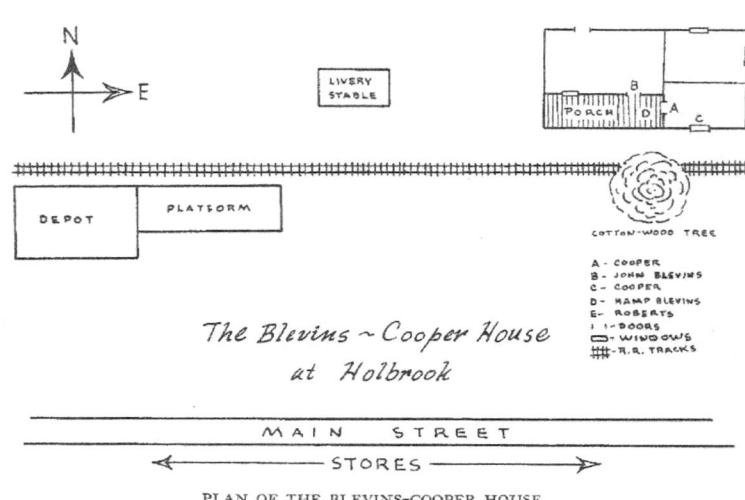

PLAN OF THE BLEVINS-COOPER HOUSE,
AS SKETCHED BY WILL C. BARNES

Chapter Thirteen
Three Men Lynched

The following information in this chapter is taken directly from Will Barnes memoirs in his book, *Apaches & Longhorns*. In this chapter the author will present Will Barnes views and involvement in several of the events relating to the Pleasant Valley War. Shortly after the Cooper Blevins shootout at Holbrook, another group of individuals were suspected of being horse thieves and cattle rustlers in Tonto Basin as well as Pleasant Valley.

Near the town of Heber, in Yavapai County, above the Mogollon Rim, Arizona Territory, which is twenty miles north of Pleasant Valley, a young chap had a horse ranch. He was a tall, handsome, red-headed lad, and a favorite fellow in and around the towns of Heber and Holbrook and the surrounding area. His language and the way he carried himself, indicated that he was well educated, came from a good family and was brought up in an above average life style. Like many young fellows who drifted into the wild and woolly West during those years, once he crossed the Rio Grande, sadly he left behind moral ideas of right and wrong, and thought most anything went in the Arizona and New Mexico Territories.

His name was James aka; "Jamie" Stott. After a while, stock detectives employed by the local association of cattlemen obtained conclusive proof that the young man's ranch was being used as headquarters for a well-organized band of horse-thieves and cattle rustlers. Bunches of horses and cattle from the north were exchanged for others stolen from the south, and kept on his ranges, while brands were changed and the hair grew out over the old brands.

An arrest warrant was issued in Apache County for the crime of horse stealing. Stott was arrested, went to trial and was acquitted for lack of evidence. The close by uninhabited portions of the Indian Reservation offered a fine region in which to hide the horses and cattle away while new brands healed over, because the place was so wild and remote, that the owners of the stolen stock turned back home after losing the trails. In common with many others, Will Barnes, an Apache County Deputy Sheriff had a strong suspicion of what was happening. Barnes writes that he liked the young fellow from Boston and tried to warn Stott of the danger he was taking. But young Jamie would not listen. When confronted by Barnes, Stott would pat the six-shooter which always hung at his hip and say;

"I can take care of myself any day. I'd love to see the color of the man's hair that can get the drop on me."

Will Barnes writes that on those occasions after warning Jamie and hearing his answer to Barnes warnings;

"Well, Jamie, my boy, I've warned you that you are playing with fire and will at some point you will get burned if you continue."

These were Will Barnes parting words to Stott as young Jamie Stott rode away one morning after having spent the night at Barnes' home in Holbrook. Ten or twelve days later, with two of his men, Barnes was up on the mountain at their Long Tom ranch ranges, as Barnes explains in his book. Early on the morning of August 10, 1888, one of his cowboys rode out to roundup one of his saddle horses. An hour later young Louis Johnson came tearing back down the trail towards their camp as if the whole Apache tribe was after him. So excited that he could scarcely talk, he managed to explain that he had found three men hanging from the limb of a large pine tree a few miles from the ranch, close to the trail leading down to the Blevins Canyon Creek ranch;

> "Did you know them?" Barnes asked.
> "Sure did! They were Jim Stott, Billy (aka: Jeff) Wilson, and Jim Scott."

Naturally there was considerable excitement in our camp. Every one of these men was well known to all of us. Young Louis Johnson explained that he was stray horse hunting when he discovered the bodies;

> "I couldn't find the horses, but did run into a lot of fresh horse tracks in the road. Thinking they might be our horses, I followed them down the road for a couple of miles. The trail led through a very rocky bit of ground. The tracks were hard to see, and I was leaning down from my saddle, trying to figure out who and where they were going. Suddenly old Pete, my horse, gave a snort and stopped dead still. When I raised my head, I found myself within ten feet of three bodies hanging from a big pine tree. Their faces were opposite mine; hands tied behind them; eyes looking up into the sky, but seeing nothing, he continued huskily, "I just whirled Pete around, jabbed both my spurs into his ribs and drug it for the ranch."

A hurried ride by Barnes and two of his wranglers to the location where the bodies of the men were still hanging corroborated young Louis Johnson's story. They were located where the trail from Canyon Creek crossed General Crook's *"Verde Road,"* *(Now called State Route 260)*, traveling south on a trail, *(that is now the road from SR260 to Bear Canyon Lake),* Barnes writes, that he and two of his wranglers found three bodies swinging from the limbs of a large pine tree limb just where Louis Johnson said they were.

Barnes recognized them right off. He writes they were Jamie Stott, Jim Scott, and Billy (Jeff) Wilson. All had been hurled into the next world. The indications were that the deed had been done not more than twenty-four hours before Barnes and his two wranglers found the bodies. Barnes goes on to say that he sent one of the men with him to Holbrook to report the incident. Leaving the bodies of the men still hanging so the coroner could complete his task, Barnes and his other wrangler left almost immediately after identifying the three men's bodies. The three bodies swung there in the bright sun for three full days before the coroner arrived. A few hardy individuals visited the scene, but nobody had the nerve to cut the bodies down. Nor did any linger around the spot. Their curiosity was quickly satisfied.

After three days from the time Barnes sent his wrangler to Holbrook to report the lynching, A. F. Banta, County Justice of the Peace at Holbrook, arrived at Barnes Ranch with three men Sam Brown, the livery stable owner; Ben Burke, a local carpenter in Holbrook; and F. A. Ames, an employee of the Aztec Cattle Company, to perform an inquest on the bodies of all three men. The three men were excited to go with Justice of the Peace Banta. One of Barnes cowboys, S. T. Frankenfield, who volunteered to guide the posse to the scene of the hanging and who was the first man to discover the bodies and was the man Barnes sent to Holbrook to give the alarming news. Justice Banta asked him to go with them, because he knew the exact location of the ugly scene. Barnes writes that Frankenfield was not very excited about going back to the scene of the hanging, but he agreed to guide them to the scene.

The party, after viewing the remains as a Coroner's Jury, started to dig graves immediately under each man, with the idea in mind of simply cutting the ropes and dropping each body into its respective grave without having to handle the three day old badly decayed bodies from exposure to the sun and the other elements. However, the spot proved so rocky that digging was out of the question.

Sam Brown, who owned and drove the wagon they brought, stood up in the vehicle, and, cutting each rope, allowing each body to drop into a large canvas wagon-sheet that was spread below it. Each body was then rolled in its wagon sheet, roped securely and loaded into the wagon, which was driven down the hill into a little open spot where the ground was easier to dig. Three separate graves were dug, each one of the sheeted forms dropped into its own grave with the earth shoveled over it. It was reported that Sam Brown said the *"Lord's Prayer"* over their bodies after they were buried.

There has always been a general belief in polite circles in Holbrook that Sam couldn't repeat the *"Lord's Prayer"* in its entirety, on a bet, but Justice of the Peace Banta declared that he did. There were many who had their doubts as to his ability and whether Banta told the truth. After the earth and stones had been hastily piled over each body to make a small mound, oak stakes were cut from a nearby sapling, one side whittled smooth, and a name was penciled on each stake. The stakes were then driven into the respective mounds, for future identification.

The official party returned to Holbrook after burying the bodies of the three men. Justice Banta was sure that the deed was not committed by a mob of murderers as thought by most folks. On the contrary, there was little doubt, after a brief investigation of the scene that the work was done by men, most of whom were reputable citizens, determined to put an end to the reign of lawlessness that for some time had terrorized the entire region. Every man in the burial party knew the three victims, and the charges against them were common knowledge all over that region.

Billy (aka: Jeff) Wilson had been a cook for the Hashknife round-up wagon for some months. He was a first-class round-up cook. Will Barnes personally knew Wilson. He quit his job for some unknown reason, and after a while became a member of Jamie Stott's household at his Bear Springs ranch. Wilson was not a bad sort, as men went in those days. But he evidently craved excitement and a little easy money. The horse stealing business furnished both. Barnes never knew him to be accused of any wrong-doing before being hung, though there was not really much known about Wilson. He drifted into Arizona from some place over in New Mexico. But there were no wanted papers on him that Barnes ever found. Wilson was just a drifting cowboy who met Jamie Stott when they both worked for the Hashknife spread. Stott was a drover and Wilson a cook.

James Scott was a Texas boy, a drifting cowpuncher, who was generally believed to have fallen into bad company and paid the penalty. Scott came to Arizona from Oregon. When news of the hanging of the three men was flashed over the wires, his relatives in Eugene, Oregon, believing their brother to be one of the men, kept the wires busy for several days, until the identity of the man who was hung was cleared up and they received assurance that their brother was not the James Scott of the necktie party.

Jamie Stott's history has already been discussed. Details of the unfortunate affair were learned from different sources later. The men involved did not, of course, talk much of their part in it; but, as the days passed, bits of information came to the surface from time to time from the lips of persons who had taken part in the deed. When pieced together, they made a fairly understandable story of what occurred on the day the execution took place. The whole plan had been worked out carefully in advance.

One party, led by well-known Gila County Sheriff Glenn Reynolds and his deputy, Tom Horn, were said to have been in Tonto Basin, carrying warrants for the arrest of the three men for horse thievery, again a hanging offense in those days.

> This author along with author Chip Carlson in his book, Tom Horn: Blood on the Moon, can place Gila County Sheriff Glenn Reynolds, and most definitely his friend and deputy sheriff at the time, Tom Horn but never proven, although Horn did admit to John Coble, years later, who was a prominent member of the Wyoming Cattlemen's association and his employer in Wyoming, where Horn worked as a stock detective, that he, Horn had been with a group of citizens who hung three horse thieves while he worked as a Deputy Gila County Sheriff.

Barnes continues to write, that before daylight, the morning of August 9, 1888, a posse of three men, who Stott recognized and probably, Apache County Deputy Sheriffs Osmer D. Flake, Jim Houck and this author and a third unknown deputy, who this author believes was Tom Horn, who were all carrying warrants for the arrest of the three men, hid near Stott's cabin at Aztec Springs, waiting for one of the men to come out from inside the cabin. Hiding and waiting for his unsuspecting prey was a very typical move that was used by Deputy Sheriffs in those days. No need for gunplay if you can catch your prey by surprise. Jamie Stott was the first man to appear. He came out half dressed, and started to the wood-pile for wood to build a fire to make their breakfast. As he stepped clear of the cabin door, unaware of anything wrong, a voice at his right snapped;

"Hands up, Jim!"

As Stott turned toward the voice, a man was holding a rifle pointed right at him, and then the man stepped out from around the corner of the cabin to his left. Turning quickly, Stott faced the muzzle of a rifle held in the hands of a man he obviously knew only too well. His reluctant hands went into the air, slowly, but as directed. Is it possible, he must have said to himself, that I am to be taken so easily? For, he had so often bragged of his ability to take care of himself. He realized the tenseness of the situation, however, and its necessities, and his need to use discretion. Under the circumstances, there could possibly be opportunity for escape later.

"Oh, well, have your way, boys! Make yourselves at home. May I go back into the cabin for my coat? It's cold and raw in this early morning air. Don't worry about your coat, Jim. We'll make things warm enough for you."

One of the men went for the saddle-horses hidden back in the timber. Stott still pleaded for his coat. The other two men went into the cabin, taking Stott with them. First they searched every nook and corner of the place, confiscating all the weapons they found. Stott volunteered to cook breakfast for the three men, which he did. When that was over, they took him outside and placed him on a horse. His feet were linked together with steel handcuffs, the chain passed under the animal's belly, and then the chain of the pair on his wrists was slipped through the arch of the saddle in which he sat, making it utterly impossible for him to escape or ride away from them. Then with Stott and Wilson, who was also inside when the lawmen entered the cabin, with two of the three prisoners with which they had warrants on, the three lawmen and their two prisoners rode off down the Verde road to the west. What happened later, nobody knows, exactly but by the large number of tracks found, it appeared they met another very large group of men on the trail, thought to be local ranchers, who joined the posse to join in the necktie party to come.

It was said, by witnesses, according to Barnes, that Stott pleaded for a chance, just a show for his life. He undoubtedly knew what was ahead of him. In due time the party arrived at the trail that came up from Tonto Basin to Pleasant Valley, here they met the large posse from that section. From the little information that leaked out subsequently, it is believed that Scott, who was with the large group of men who met Horn and Reynolds, along with Wilson broke down and begged for mercy, when they found themselves sitting on their horses under a pine tree, faces uncovered, each with the noose of a rope around his neck, the other end of which was tied hard and fast to a limb above them. But the Vigilantes were hard-boiled, they were not going to allow these men to escape justice through the legal system since Stott had too many friends in high places and a family with enough money to get him off almost any crime. The chains fastening the prisoners' feet beneath the bellies of their horses were opened.

Oblivious to the part they were to play, the horses stood quietly. A man stood behind each animal. At a signal, each delivered a crashing blow with a rope on the hips of the horse in front of him. A wild plunge forward and the riders were left swinging in the air. Their faces twitched, their bodies turned round and round in the bright sunlight, their manacled hands dragged in vain at the steel shackles behind them which held them securely.

Then the Vigilantes turned to Stott. Unafraid and undaunted, he faced them all and dared them to do their worst. He declared that if they would turn him loose he would fight them all, single-handed and alone. He addressed each one by name, and called down on his head every curse and malediction his trembling lips could utter. As he talked, the horse he was on jumped from under him, and Stott, too, was swinging back and forth with his two comrades, *"dancing a dead man's jig,"* it was called in those lively days.

The Associated Press carried the news of the triple hanging all over the country. To Holbrook, from their home in Massachusetts came the aged parents of Stott, to demand that the perpetrators of the deed be arrested and punished by the authorities.

According to Will Barnes, the day before Stott's parents arrived, a telegram reached Holbrook from Albuquerque, New Mexico, to *"The Master of the Masonic Lodge at Holbrook,"* requesting that the official meet Mr. James Stott, Jamie's parents, on the arrival of the noon train from the East. As the Master was absent from town that day, the message was delivered to me *(Will Barnes)*, as the next official in rank. With my mother, Barnes writes, they went to the station to meet the train. Barnes writes that he will never forget the shock, they both experienced when two very elderly people stepped from one of the cars. We took them both to the local hotel, and after they had had a short rest, then we escorted them over to our house, where everything humanly possible was done to comfort them in their time of great sorrow.

Believing that any action looking toward the punishment of the Vigilantes would probably create a difficult situation in the region, one that might bring reprisals on citizens who were willing to make an effort to help them, Barnes advised them against any such attempt; and the two sorrowing ones went back to their eastern home convinced that their only son had been murdered and that justice had been denied them. Will Barnes writes, that he promised Stott's parents that he would see to it that their son's body was dug up and shipped back to them, whenever they should write and ask that this be done. But they never wrote to Barnes with instructions. The time between Sott's parents left Barnes home and went back to their hotel before leaving to go back home will be discussed later with testimony from another witness, that will clear up why they did not write Barnes.

Below is a picture of the gravesite and location that suspected horse thieves and cattle rustlers Jamie Stott, Jim Scott and Billy Wilson were hung and buried, located near SR60 and the Sharps Creek intersection. This picture was taken by Marian Hensley. The author is standing on the right of friend, Don Hensley. April 23, 2016

The three men's bodies are still lying there, where they were originally buried. An uncle of Jim Scott, who was once a territorial official in Arizona, and, at the time of the execution of his nephew, a prominent

Pacific Coast lawyer, asked Barnes soon after the affair to come to Los Angeles at his expense and advise him as to what (if any) steps he could take against the men concerned with the hanging. The victim was the son of his only sister, who lived in eastern Texas. She had asked her brother to do what he could in the matter. Things in northern Arizona at that time were mighty tense.

The photos of Stott and Wilson below were found in our National Archives, both photos are Circa 1880's.

Jamie Stott **Billy (Jeff) Wilson**

Chapter Fourteen
Frederick Russell Burnham

In this chapter the Author will present a biography of Frederick Russell Burnham, a very reputable resource with regard to his involvement in the Pleasant Valley War. This biography is presented to bring credibility to young Fred Burnham as a great resource, since he recorded his firsthand experiences during the Pleasant Valley War, written from his own memoirs, his book called *"Scouting on Two Continents."*

The Author believes that Burnham's biography and credibility is very important because of his direct involvement in the Pleasant Valley War. Fred Burnham's biography is a little lengthy, but he was an amazing man and his written word concerning his involvement in the feud has been overlooked by most of historians.

Frederick Russell Burnham was the first man to come forward that he was drawn into the feud and having been on the Graham faction side of the feud, and he believed that he was on the wrong side of the Pleasant Valley War or the Graham-Tewksbury Feud. Fred Burnham's credibility having been directly involved in this feud is really an eye opener.

Frederick Russell "Fred" Burnham was born May 11, 1861, on a Sioux Indian Reservation in Minnesota, to a missionary family living in the small pioneer town of Tivoli *(now gone),* about twenty miles outside the village of Mankato. His father, the Reverend Edwin Otway Burnham, was a Presbyterian minister, educated and ordained in New York, but originally from Ghent, Kentucky. Fred's mother, Rebecca Russell Burnham, spent most of her childhood in Iowa, having emigrated with her family from Westminster, England at the age of three.

In the Dakota War of 1862, Chief Little Crow and his Sioux warriors attacked the nearby town of New Ulm, Minnesota. Burnham's father was in Mankato buying ammunition at the time, so when Burnham's mother saw Sioux approaching her cabin dressed in war paint, she knew she had to leave and could never escape carrying her baby. She hid baby Fred in a basket of green corn husks in a corn field and fled for her life. When she returned she found their house burned down, but baby Fred was found safe and sound, sound asleep hidden in the basket of husks, still in the corn field, where his mom left him.

The family decided to move back to Iowa where young Fred grew up and attended local schools. It was there that he met Blanche Blick, who would later become his wife. The Burnham family moved to Los Angeles, California in 1870, in search of easier living conditions, soon after Fred's father Edwin was seriously injured in an accident while rebuilding the family homestead. Two years later, Edwin died, leaving the family destitute. Burnham's mother along with his three-year old younger brother Howard moved back to Iowa to live with her parents; Twelve-year old Fred remained in California alone tasked with having to repay his family's debts and ultimately to make his own way.

For the next few years, young Fred worked as a mounted messenger for the Western Union Telegraph Company in California and in the Arizona Territory. On one occasion his horse was stolen from him by Tiburcio Vasquez, the famous Mexican Southern California bandit. At the age of 14, Fred Burnham began his life as a scout and tracker in the Apache Wars, during which he took part of the last United States Army expedition to find capture or kill the Apache renegade Geronimo.

The U.S. Army Arizona Territorial office was at Fort Whipple near the town of in Prescott, Arizona in

1875 when Fred arrived. Fred met an old scout by the name of Lee, who served under General George Crook, the Arizona U.S. Army Commander. Lee taught Burnham how to track Apache by many different means but the most important skill was by detecting the odor of burning mescal, a species of the aloe plants the Apache often cooked and ate. With a careful study of the local air currents and canyons, he was taught to track them by following the burning odor of the plant, to Apache hiding places from as far away as six miles.

The photo below of an aloe mescal plant was taken by the author

During the Apache uprisings, young Fred also learned a lot about scouting and trailing from Al Sieber, the Chief of Scouts for the U.S. Army under General Crook while living in Prescott and his assistant Archie McIntosh, who had been a lead scout in Crook's previous two Geronimo campaigns. Fred also learned even more about scouting techniques from the Apache scouts with Crooks scouting unit, who were older and in their twilight years. But he was taught by them the most important scouting skill a vital lesson, that it is imperative that a scout know the history, tradition, religion, social customs, and superstitions of whatever country or people, he is called on to work with or among. But the scout, who was to have perhaps the greatest influence on Burnham during his formative years, was an old army scout by the name of Holmes.

Holmes served under Kit Carson and John C. Freemont, but he was an old man and physically impaired, by the time Fred met him. He lost all his family in the Indian wars and before he died he wanted to impart his knowledge of the frontier to young Fred Burnham. The two men traveled throughout the American Southwest and Northern Mexico, with Holmes teaching Fred many scouting skills, such as how to track a trail, to double and cover one's own trail, to properly ascend and descend precipices, and how to tell the time at night. Burnham also learned survival skills from Holmes, such as where to find water in the desert, how to protect himself from snakes, and what to do in case of forest fires or floods. The buffalo were by that time disappearing from Texas, and the plains, at the same time the silver & gold mining camps in the Arizona Territory were drawing national attention. Fred decided to go to the Arizona Territory. He earned a small stake by driving a bunch of wild Texas ponies up to Missouri and selling them, and for a time thereafter reveled in spurs, sombreros, and all the picturesque equipment and life of a cowpuncher

Fearing his end was near and having lost his entire family in the Indian wars, Holmes was looking for a pupil to whom he might impart the frontier knowledge he had gathered throughout his long life. He chose Fred as his companion and his eager pupil. For six months they traveled into the mountains in Arizona, New Mexico and Sonora, Old Mexico. With infinite patience Holmes taught Fred the details of trailing and hunting that make up a scout's work.

Holmes impressed upon Fred that in the simplest jobs there is a right way and a wrong way. He showed Fred the right way to take off a saddle, hobble a horse, to draw a nail, to braid a rope, to make a bed, as well as how to protect oneself from snakes, forest fires, falling trees or floods. According to Fred, Holmes showed him how to ascend and descend precipices, how to double and cover a trail, how to time himself at night, how to travel in the direction intended either day or night and how to find water in the deserts. All this instruction was given to Fred in endless detail.

The two men spent many hours around their campfires while Holmes related tales and incidents, all bearing on the scout's life that he had lead from his boyhood days. According to Fred there was so much information, that unfortunately, he was not able to absorb it all but many of the main skills Holmes patiently offered, stuck in Fred's mind. Many times, in emergencies, Fred remembered Holmes words that proved to be the deciding factor between Fred's death and his ability to survive all of which Burnham gratefully gave credit to the wisdom and leadership that was bestowed on him by Holmes.

After departing from Holmes with a vast knowledge of scouting, Fred decided to go to Prescott and see if he could land a job as a scout for the Army there in Prescott he met an old friend of Holmes, a scout by the name of Lee. Lee had a gold mine claim in the Santa Maria River country, which is located a little east of Bagdad, Arizona eighty miles west of Prescott. He wanted to gather samples to be assayed. It was rough desert land of wide mesas covered with boulders or lava and cleft by torturous canyons hundreds of feet deep. According to Fred, he and Lee were only there for a few days gathering rock samples, then they headed back to Prescott but while they were there, Lee pointed out the acres of wild mescal which were a major part of the Apache's food and medicinal life support.

Lee was one of General George Crook's best scouts and his success in locating Apache's was due to his intimate knowledge of their lifestyle, eating habits and especially their method of preparing mescal. Mescal is a species of the aloe plant family, with a heart about the size of a large turnip. It is the duty of the Apache squaw to gather the mescal, trim off the thorny leaves, and pile bushels of the hearts into great mounts of boulders on which a fire is kept burning for five days. The heat of the boulders gradually roasts the mescal, bringing out the sweetness and nourishment. These baked hearts are then patted out in cakes, dried on racks of small cedar poles or willow sticks, and made ready for carrying in fiber bags or rawhide lacings. They taste somewhat like a turnip, but mescal hearts are sweeter than a sweet potato. They are very nourishing, but are full of natural fine fibers, which the Apache chews and spits out, much as sugar cane or sorghum is eaten and disposed of by the natives of those countries. It is also a custom of the Apaches to gather one big pit full of mescal each year to be fermented into a strong drink for one glorious drunk.

Lee made a careful study of the air currents that sweep through the deep canyons, and although the Apaches found ways to conceal the telltale smoke clouds, they could not prevent the odor of burning mescal from hanging in the air and drifting for miles up and down the canyons. By tracing these odors, Lee could mark the most secret hiding places of the Apaches. Because they could not do without the harvest of the mescal or be content to live without it, they were inevitably spied upon by him, then surrounded by government troops and captured. In many cases the odor of the mescal could be detected as far as five to six miles from its source. With a little dried venison, beef or horse meat and a roast of mescal, the Apache seemed to be supplied with a balance ration of food. With this food supply, the Apaches could lead their enemies on a maddening chase and to inflict many defeats in the hot dry deserts of the southwest Arizona Territory.

Lee impressed upon young Fred Burnham the importance that a scout should know the history, tradition, religion, social customs and superstitions of whatever country or people he was called to work in and among. Lee taught young Fred that those factors were almost as important as the physical character of the country, its climate and food sources. Certain people will do certain things without fail. Certain other things, depending upon where they lived, that seemed obvious would be something they might not do. There is no danger of knowing too much of the mental habits of an enemy, that one should neither underestimate the enemy nor credit him with superhuman powers. Fear and courage are latent in every human being, though roused into activity by very diverse means, were some of the lessons Lee taught young Fred. Burnham did not drink or smoke. It was his belief that as a scout he needed all five senses and every faculty of mind at the highest efficiency at all times. There is nothing that sharpens a man's senses so acutely as to know that bitter and determined enemies were in pursuit of him both day and night. Burnham mentions an incident that bears out this very belief;

> "I recall one scout I worked with who forfeited his life by his neglect for one instant to keep in the shade of a small oak tree. He was safe from sight so long as he kept in the shadow, but he became so intent on using his field glasses that he allowed a shaft of sunlight to betray him to the enemy."

Fred was asked many times how it was possible for a scout to live for months in an enemy's country, and how horses can travel the astounding distance they do. Volumes have been written on the care of horses but not of the training of a scout to live in such conditions.

In every country, food can be found if the scout knows how to get it and if his stomach will lend itself to such adjustment as are sometimes necessary. When changing from a cereal diet to a diet of meat, there is likely to be a constant desire for meat or fats in some form. But a man's stomach, like his hand, can be trained to many strange habits. In Arizona, one of the favorite ways of preparing food for long hard rides without lighting a fire in dangerous country was to dry venison, then grind it into a powder form, then mix it, about half and half with flour and then bake in a loaf that would fit in our saddle bags. Ten pounds of this concentrated food would last a man ten days and keep up his strength, also allowing him to not feel hunger.

A scout knows that a horse can thrive on most of the food that a man eats, even cooked food. One of the reasons why a good scout could outride the cowboys and frontiersman of the west was that he gave infinite care to his mount. He fed him raw eggs when available as well as dried milk, dried bread, dried fruit, vegetables, crackers, prunes, raisins, dried milk as well as bacon and dried meat. The twig ends cut from the desert willow and cottonwood gave the horse roughage. In the deserts the scout would also feed his horse the fig like fruit from the tops of Pitahaya, Saguaro cactus and Spanish bayonet. Horses will also eat crushed mesquite beans, acorns soaked and ground as well as other desert shrubs and seeds in season.

Water is sometimes found in deep, almost impenetrable canyons. It can be carried to the horse in a hat, Navajo blanket, a piece of good canvass or even a bit of a rubber cloth. A saddle blanket will absorb a gallon or two of water, and by turning it over and over in a ball as one walks or climbs, not much water will be lost, then the blanket can be rung out into a hat or cavity in a rock. The horse can also be taught to drink from a canteen or a bottle.

At last Burnham found himself in Santa Fe, New Mexico Territory. The action in Santa Fe was pretty slow and sometimes work was hard to find. It wasn't long before Fred had spent his grubstake. With only enough money to buy food for himself and his mount, Fred started out on his last pony into the bad country that lay between Santa Fe and Prescott, Arizona. Through his own carelessness, his horse, saddle and gear were stolen from him in broad daylight just on the outskirts of town.

Fred made the five-hundred-mile trek on foot and alone from Santa Fe to Prescott, Arizona, most of the time traveling by night and sleeping by day, because the Indians all along the trail from Santa Fe to Prescott were on the warpath. The Mogollon Mountains were covered with snow by the time Fred reached the Mogollon Plateau. It was winter and food was scarce. The Indians raided and drove off most of the settlers and their stock. They almost caught Fred on a couple close calls, and the snow and the cold gave him a harder time than the Indians. At a little creek filled with melted snow water along the trail even in the freezing cold, Fred enjoyed a swim and filled his canteen with fresh water. It was only twenty feet wide, but in his famished and exhausted condition made the feat seem as arduous as swimming in the dangerous Hellesport River, near his home town in Iowa. In spite of the hardships of the journey, Fred found a lot of beauty in that wilderness that interested him, including the Painted Desert, the forests of solid stone, the Little Colorado River and the curious cliff dwellings in the Verde River basin.

When he reached Prescott, Fred hooked up with his old scout friend Lee again, and stayed with Lee for a couple of months. While there in Prescott Fred heard about a great silver strike in Globe, Arizona, so he figured he would work his way to Globe, some two hundred and fifty miles from Prescott. Fred headed south to the Salt River Basin near the town of Phoenix, figuring he would find work there and then when he had a grubstake he would go East to Globe. Once he arrived near the Salt River Valley town of Tempe, he befriended a family by the name of Wells. Burnham does not mention the family by name in his book, but through this author's investigation, the name of the family was Wells, so from here on out the author will use their name in this book.

In nearby Globe, Arizona, Burnham unwittingly joined the Graham faction of the Pleasant Valley War before the mass killing started, and barely escaped death, himself, from his enemies the Tewksbury faction in the feud. Fred had no stake in the feud to start, but he was drawn into the conflict by his association with his friends, the John Wells family. Once the killing started, he had no choice but to join a faction as a hired gun even though, in his own words, it put him on the wrong side of the law. In between raids and forays, he practiced incessantly with his pistol and he learned to shoot using either hand and from the back of a galloping horse. Burnham began to see that even though he joined the feud to help his friends, he had been on the wrong side, in his own written word from his book, Scouting on two Continents, he writes;

> *"Avenging only led to more vengeance and to even greater injustice than that suffered through the often unjustly administered laws of the land,"*

The balance of Fred's life here in Arizona, will be discussed in detail in the next chapter, but suffice to say, his life got better after his friend Judge Hackney helped clear up his issues with the law, which will be discussed in the next chapter.

After Judge Hackney helped Fred clear his name, Fred went back to California but when he returned again to Arizona several years later he was appointed Deputy Sheriff of Pinal County, but he soon went back to herding cattle and prospecting. From their a couple years later Fred went back to Prescott, to find work. Having no luck he traveled back Iowa to visit his childhood sweetheart, Blanche, while there the two were married on February 6, 1884. Fred and Blanche Burnham settled down soon after and moved to California where they owned an orange grove in Pasadena, from which they made a menial living. Frustrated with being a farmer and orange grower, and boredom of farming and growing oranges, Fred was soon back doing prospecting and scouting but now he his wife Blanche and their young son Roderick moved to South Africa, after hearing that it was a great place to make a living and raise a family.

From this point until the end of this chapter, the author will present a brief description of Fred Burnham's life and experience as a scout in South Africa. The author believes it is important for the reader to understand the depth of this amazing man's scouting skills and the quality person that he was, as it solidifies the fact that his written experience during the Pleasant Valley War along with Will Barnes, and their involvement in the Pleasant Valley War or the Graham vs Tewksbury Feud, both are two of the most important pieces in solving the puzzle of the most brutal and murderous feud in United States History.

Fred Burnham was done with the Southwest and being a soldier of fortune, as his friend Richard Harding Davis later called him. So, Fred began to look elsewhere for the next undeveloped frontier, feeling that the American West was becoming tame and unchallenging. When he heard of the work of Cecil Rhodes and his pioneers in South Africa, who were attempting to build a railway across Africa from Cape to Cairo, Burnham sold what little he owned and, in 1893, he and Blanche set sail for Durban in South Africa with their young son, Frederick Russell with the intention to join Rhodes's pioneers in Matabeleland and Mashonaland.

Burnham was trekking a 1,000 miles north from Durban to Matabeleland with his wife and son, Roderick in an American built Conestoga wagon pulled by six burros, when war broke out between Rhodes's British South Africa and the Matabele in 1893. Fred signed up to scout for the British South African Army. Immediately upon arriving at Matabeleland, Fred joined the fighting. Leander Starr Jameson, the Company's Chief Magistrate in Mashonaland, hoped to defeat the Matabele quickly by capturing their Chief Lobengula, at his main headquarters. So, Jameson sent Burnham and a small group of scouts ahead to report on the situation there. Fred and his group of scouts were able to sneak into Chief Lobengula's camp, capture the chief without a sound, escape and bring him back to his leader Leander Jameson. With the capture of their chief the war with the Matabele was over. Fred was promoted to Chief of Scouts by Leander Starr Jameson.

Then a few years later Fred Burnham got involved in the Boar Wars and for his outstanding service in the first Boar War, Fred Burnham was presented the British South Africa Company Medal, a gold watch, and a share of a 300 acre tract of land in Matabeleland. It was there on his own land, that Burnham uncovered a cache of artifacts in the huge granite ruins, of the ancient civilization of the Great

Zimbabwe. Matabeleland became part of the Company domain, which was formally named Rhodesia in 1895.

In 1896, Fred Burnham led an expedition for Northern Territories British South Africa Exploration Company into the Zambezi Desert, in Northern Rhodesia, where they discovered a major copper deposit. Along the Kafue River, Burnham saw many similarities to copper deposits he had worked in the United States, and he encountered native people who wearing copper bracelets. After this expedition, he was elected to the Royal Geographical Society.

In 1897 Burnham was back in Matabeleland. The troop he was assigned to was undermanned due to the ill-fated Jameson Raid into the South African Republic, that took the lives of 80% of the troop, and in the first few months of the war alone, hundreds of white settlers were killed. With a few troops to support them, the settlers quickly built a fortress in the center of Bulawayo on their own and mounted patrols under famous scouts Robert Baden-Powell, and Frederick Selous. It was also during this war that two scouts of very different backgrounds, Burnham and Baden-Powell, would first meet and discuss ideas for training youth that would eventually become the plan for the program and the code of honor for the Boy Scouts.

The turning point in the war came when Burnham found a way through the Matopos Hills to a sacred cave not many miles from the Mangwe district, to a sanctuary then known only to the Matabele where Chief Mlimo had been hiding. Not far from the cave was a village (now gone) of about 100 huts filled with many warriors.

For Fred's outstanding service in capturing and killing Chief Mlimo, that officially ended the war. So Burnham's boss, General Carrington, the British Army commander during the Second Matabele War was quoted;

> "Frederick Burnham is the finest scout whoever scouted Africa. He was my Chief of Scouts in 1896 in the Matabeleland war, along with being the eyes and ears of my force."

With the Matabele wars over, Burnham decided it was time to leave Africa and move on to other adventures. The family returned to California. Soon after, Fred traveled to Alaska and the Yukon to prospect in the Klondike Gold Rush, taking with him his eldest son Roderick, who was then 12 years old. Upon hearing of the Spanish-American War, Burnham rushed home to volunteer his services, but the war had ended before he could get to the fighting. Burnham returned to the Klondike having played no part in the war.

Roberts asked General Frederick Carrington, who had commanded the British forces in Matabeleland three years earlier, who he should appoint as his Chief of Scouts in South Africa. Carrington, who had selected Burnham for this role, advised Roberts to do the same, describing Burnham as;

> "The finest scout who ever scouted in Africa."

Soon after arriving in South Africa on the RMS Dunottar Castle, Roberts sent for Burnham. The American scout was prospecting near Skagway, Alaska, when he received the following telegram in January 1900;

> "Lord Roberts appoints you on his personal staff as Chief of Scouts. If you accept, come at once the quickest way possible."

Cape Town South Africa is at the opposite end of the globe from the Klondike, so Burnham left immediately. In an unusual step for a foreigner,

Burnham received a command post from Roberts and the British Army rank of captain. Burnham reached the front just before the Battle of Paardeberg (February 1900). During the war, Burnham spent much time behind the Boer lines gathering information and blowing up railway bridges and tracks. He was captured twice (escaping both times), and also temporarily disabled at one point by near-fatal wounds.

Burnham was first captured during the fighting at Sanna's Post in the Orange Free State. He gave himself up in order to obtain information on the enemy, which he did, and then he escaped from his guards and succeeded in reaching British occupied Bloemfontein safely after two days and nights on the run. The second time he was captured was while trying to warn a British column approaching Thaba Nchu. He came upon a group of Boers hiding on the banks of the river, toward which the British were even then advancing. Cut off from his own side, Burnham chose to signal the approaching soldiers even though it would expose him to capture. With a red kerchief, Burnham signaled the soldiers to turn back, but the column paid no attention and plodded steadily on into the ambush, while Burnham was at once taken prisoner.

In the fight that followed, Burnham pretended to receive a wound in the knee. Limping heavily and groaning with pain, he was placed in a wagon with the officers who really were wounded, and who, in consequence, were not closely guarded. Later that evening, Burnham slipped over the driver's seat, dropped between the two wheels of the wagon, lowered himself and fell between the legs of the oxen on his back in the road. In an instant the wagon had passed over him safely, and while the dust still hung above the trail he rolled rapidly over into the ditch at the side of the road and lay motionless. It was four days before he was able to re-enter the British lines, during which time he had been lying in the open field. He had subsisted on one biscuit and two handfuls of "mielies," (Mielies are biscuits made from a coarse type of flour made from the maize plant, also known as mielies or mealies in southern Africa). Lord Roberts, Commander of all British troops fighting in the Second Boer War was quoted as saying:

> *"I take this opportunity to thank you, Frederick Russell Burnham, for your valuable services you rendered since you joined my head-quarters at Paardeburg last February. I doubt if any other man in the force could have successfully carried out such perilous enterprises in which you have from time to time been engaged, demanding as they did the training of a lifetime, combined with exceptional courage, caution and powers of endurance."*

On June 2, 1900, during the British march on Pretoria, Burnham was wounded, almost fatally. He was on a mission to cut off the flow of Boer gold and supplies to and from the sea and to halt the transportation of British prisoners of war out of the Pretoria. He scouted alone far to the east behind enemy lines trying to identify the best choke point along the Pretoria-Delagoa Bay railway line. He came upon an underpass of a railway bridge, an ideal location to disrupt the trains, but was immediately surrounded by a party of Boer soldiers. Burnham instantly fled and he had almost escaped when his horse was shot and fell, knocking him senseless and pinning him under its dead body. It was night and he was already far away from the troop when his horse was shot, so the Boer troopers apparently did not check to see if Burnham had been injured or killed.

When he awoke hours later, Burnham was alone and in a dazed state having sustained serious injuries. Despite his acute agony, Burnham proceeded to creep back to the railway, placed his charges, and blew up the line in two places. He then crept on his hands and knees to an empty animal enclosure to avoid capture and stayed there for two days and nights insensible. The next day, Burnham heard fighting in the distance so he crawled in that direction. By this time he was indifferent as to the source of the gunshots and by chance it was a British patrol that found him.

Once back at the army camp in Pretoria the surgeons discovered that Burnham had torn apart his stomach muscles and burst a blood-vessel. His very survival was due only to the fact that he had been without food or water for three days. Burnham's injuries were so serious that he was ordered to England by Lord Roberts. Two days before leaving for London, he was promoted to the rank of major, having received letters of commendation or congratulations from Baden-Powell, Rhodes, and Field Marshal Roberts. On his arrival in England, Burnham was commanded to dine with Queen Victoria and to spend the night at Osborne House.

A few months later, after the Queen's death, King Edward VII personally presented Burnham with the Queen's South Africa Medal with four bars for the battles at Driefontein (March 10, 1900), Johannesburg (May 31, 1900), Paardeberg (February 17–26, 1900), and Cape Colony (October 11, 1899 - May 31, 1902), in addition to the cross of the Distinguished Service Order, the second highest decoration in the British Army, for his heroism during the "victorious" march to Pretoria (June 2-5, 1900). The King also made his British Army appointment and rank permanent, despite his U.S. citizenship. Burnham received the highest awards of any soldier and the King pronounced Frederick Russell Burnham;

"The King of Army Scouts."

Burnham was already a celebrated scout when he first befriended Baden-Powell during the Second Matabele War, but the backgrounds of these two scouts was as strange a contrast as it is possible to imagine. From his youth on the open plains, Burnham's earliest playmates were Sioux Indian boys and their ambitions pointed to excelling in the lore and arts of the trail and together they dreamed of someday becoming great scouts. When Burnham was a teenager he supported himself by hunting game and making long rides for Western Union through the California deserts, his early mentors were wise old scouts of the American West, and by nineteen years of age Fred was a seasoned scout chasing and being chased by Apache.

The British scout he would later befriend and serve with in Matabeleland, Baden-Powell, was born in London and had graduated from Charterhouse, one of England's most famous public schools. Baden-Powell developed an ambition to become a scout at an early age. He passed an exam that gave him an immediate commission into the British Army when he was 19, but it would take several years before he was engaged in any active service. When the two men met in 1896, Baden-Powell was an army intelligence officer and a brilliant outdoorsman who had organized a small scouting section in his regiment, and also wrote the book, *"Reconnaissance and Scouting" (published in 1884),* then he served as a scout in the British Army in India, Afghanistan, Natal and Ashanti. Fred Burnham at the same time was General Carrington's Chief of Scouts.

During the siege of Bulawayo, these two men rode many times into the Matopos Hills on patrol, and it was in these hills that Burnham first introduced

Baden-Powell to the ways and methods of the Native Americans, and taught him "woodcraft" (better known today as scout craft). Baden-Powell had written at length about reconnaissance and tracking, but from Burnham he learned many new dimensions such as how to travel in wild country without either a compass or map, how to discover nearby dangers by observing animals, and the many techniques for finding potable water. So impressed was Baden-Powell by Burnham's scouting spirit and knowledge that he closely listened to all Fred had to tell. It was also then that Baden-Powell began to wear his signature Stetson campaign hat and neckerchief, like those worn by Burnham, for the first time. Both men recognized that wars were changing markedly and that the British Army needed to adapt. During their joint scouting missions, Baden-Powell and Burnham discussed the concept of a broad training program in woodcraft for young men, rich in exploration, tracking, field craft, and self-reliance. In Africa, no scout embodied these traits more than Burnham.

In his first scouting handbook, Aids to scouting (1899), Baden-Powell published many of the lessons he learned from Burnham and this book was later used by boys' groups as a guide to outdoor fun. At the urging of several youth leaders, Baden-Powell decided to adapt his scouting handbook specifically to training boys. While Baden-Powell went on to refine the concept of Scouting, publish Scouting for boys (1908), and become the founder of the international Scouting movement, Burnham has been called the movement's father. James E. West, Chief Scout Executive for the Boy Scouts of America (BSA), summarized Burnham's historical relevance to Scouting:

> *"There is a special significance for those of us in Scouting for Fred Burnham was enthroned for this work by*

> Lord Baden Powell, who was then connected with the British Army in Africa, and who had unbounded admiration for the scouting methods of Frederick Russell Burnham. So these two pioneers, each of whom was to have such immeasurable influence in restoring the old traditions of American youth, met in Africa, years before the Scouting movement began."

Burnham later became close friends with others involved in the Scouting movement in the United States, such as Theodore Roosevelt, the Chief Scout Citizen, and Gifford Pinchot, the Chief Scout Forester, and E.B. DeGroot, BSA Scout Executive of Los Angeles. DeGroot said of Burnham:

> "Frederick Russell Burnham is a sufficient and heroic figure, model and living example, who inspired and gave Baden-Powell the plan for the program and the code of honor of Scouting for Boys."

Fred Burnham returned to North America and for the next few years became associated with the Yaqui River irrigation project in Mexico. While investigating the Yaqui valley for mineral and agricultural resources, Burnham figured that a dam could provide year-round water to the rich soil in the valley; turning the region into one of the garden spots of the world and generate much needed electricity. He purchased water rights and some 300 acres of land in this region and contacted an old friend from his time in Africa, John Hays Hammond, who conducted his own studies and then purchased an additional 900,000 acres of this land, an area the size of Rhode Island. Burnham together with Charles Frederick Holder made important archaeological discoveries of Mayan civilization in this region, including the Esperanza Stone.

In 1909, at the request of the U.S. Secret Service, Burnham was assigned as chief guard and sharpshooter for a dangerous meeting between U.S. President Taft and Mexican President Porfirio Diaz in El Paso, Texas. In 1912, he led a team of 500 men to guide the mining properties owned by Hammond, J.P. Morgan, and the Guggenheims in the Mexican state of Sonora. Just as the irrigation and mining projects were nearing completion in 1912, a long series of Mexican revolutions began. The final blow to these efforts came in 1917 when Mexico passed laws prohibiting the sale of land to foreigners. Burnham and Hammond carried their properties until 1930 then they sold them to the Mexican government.

Frederick Russell Burnham joined the U.S. Army in 1917 just before the First World War broke out. During this period, Burnham was one of the 18 officers selected by former U.S. President Theodore Roosevelt to raise a volunteer infantry division for service in France shortly after the United States entered the war. A plan to raise volunteer soldiers from the Western U.S. came out of a meeting of the New York based Rocky Mountain Club and Fred Burnham was put in charge of both the general organization and recruitment. Congress gave Roosevelt the authority to engage up to four divisions similar to the Rough Riders of 1st United States Volunteer Cavalry Regiment and also to the British Army 25th (Frontiersmen) Battalion, Royal Fusiliers; however, as Commander in chief, President Woodrow Wilson refused to make use of Roosevelt's volunteers. President Theodore Roosevelt said of Burnham when he was told that Burnham had enlisted in the Army to fight in France;

"I know Frederick Russell Burnham. He is a scout and a hunter of courage

and ability, a man totally without fear, a sure shot, and a fighter. He is the ideal scout, and when enlisted in the military service of any country, he would be of the greatest benefit possible."

Roosevelt had been an outspoken critic of Wilson's neutrality policies, so even though Roosevelt had made several attempts to come to an agreement with Wilson, the President was unwilling to accept any compromise. In an astute display of political trickery, Wilson announced to the press that he would not send Roosevelt and his volunteers to France, but instead would send an American Expeditionary Force under the command of General Jack Pershing. Roosevelt was left with no option except to disband the volunteers. He never forgave Wilson, and quickly published "The Foes of our Own Household," a harsh indictment of the sitting president. These relentless attacks helped the Republicans win control of Congress in 1918. Roosevelt might have been a serious candidate for president in 1920, but lingering malaria kept him out of the race.

During World War 1, Burnham was living in California and was active in counterespionage for Britain. Much of it involved a famous Boer spy, Captain Fritz Joubert Duquesne, who became a German spy in both World War One and World War Two and claimed to have killed Field Marshal Kitchener while in route to meet with the Russians. During the Second Boer War, Burnham and Duquesne were each under orders to assassinate the other, but it was not until 1910 that the two men first met while both were in Washington, D.C., separately lobbying Congress to pass a bill in favor of the importation of African game animals into the United States. Duquesne was twice arrested by the FBI and in 1942 he and 32 other Nazi agents (the Duquesne Spy Ring) were jailed for espionage in the largest spy ring conviction in U.S. history. An interesting statement from one warrior to another, made by Duquesne between the 1st and 2nd World Wars regarding Burnham;

> "To my friendly enemy, Major Frederick Russell Burnham, the greatest scout of the world, whose eyes were that of an Empire. I once craved the honor of killing him, but failing that, I extend my heartiest admiration."

Although Burnham had lived all over the world, he never had a great deal of wealth to show for his efforts. It was not until he returned to California, the place of his youth, that he found great affluence. In November 1923, he struck oil in Dominguez Hills, near Carson, California. In a field that covered just two square miles, over 150 wells from Union Oil were soon producing 37,000 barrels a day, with 10,000 barrels a day going to the Burnham Exploration Company, a syndicate formed in 1919 between Frederick Burnham, son Roderick, John Hayes Hammond, and son Harris Hammond. In the first 10 years of operation, the Burnham Exploration Company paid out $10.2 million in dividends. The spot where Burnham found oil was land where;

"As a small boy he used to graze cattle, and shoot game, that he sold to the neighboring mining districts to support his widowed mother and infant brother."

Many years after the oil was depleted, the land near the Dominguez field was re-developed and became the site of the California State University, Dominguez Hills. In 2010, Occidental Petroleum Corporation expressed interest in redeveloping the former Dominguez oil field using modern extraction technologies.

An avid conservationist and hunter, Burnham supported the early conservation programs of his friends Theodore Roosevelt and Gifford Pinchot. He and his associate John Hayes Hammond led novel game expeditions to Africa with the goal of finding large animals such as Giant Eland, hippopotamus, zebra, and various bird species that might be bred in the United States and become game for future American sportsmen. Burnham, Hammond, and Duquesne appeared several times before the House Committee on Agriculture to ask for help in importing large African animals. In 1914, he helped establish the Wild Life Protective League of America, Department of Southern California, and served as its first Secretary.

In his later years, Burnham filled various public offices and also served as a member of the Boone & Crockett Club of New York, and also as a founding member of the American Committee for International Wildlife Protection (now a committee of the World Conservation Union). He was one of the original members of the first California State Parks Commission (serving from 1927 to 1934), a founding member of the Save the Redwoods League and president of the Southwest Museum of Los Angeles from 1938 until 1940, and he served as both the Honorary President of the Arizona Boy Scouts and as a regional executive for the BSA throughout the 1940s until his death in 1947.

The BSA made Burnham an Honorary Scout in 1927, and for his noteworthy and extraordinary service to the Scouting movement, Burnham was bestowed the highest commendation given by the BSA, the Silver Buffalo Award, in 1936. Throughout his life Fred Burnham remained active in Scouting at both the regional and national level in the U.S.A. and corresponded regularly with Baden-Powell on scouting topics.

Burnham and Baden-Powell remained close friends for their long lives. Burnham called Baden-

Powell a *"wonderfully able scout,"* and nicknamed him *"Sherlock Holmes."* Baden-Powell considered Fred Burnham to be *"the greatest to ever live."* The seal on the Burnham–Baden-Powell letters at Yale and Stanford expired in 2000 and the true depth of their friendship and love of Scouting has again been revealed. In 1931, Burnham read the speech dedicating Mount Baden-Powell, California, to his old scouting friend. Their friendship, and equal status in the world of scouting and conservation, was honored in 1951 with the dedication of the adjoining peak as Mount Burnham.

In 1936, Burnham enlisted the Arizona Boy Scouts in a campaign to save the Desert Bighorn Sheep from probable extinction. Several other prominent Arizonans and environmental groups joined the movement and a "Save the Bighorns" poster contest was started in schools throughout the state. Burnham provided prizes and appeared in store windows from one end of Arizona to the other. The contest-winning bighorn emblem was made into a neckerchief slide for the Boy Scouts of America. Burnham gave talks and presentations on the, "Save the Bighorns" subject at school assemblies and on radio shows. On January 18, 1939, over 1.5 million acres were set aside in Arizona to establish the Kofa National Wildlife Refuge and the Cabeza Prieta National Wildlife Refuge. Burnham gave the dedication speech.

Fred Burnham never smoked and seldom drank alcohol, fearing these habits would injure the acuteness of his sense of smell. He found ways to train himself mentally. He took power naps instead of indulging in periods of long sleep, and drank very little liquid. He trained himself to accept these abstinences in order to endure the most appalling fatigues, hunger, thirst, and wounds, so that when scouting or traveling where there was no water, he might still be able to survive. On more than one occasion he survived in environments where others would have died, or were in fact dying, of exhaustion. He was quiet-mannered and courteous, according to contemporaries. Their reports describe a man who was not shy, nor self-conscious, along with the fact that he was extremely modest, and seldom spoke of his many adventures.

Frederick Russell Burnham died of heart failure at the age of 86, on September 1, 1947 at his home in Santa, Barbara, California. He was buried at a private ceremony at Three Rivers, California, near his old cattle ranch, La Cuesta. His memorial stone was designed by his only surviving child, Roderick. Also buried at Three Rivers are his first wife, Blanche, several members of the Blick family who had also pioneered 1890s Rhodesia with Burnham, Roderick, and his granddaughter Martha Burnham Burleigh, and "Pete" Ingram, the Montana cowboy who had survived the Shangani Patrol massacre along with Burnham.

Frederick R. Burnham **British Army Major**
Circa 1880 **Circa 1901**

Chapter Fifteen
Burnham and the Pleasant Valley War

In this chapter the author will present Frederick Russell Burnham's involvement in the Pleasant Valley War. This chapter is taken directly from Burnham's published memoirs, *"Scouting on Two Continents"*. In it, Fred mentions his involvement in the *"The Pleasant Valley War,"* sometimes called the Graham vs Tewksbury Feud, or Tonto Basin War. It was commonly thought over the years, to be a sheep vs cattle range war, between two feuding families, the cattle-herding Grahams and the sheep-herding Tewksbury's. Most of this information has already been shared by the author but like all history, the reader will find new information, and another view of the Pleasant Valley War in this chapter, as all history is like a jigsaw puzzle with each piece of history found helps the reader to get a better picture of our past. With that in mind the author presents Fred Burnham's experience in the feud, since he was involved in the feud in the beginning.

Other eyewitness reports as well as Burnham's personal experience indicate that sheep were not brought into Pleasant Valley until 1885, two years after the feuding between the Tewksbury and Graham factions began. Although Pleasant Valley is physically located in Gila County, Arizona, at the time of the Pleasant Valley War, Young, Arizona, located in the center of the valley was in Eastern Yavapai County. But many of the events in the feud took place in nearby Apache and Navajo Counties. The Graham vs Tewksbury Feud lasted almost a decade, from 1883 to 1892, with the deadliest incidents occurring between the years 1886 and 1887, the last known killing occurring in 1892. In all the feuds that have taken place throughout American History, the Pleasant Valley War was the most brutal and deadly feud, resulting in an almost complete annihilation of one of the two families involved.

During the late 1880s, throughout the Western portion of the United States, there were a number of range wars, or informal undeclared violent conflicts, erupting between cattlemen and sheep men over water rights, grazing rights, or property and border disagreements. In the case of the Tewksbury's and the Graham's, there had been quarrels between the work hands of both factions as far back as 1882. The early clashes stemmed from accusations of cattle and horse rustling leveled at both parties, and some of both the Tewksbury's and Grahams were arrested on charges made by the largest rancher in Pleasant Valley, James Stinson, declaring that both the Tewksbury's and the Grahams, together or separately had all taken part in rustling cattle and horse stealing from Stinson's stock.

There was also an undercurrent of racial prejudice against the Tewksbury's who were half-Indian and Irish, and were referred to as *"damn blacks"* by the Grahams and Stinson. James Stinson made a deal with the Grahams to pay them each fifty head of cattle for any of the Tewksbury Faction that was caught and sentenced for stealing his cattle. Earning their reward by turning states evidence against the Tewksbury brothers, with whom the Grahams had worked with and had been friends. Stinson figured they all were going to continue raiding his stock but if he at least got one of them on his side, he might be able to stop the other side from rustling. He approached the Grahams and shared his idea. The Grahams took the deal and went to work for Stinson with an expressed vow to drive the Tewksbury's out of Pleasant Valley, but the case of cattle rustling against the Tewksbury's was thrown out of court in Prescott for lack of evidence.

Once partisan feelings became tense and hostilities began, Frederick Russell Burnham was drawn into the conflict in 1884. Initially he was not involved but was dragged into it and subsequently marked for death. Burnham hid for many days before he could escape from the valley. With the help of friends, he managed to get out of the feud district after several months during which he had several narrow death escapes, accounts that he recalls in his memoirs, Scouting on Two Continents.

A local cattleman, John Wells Sr., and his family became close friends of Fred Burnham, when he showed up at their ranch in the Salt River area, cold and hungry. Down in his luck and hopes to grow his cattle herd, Wells Sr. borrowed money from a banker in Globe, Arizona to move his cattle from the Salt River Area to Pleasant Valley. With help from their new friend Fred, John Wells Sr. and his family planned to move their herd of cattle to the abandoned Middleton ranch in Pleasant Valley that would allow their cattle good grazing year round. At this point in time the Wells clan had no stake in the feud, but John Wells' creditors, *(the Graham brothers, John and Tom, who bought the loan paper from a Globe banker, were two of the leading men on one side of the feud)*, so they had something to say about Wells debt.

John Wells Sr. was told by Tom Graham to join their forces in driving off the Tewksbury's cattle and sheep or forfeit his own stock. When Wells refused, his creditors demanded immediate payment of the loan and petitioned the sheriff to send two deputies to seize his cattle. Wells gathered his clan and cattle together along with a young ranch hand Frederick Russell Burnham, who Wells had trained in long rifle marksmanship, and who the Wells family considered a part of their family and began driving their herd along the trail to Pleasant Valley and their new home, hotly pursued by the two Gila County Deputy Sheriff's Deputies, sent to confiscate their cattle for the Grahams.

It was slow going to drive the cattle into the mountains and the deputies had no trouble catching up to the Wells clan and their herd. The deputies forced the Wells girls and their mother to halt, which then set off the barking dogs as they were trailing the herd. Burnham and John Wells Jr., Burnham's close friend and the son of John Wells Sr., were working the front of the herd when they herd the commotion coming from the rear so they rushed back to see what was causing the commotion. Just when they arrived one of the dogs bit a deputy as he was dismounting. The deputy drew and shot the dog, which then caused Burnham, John Jr., and two of the girls to draw their weapons.

The deputy who shot the dog began to dismount, but his feet no more than hit the ground when he fell dead. It was not shot a shot coming from Fred, John Jr. or the girls. The shot came from a long distance by John Wells Sr., who was watching the family and the cattle from a high point some 800 yards or more away. The other deputy immediately raised his hands. The group continued their journey into the mountains, taking the captured deputy with them. Once they arrived at their destination they released the living deputy and the body of the other dead deputy.

The surviving deputy returned to Globe and reported the incident. In Globe, a meeting was held to discuss the elimination of John Wells Senior, Fred Burnham and John Wells Jr. Several posses were raised to go after the killers of the deputy. Killings and counter-killings became a weekly occurrence. For the Wells' outfit it became a sheer waste of human life in a struggle without honor or profit in another man's feud, and seemingly with no end in sight.

For young Fred Burnham, it became apparent that he had the worst of two worlds. The Graham faction was losing the war and every man he killed created a new feud, a personal one, not winner take all, but winner take on all. Only nineteen years old and facing a grim future as a nameless gunslinger whose only *"crime"* had been simply to stand by his friends the Wells family. So young Fred Burnham went to Globe and looked up an old family friend, Judge Hackney, the editor of the Silver Belt newspaper that was published in Globe.

Once Fred arrived in Globe, scared to death, he contacted his friend the Silver Belt editor, Aaron Hackney, who let him stay hidden in his house. With Hackney's help, Fred Burnham assumed several aliases and made the difficult journey out of Globe. Fred eventually made his way out of the territory arriving in Tombstone, Arizona, and stayed with friends that Judge Hackney, referred him too. At this point Fred began to reflect on the feud:

> *"Now my mind began to clarify. I saw that my sentimental siding with the young herder's cause (John Wells) was all wrong; that avenging only led to more vengeance and to even greater injustice than that suffered through the often unjustly administered laws of the land. I realized that I was in the wrong and had been for a long time, without knowing it."*

The Wells family had been driven out of their ranch in Tonto Basin earlier, because of cattle rustlers, who were running rampant all over northern Arizona. Wells was able to salvage a hundred head of cattle when they moved out and settled near the town of Tempe, in the Salt River Valley. On this piece of government land the family built a brush home and a few corrals. As poor as they were, Burnham's wretched condition stirred their sympathy and he was cordially invited to camp with them, feed, water and rest his horse.

The Wells family's hospitality and their friendship led to the first link in a chain of events in Fred's life, that for years he was not able to break. Burnham became a thread woven into a strange and intricate pattern. A pattern sometimes bright and cheerful, but never altogether free of the black wrap of crime and bloodshed, that made up so much of the fabric of life in the Arizona and New Mexico Territories in those days. Trouble had been brewing for quite a while. Not only were the Apaches always sullen and often at war, but the cattlemen were trying to drive the sheep men out of the country and of course the lack of lawmen in that area made the area very attractive to cattle rustlers and horse thieves.

The Wells family soon became Fred Burnham's good friends. John Wells Sr., the father and the mother were elderly folks, but rugged seasoned pioneers. There were a number of daughters but only one son, John Jr. The main cattle range riding, branding and caring was done by John Jr., with as much assistance from his two oldest sisters were able to provide. The girls were quite competent cowgirls, though and their aid was at times necessary to protect or to save the herd, for in those days, free grazing ranges were held by the strong.

Wells Sr. decided to move his family and his cattle herd back to their ranch in Tonto Basin, where they had a 160-acre parcel of land that belonged to them and they knew the Indians had been all but driven out of Tonto Basin and nearby Pleasant Valley. So they began to move their herd east from Tempe to outside Globe with the intention of going from Globe north to Pleasant Valley, that lay about sixty miles north of Globe. Burnham wrote in his memoirs that he soon became aware of a strange undercurrent of mischief at the roundups or in the saloons and dance halls in

Globe, Arizona. Fred sensed the growing struggle among the territorial officials and politicians, as to whether Arizona should be run by a few great cattle barons or by the Daggs brothers, who were Arizona's largest and wealthiest sheep men and their friends, who were all located in the towns around the northeastern part of the Arizona Territory.

Fred went on to write in his memoirs that he became very close friends with old man Wells, who Fred Burnham writes in his biography, was the greatest long range shooter with a double-trigger, 45/70 caliber buffalo gun he ever met. Fred was constantly practicing with his rifle, and his pistols. Old man Wells taught Fred the value of knowing the effect of light, as well as shadows and windage, two factors that are most important when it came to long range shooting. While his horse was recuperating in the pasture from an injury, Fred borrowed a mount from the old buffalo hunter and pushed on to Globe, saying goodbye to his friends, who continued on to Pleasant Valley. Fred worked from time to time in some mining developments, but every couple of weeks he would return to the Salt River and Tonto Basin to see his friends, the Wells family. The feud between the Tewksbury's and the Graham's by that time was in full swing, with the frequency of killings at an all-time high. Fred wrote that his friends tried to remain neutral but at last it became impossible to stay out of the Pleasant Valley War.

Their involvement started when John Wells Sr. borrowed money from a banker in Globe to help finance his cattle drive and to help the family and his herd get through the winter on their drive back to their ranch. He knew that he would be able to pay back the loan in the spring, when his cattle were ready for market. He was told by the banker who loaned him the money, that they wanted him to join the Graham side of the feud, and to help drive off the Tewksbury's band of sheep. Wells refused to obey telling the banker the terms of the loan were that he had one year to repay the loan.

Enter John and Tom Graham, who bought the paper on the loan from the banker with the intent of compelling old man Wells to join their side of the feud or else they would call in the loan if he would not join them and confiscate the cattle to pay the balance of the loan. After John Wells failed to pay the remainder of the debt the Graham's called in the loan. Wells was never served with a written notice, but heard through the grapevine, that the Grahams held the paper on his loan. Wells decided to stash his cattle in the mountains until he could figure out a solution.

When Fred Burnham heard about the predicament his friends were in, he left Globe and went back to help them move the cattle the rest of the way to their new home in Pleasant Valley. According to Burnham, old man Wells had a box canyon picked out in the Sierra Ancha Mountains south of Pleasant Valley. He knew it would be a perfect place to cache the herd and keep it in tack. As they drove the cattle to the place, John Wells Jr. and Fred rode point on the drive and the girls, with their mother and the dogs brought up the rear, while John Sr. covered their trail from high points with his long rifle.

Two deputy sheriffs' from Globe either on official or unofficial business were spotted by old man Wells, following the herd, either looking to make a name for themselves or possibly get a bunch of cattle for themselves, the purpose was unknown. When they finally caught up to the girls in the rear of the herd, the barking of the dogs reached the ears of John Jr. and Fred, so they headed back to the rear of the herd with the intention of not letting anyone take the cattle. They informed the deputies that the cattle belonged to the girls and that old man Wells was not with them. Burnham writes;

"When we got there, we heard the girls tell the deputies in no uncertain terms that they were not about to give up the herd to anyone. John and Fred, according to Burnham, had a wordy war with the deputies and while they were arguing, one of the deputies dismounted as the girls informed the deputies again, that the cattle were theirs and they were not about to let anyone take them. One of the dogs promptly attacked and bit the deputy, who pulled his pistol and shot the dog. Everybody drew their pistols but there was only one shot fired. The deputy on the ground dropped dead. The other deputy threw up his hands. It was not known to them at that time, who fired the shot that killed the deputy, maybe one of the girls or John Jr., but for sure Fred new he did not fire his gun. And he did not see any of the girls or John Jr's pistols fire a shot"

It turned out that it was none of the girls, John Jr. or Fred, who fired the fatal shot. It was actually old man Wells, who had been trailing the deputies from his high point and when the deputies pulled their pistols. The man who shot the dog was killed with one shot from an astounding distance of eight hundred yards from a slug shot from Well's 45/70 caliber Sharps long distance, black powder buffalo rifle. It would have been a great shot with a modern flat trajectory high powered rifle equipped with a scope but it was even a more amazing feat, since it was shot from a black powder buffalo gun with and old long scope. According to Fred Burnham, Wells was the best long distance shot he ever met.

Killing the law officer dealt them all a terrible blow. In that one act, a whole family and their best friend,

Fred Burnham, crossed the divide of law abiding citizens to live on the other side of the law. The hour had now struck, when to gain protection from the law, they simply had to join the Graham faction of the Graham vs Tewksbury Feud. The Wells family along with their friend Fred Burnham agreed to join the Graham faction and so arrangements were made to give up some of the cattle to the captured deputy, and a tale was built up for the officials in Globe by the Graham brothers. It was not long before help was needed by the feudists and had to be given, both in money and in personal service. Fred writes that he spent all of his non-working time practicing incessantly with his pistol, becoming a crack shot with both his right and left hand and especially from a galloping horse.

Fred continued to write, that his friends were being killed off on a regular basis. Sadly, he found out that many of them deserved it. Sordid motives and black treachery run rampant in every gang of feudists, cattle thieves, horse thieves and outlaws. Although here and there great characters stood out, both good and evil. A feud is a terrible eye opener to a young man. It reveals the seamy side of life at the time of a boy's highest enthusiasm, and is very apt to make him cynical and pessimistic. Fred began to see cowardice amongst the politicians in the territory but especially in and around Globe, Arizona, that was the capital of Gila County, Arizona. Burnham called his intense situation

> *"The secret dread that follows a man like his shadow but, unlike the shadow, does not depart after the sun goes down."*

A feud is hard on the women folk involved, and even the little children absorb the fear around them and show pathetic furtiveness. Burnham recalled a day when John Sr., John Jr., and he, all heavily armed, rode up to a cabin on Tonto Creek, *(which at that time, would have probably been either the Horton or Colcord ranch house).* As they approached the cabin, Fred saw a little girl, about five years old, carrying a white pitcher of water from their nearby spring on her way to the house. When the child saw Fred, John Wells Sr. and John Jr. approaching their family cabin, she gave a scream, dropped the pitcher, and ran, not to the house, as a child ordinarily would do, but to the creek bottom, shouting at the top of her voice;

"Daddy, Daddy! Here they come to kill you!"

She already understood or had been trained to understand the danger that existed living in Tonto Basin or Pleasant Valley, during that time period, and that her own presence in the cabin might deter her father from shooting an enemy or an enemy from shooting him. Fortunately, her father was not an impulsive man and did not open fire until quite satisfied that it was against a foe, but the little girl refused to come out of her hiding spot until her mother's voice called her with just the right ring of assurance.

In the Tonto Basin or Pleasant Valley Feud, Fred Burnham, in his own words, found himself on the losing side. After a time, as the legal authorities got control of things, and some of the treacherous deputies were ousted, matters began to swing back to their normal status; but the scars of the feud, to this day *(1936 the date that Burnham published his memoirs)* mark the second generation of those folks involved. Fearing that it might even now bring tears to some and rage to others, Burnham chose not to repeat names. It was a harsh school of life, yet from this same belt of the Southwest, Teddy Roosevelt's immortal Rough Riders were largely recruited. All that was really needed was a good cause and a good leader to transform outlaws into heroes.

Most of the men in the Southwest in those days were survivors of the Civil War and moved into Arizona from the Midwest and Texas looking for the excitement of the last frontier in the United States continent. They found all they wanted in the New Mexico and Arizona Territories from gold and silver mining to raising cattle and horses, and to outlawry. There wasn't much need for men trained to hunt and kill other men, by the North or the South anywhere after the civil war. The Arizona and New Mexico Territories were the only places left in the United States, where common folks could go, claim the rights to 160 acres of prime land and build a life for themselves and their families.

A new dilemma confronted Fred. Even in defeat, he still had enemies. A cloud hung over him. He moved from place to place very secretly, rarely being out during the day and he changed his name quite regularly. Throughout the Pleasant Valley feud, Burnham kept one complete outfit in Prescott, where he had a change of clothes cached, with loyal friends and a place where he could safely disarm and rest. Burnham became a liaison to certain major players in Prescott, Globe and the Tonto Basin including Pleasant Valley. Here and there, he had glimpses of the highest powers of government in the Arizona Territory, and saw how everyone else in the territory were just pawns in a game of high stakes chess.

Burnham made use of the craftiness and cunning he had learned among the Indians, as well as all the scouting tricks he learned from Lee and Holmes, along with the methods employed by the bandit Vasquez. In those days, every little detail of a man's equipment was observed and remembered by those he met, and of course, this included a rider's horse, saddle and its brand were especially noted. Burnham took care to never ride a horse from one district to another district, and established a cache and a friend in each district. He found that he could travel long distances on foot and very swiftly. He worked in mining camps, because he knew the mining lingo. He could drive oxen teams well enough to get work with teamsters. Burnham learned by bitter experience to conceal whatever skill he had with his pistols and his rifle. On more than one occasion, his boyish boasting nearly cost him his life. The hardest thing for him to disguise were his height and the color of his eyes. Being so young and slightly undersized, his best role was that of a tenderfoot from back east, or a simple mere careless, harmless kid.

During this time of Burnham's life, he had many hours to think about his future, he saw a far different life from what he pictured, when he lived in California with his family. Life in California was free and easy as well as the presence of law enforcement officers everywhere. In the Arizona Territory on the other hand lawmen were still scarce or even non-existent in some areas, so if a crime was committed and the offender captured, usually by a mob and punished on the spot. Sadly, according to Burnham, he fell in by accident with rustlers, smugglers or feudists.

It seemed like everywhere he turned there was trouble, seeing Fred in this life struggle and knowing that he had good upbringing and wanted to be on the right side of the law, his friend, Judge Aaron Hackney, an old family friend, kept in touch with one of Fred's uncle's, and received a letter from Fred's uncle that Hackney passed on to Fred. The message was short and to the point;

> *"Above all, duty comes before all Fred. You come from the wrong stock to make a villain."*

After reading the message, Burnham figured out that he had been on the wrong side of the law for a long time, without even realizing it. Then young Fred Burnham had a long talk with Judge Hackney, who suggested Burnham rid himself of all of his Pleasant Valley connections. He suggested that Fred leave Globe and start a new life in Tombstone. Judge Hackney, being the publisher of the Silver Belt Newspaper in Globe was able to pull some strings and made arrangements with a couple of his close friends in Tucson to help young Fred. Judge Hackney gave Fred a personal letter of recommendation that he was to present his friends in Tucson and his other friends, when he arrived at his destination, which was Tombstone.

The Gunfight at the O.K. Corral occurred only a few months earlier, when Fred arrived in Tombstone in late December of the year 1881. Tombstone was a new boomtown attracting silver miners from all parts and made it an ideal location to hide out. Burnham assumed several aliases and occasionally delivered messages for a friend he met in Tombstone by the name of Neil McLeod, who was a retired prize fighter, and who once fought the Heavyweight World Champion John L. Sullivan for the world boxing championship. McLoed had smuggling partners in Sonora, Mexico. From Neil McLeod, young Fred learned many valuable tricks for avoiding detection, passing coded messages, and throwing off pursuers.

At that point, Fred realized that he needed to take the advice of his friend Judge Hackney and try to straighten out his life, working with McLeod was a good experience, but Fred realized that he was still going in the wrong direction. So he looked up the friend of Judge Hackney there in Tombstone, who he was meant to meet and visit when he first arrived. Upon presenting the letter of recommendation from Judge Hackney to his friend in town, Burnham found himself in touch with a quiet, soft-voiced man, who made his living as a gambler. His games were all of skill and chance; his word was his bond; his percentage of profit was measured like any broker working at the New York Stock Exchange. His vaults held money in safe keeping for many friends and customers who did not trust the banks in those days.

Fred stayed with the gambler for several months, while the gambler spent time with him explaining and showing him the practical, common sense and honest way of looking at life. The gambler convinced Fred there were many decent, law abiding folks who were getting a lot more out of life than at first glance. Finally, the old gambler won Fred's confidence over completely, by telling him how close he had come once to becoming a bandit and stage robber himself. He described the mental turmoil that Burnham was dealing with because he, himself had to deal with it at one time in his own life, regarding Fred's involvement on the wrong side of the Pleasant Valley War. After many long talks with Judge Hackney in Globe and his friend the gambler in Tombstone, Fred was taught how to avoid trouble, and the judge provided him with the means for him to join the forces of good, convincing young Fred the importance of how law and order actually protected the good, honest folk's lives and property.

Through the grapevine, Fred learned that his good friends, the Wells family, from Pleasant Valley, needed him and that one of the Graham faction, maybe the Tewksbury's or even a law officer that he made an enemy, was out to get him and hot on his trail. His friend Judge Hackney, the editor of the Silver Belt newspaper suggested that he should seek sanctuary in the Dripping Springs area on the trail between Florence and Globe, and if he was to remain in Tombstone, it could be perilous or even fatal. Burnham knew the men that were after him were hard-riding and relentless.

The chances of obtaining a re-mount for a trip from Tombstone to Globe were not good, for it was the dry season, when range horses were generally in poor condition and unshod horses cannot stand hard ground. Fred's gambler friend gave him a horse and added a second rather poor one. But between the two horses, along with a canteen, enough jerky and Pinole, enough for him to make the journey to Dripping Springs that was halfway between Tucson and Globe, without stopping for any reason other than trouble.

It is difficult to explain and perhaps more tedious to read all the details of a long, serious chase, when both parties to the affair are skilled and determined. To the hunted the first question is, *"Who is pursuing me?"* According to Fred, if they are white men and come from towns, they may be counted on to do certain things from habit; if a plains Indian was on his trail, they would do other things; if his pursuer is a frontiersman, his actions and movements will be quite apparent, and if an Apache, he or they will employ yet another strategy.

In this instance Burnham knew he was being pursued by two very keen white frontiersmen. The inciting motive of one of the men was to get him before Burnham could provide evidence in court concerning the sale of stock of a certain brand. Burnham was an inconvenient connecting link, and his demise would in all probability save the pursuer from a prison sentence. The fact that Fred had been a close friend of this bitter enemy added zest for the pursuer. Besides, he had to make good his frequent boast that, when he once took the trail he always got his man. The other pursuer had still a stronger driving power to send Fred over the mountains and deserts, he was insanely jealous, which is almost as enduring and potent as inherited hate.

It was fortunate for Burnham that at this juncture his gambler friend knew the hearts of the men pursuing Fred and their weaknesses. His instinctive acuteness was similar to that possessed by famous scouts of the past. Some of the gamblers methods were very simple but effective. Fred's friend the gambler instructed Burnham to make it entirely open as to the road he intended to take and secretly about the one he did not intend to take, for his trailers had many sources of information and would probably find out Fred's secret inquiries. In any case, they would not suspect a youngster like Burnham of taking the trail over an openly widely used route. His gambler friend stressed the importance of Burnham being able to gain a few hours traveling during the night on a main road ahead of his followers. The darkness would cover Fred's movements till morning, as Fred would not leave a trail that could be picked up by a match, lantern or torch.

Burnham was given further instruction regarding how to make use of his lead horse. The animal's home was in Tucson and the horse, if turned loose, would travel directly to his home corral. Fred was instructed by the gambler to take the road toward Pantano until break of day then he was to pick up a rough graveled ridge where Fred could feed his horse, cook and eat a meal. After eating, Fred was to take the shoes from his good horse and put them on the unshod and inferior steed. After this was done, Burnham was to tie a few bits of cactus in a stout piece of canvas, fasten it securely to the animal's tail and head him toward Tucson. His friend went on to give further instruction;

> *"As the cactus hits against the horse, he will give a series of mad jumps, then he will settle into a run and finally slow down to walk without stopping until he reaches his corral in Tucson."*

Burnham's gambler friend went on with the instruction by instructing Fred to allow three hours to change the horse's shoes and eat lunch. By seven in the morning, you should have sent your spare horse on his way to Tucson. He went on to tell Burnham that he was to mount his own horse, which would be by then barefoot, set spur to him, and jump him off down a little canyon and into a sandy wash for about a mile. Then he was to stop. At that point Burnham was to look in his pack and find a set of horse shoes quite different from the ones he just took off this horse, yet made to fit him. Put the new shoes on his mount, then make a detour and turn toward the San Pedro River. Hopefully, this action would gain Fred, with luck, two to four day's head start.

In doing exactly what his friend told him, it would look like Fred had been surprised by Indians, just as he saddled up after resting and his barefoot unshod horse had bolted, while he had barely been able to head his own horse, plunging with fear toward Tucson. The old gambler went on to tell Fred that he needed to pick a discernable change in the shape of the unshod horses tracks, and yet a clear tale of all that happened to the shod horses tracks.

Burnham carried out his friend's instructions to the letter. Fred kept the extra food and barley left over from his first meal, and the next night he camped on the San Pedro River. His trailers did precisely as his friend predicted. They did not consider Burnham old enough or wise enough to make use of the shoe-changing trick, and all that seemed written at the camp could be accounted for by a fright from Indians, or any other cause, for even a pot of coffee spilled on a camp fire will sometimes stampede a pack train. They followed Burnham's runaway horse all the way to Tucson.

It was at this point in his journey that a bounty hunter by the name of John Dixon caught up to Fred while he was hiding in a cave in the mountains north of Tucson. Fred was actually relieved and figured maybe his trouble with the law and his enemies might come to an end. As they stepped outside the entrance to the cave a shot rang out and Dixon fell dead in front of Fred. Fred grabbed a gun and shot back at the man who shot Dixon, killing the Indian who killed Dixon. It was an Apache by the name of Coyotero, of whom Fred was familiar, who was also on Fred's trail for a different reason.

After a long and careful ride, with great vigilance, Fred Burnham arrived in the Dripping Springs country, located just a little north of the mining ghost town of Christmas. He hid his horse and put up a smoke signal as instructed by his friend in Tombstone. He was to meet his friend John Wells Jr., from Tonto Basin. He saw a return smoke signal, so he knew his friend John would be on his way to meet up with him. Fred waited patiently in the brush near his campfire that was used to send the smoke signal. Low and behold, when he turned around, instead of John Jr., one of his sisters was the person who met him and not John, who he expected to meet.

She had ridden across the Pinal Mountains to reach Fred and on the way a bear frightened her horse, which plunged down the side of a mountain through heavy brush, driving a dry pine stub clear through her calf. She was in a lot of pain and the leg was terribly swollen. To add to her woes, she told Burnham that her brother, John Jr., was under arrest and being sent by railroad to Yuma convicted of cattle stealing. Her brother John, instructed her to meet Burnham. She told him that she had lain in hiding for three days, while waiting for his smoke signal.

Burnham treated the girl's wound and took her out of the mountains to the main road where, as luck would have it, they ran into a freighter, who he had worked with in the past. Together with the freighter, they made a canvas stretcher to transport the wounded girl. Lucky for them a stagecoach came by on its way from Tombstone to Globe. The stagecoach stopped and two sporting ladies riding in the coach took the wounded girl with them to Globe.

Burnham joined the freighter and went on to Globe with him. When he got there he checked on the girl and found that the two prostitutes had nursed her back to health. Sadly, he found out from the girl that his friend John Jr. had died in the Yuma prison. She told Fred that her father had died suddenly and that her mother died a short time after her father passed. She told Burnham that her younger sister married a freighter there in Globe but she died giving birth to a son. She was now the last surviving member of her family. She ended up marrying the freighter that picked her up with Burnham and they moved to California where they prospered in the ranching business. She was the only happy ending Burnham could remember for any member of that unfortunate Wells family caught up in the toils of the Pleasant Valley Feud.

While there in Globe, Burnham visited his friend Judge Aaron Hackney, and explained what had happened to the bounty hunter and the Apache during their meeting. Hackney had arranged a meeting between Fred and his enemies in order to make a truce and the dogs of the vendetta to end. Burnham knew this was not an easy task to accomplish. Burnham had been hunted for such a long time, living in fear of his life, that his lust for finishing his foes became stronger every day. The final settlement gave him still a deeper view of the pit he had lived in every day of his life. It took a couple of months for Fred to realize he would no longer have to look over his shoulder and would be able to live a normal life.

It wasn't but a week or two the truce, that Burnham's friend Judge Hackney introduced him to a couple of local sheriffs' deputies, who needed a man with tracking skills. This was the first job of the young man's life with a new legitimate direction in his life. Young Fred Burnham's past was never exploited, discussed or revealed again.

At that point in time, Fred began to see life from a whole different angle. A life worth living depended on the legal ownership of property, the laws to protect one's property and those folks who own that property. It was necessary to remove men who created chaos, savagery and theft of property. The county taxes were hard to collect, the territory was vast and trailing criminals was difficult and expensive. By preliminary scouting Burnham could often save a posse from wasting their time, in fact he was able to do most of the work finding outlaws. His youthful training had become a real asset, which he gladly used to his benefit.

Having resolved any issues with the Tewksbury faction of the Pleasant Valley Feud, Burnham could move freely in the Territory, especially now that he was working on the right side of the law. Burnham was moving in the opposite circles of his past. His tracking skills were widely accepted as the best in the territory. He worked as a deputy for Pima County Sheriff Bob Paul in Tucson, Yavapai County Sheriff Buckey O'Neill of Prescott and Cochise County Sheriff John Slaughter. Looking for the excitement of scouting during a war and having had enough of the Southwest, Frederick Russell Burnham headed for South Africa and worked for the English Army as discussed in the previous chapter.

Chapter Sixteen
Roscoe Willson-AZ Republic Journalist

In this chapter the author will dedicate to the biography of Roscoe George Willson, a noted journalist in Phoenix who wrote a series of articles in the Sunday morning Arizona Republic Newspaper, in a section called Arizona Days and Ways. It was a magazine type section of the Sunday editions from 1953 to 1976. Roscoe Willson also authored some books filled with Arizona, crazy or bizarre true stories, "No Place for Angels," and two volumes of a book called, "Pioneer and Well Known Cattlemen of Arizona."

Of special interest to the author and the reader are Willson's published articles written on the Pleasant Valley War that will be presented as they appeared in the newspaper on the dates they were published. Along with these newspaper articles the author will present letters from and to Earle B. Forrest, the writer of the first book published about the Pleasant Valley War, called, "Arizona's Dark and Bloody Ground." The newspaper articles present Willson's perspective as taken from conversations and notes about the Pleasant Valley War from Willson's friend William Colcord, who was one of the last survivors and founding ranchers in Tonto Basin and who was also able to stay neutral during the Graham vs Tewksbury Feud so often called the Pleasant Valley War. This series of articles, along with L.J. Horton, who also stayed neutral, in this author's opinion are the most accurate, unbiased, versions of the Tonto Basin War that have been found.

The dialogue in the letters written between Earle B. Forrest and Roscoe Willson are priceless. There is no doubt they both had different opinions and views of some of the circumstances involving these two families and some of the events that occurred between the Tewksbury and Graham factions of the feud. By this time even though some of the event's facts have already been presented several times in previous chapters, by now the reader should be pretty familiar with all of the incidents that happened. But there are some new facts presented along with all of the repeated information.

Roscoe G. Willson was born in Granite Falls, Minnesota, July 13, 1879. His family moved to the Dakota Territory in 1881. During the construction of the Great Northern Railroad, Roscoe's father ran a farm machinery business and started the Pembina County Democratic Weekly Newspaper. Roscoe graduated from high school in Bathgate, North Dakota at the age of sixteen and began working at his father's newspaper.

In 1898 Roscoe Willson went to Minneapolis to work at his uncle's printing plant. His job was to do police court reporting for the Minneapolis Tribune. That same year Roscoe became restless, he sold all his possessions and rode a bicycle from North Dakota to Mexico. Roscoe spent over three years wandering around Mexico and Guatemala. He worked for the railroads, construction companies, coffee and rubber plantations, harbor works, and other odd jobs.

When a Yellow Fever epidemic broke out in Tampico, Mexico Roscoe returned to the United States through El Paso, narrowly escaping a major quarantine. He again went to work for a railroad construction team, and found jobs along the way through Texas, New Mexico, and finally into Prescott, Arizona on July 1, 1902. From Prescott, Roscoe went to Crown King, Arizona, at that time booming silver and gold mining camp at the time and took a job at the Crown King Mine. He bought a burro and went out prospecting on his own, which was his lifelong passion.

Roscoe Willson joined the U.S. Forest Service in 1905 after he was burnt out from prospecting. His job with the Forest Service was to inventory the timber in Horsethief Basin, located near Crown King, and where he earned the nickname name *"Horsethief Willson."* His assignments took him to Fort Huachuca, Tumacacori, and the Baboquivari Forests in Southern Arizona.

In May of 1907 Roscoe met Maude Hudgin, in Nogales, Arizona. The two were married January 6, 1909 and the newlyweds moved to Albuquerque, New Mexico. In May of that year Roscoe was appointed supervisor of the Tonto National Forest in north central Arizona, with its headquarters at Roosevelt. So, Roscoe and Maude moved to the town of Roosevelt, Arizona and lived there for five years during the construction and the ultimate dedication of the Theodore Roosevelt Dam. After several years of working for the National Forest Service at Roosevelt, Roscoe Willson was promoted to a supervisor of the Madison National Forest in Clearwater, Idaho near Yellowstone National Park.

By 1919, Roscoe resigned from the Forest Service to pursue sheep ranching in Montana. He went broke after the 1929 stock market crash and gave up ranching to run a lumber yard at the Cat Creek Oil Field in Montana. Willson sold oil well supplies and wrote articles about the oil field news for the Montana newspapers. This led Roscoe Willson to enter a partnership in the oil rig business. Roscoe built the first oil rig in the Kevin-Sunburst Field just north of Shelby, Montana. He sold the business for a tidy profit in 1923 and from there he and Maude drove to California to spend the winter, after the cold winters in Montana, the beautiful California climate was certainly a welcome change.

Roscoe and Maude Willson returned to Arizona in the spring of 1924. The Willson's opened a business called the Arizona Specialty Company, here in Phoenix, becoming one of the first tenants of the Luhrs Building in downtown Phoenix. Maude ran the office and Roscoe sold advertising. Willson also went back to prospecting in the nearby Sonoran Desert. Roscoe claimed he never found any rich mines but thoroughly enjoyed the hunt. The Willsons' sold the business in 1945 and retired.

In 1947, Roscoe Willson, bored of retirement, took a job with the Arizona Republic newspaper and began writing his Arizona Days and Ways articles in what was a magazine section of the Sunday morning edition. The magazine was dedicated to travel and commerce in Arizona, Willson's column was dedicated to the unique and bizarre Arizona Historical stories. Willson researched each article and wrote each story in his weekly article every Sunday from 1947 until his death on August 25, 1976 at age 97.

Starting below, the author will present each one of Willson's articles concerning the Pleasant Valley War. They are copies of the articles that Roscoe wrote from his notes and conversation with William Colcord, who was an original settler in Tonto Basin a few miles north of Young, Arizona, in the center of Pleasant Valley. Of the many interesting articles this author has read that Willson wrote, the following articles will have special meaning to the reader. Following these articles, of special interest to the author will present the letters written from Earle B. Forrest and Roscoe Willson concerning their debate about some of the facts about the Pleasant Valley War.

The first article Roscoe Willson wrote regarding the Pleasant Valley War was published in the Arizona Republic, Arizona Days and Ways section of the weekly newspaper on February 25, 1951;

Pleasant Valley War Witness Talks
Old Timer to Correct Feud Tales

In the year 1887, at a time Arizona cattle ranges were being stocked by cattlemen from Texas, Colorado, Kansas and other states, a feud developed between two cattle outfits in what is now northeastern Gila County. The feud became famous in the annals of western gun-fighting as the Pleasant Valley War, or the Graham-Tewksbury Feud, in which some thirty-five men were killed and another fifteen disappeared, never to be seen or heard from again.

Only a few brief paragraphs concerning it were written in the territorial newspaper in all probability because the editors in those days were having "a man for breakfast," every morning and thought nothing of it. Years later, long after most of those conversant with the affair were either dead or removed to distant parts, writers from the East scenting out tales of the old west came into the country and produced a flock of books and magazine articles purporting to tell the story of the Pleasant Valley War.

Most of these authors were never able to talk with survivors of the feud but the age of 83 just a year ago this reporter was introduced to William C. Colcord who opened up and discussed how he was able stay friends with both the Tewksbury and Graham factions while he lived in Pleasant Valley during the feud.

William C. "Bill" Colcord was born in Louisiana in 1867. His father, Col.

William Rogers Colcord, returned home from the Civil War and found his Louisiana sugar plantation in ruins, so he moved his family to Oklahoma Territory. After the death of his father, Bill, and his younger brother, Harvey, moved to Arizona Territory. They arrived in Flagstaff in 1885 with a herd of cattle. There, Bill worked for Babbitt Brothers Cattle Company, and Harvey tended the Colcord cattle. After a year, they moved to Walnut Creek, west of Pleasant Valley.

When he was 32 years old, Wayne Colcord married Pauline Merritt of Prescott. While in Pleasant Valley, Bill and Harvey became acquainted with both factions of the Pleasant Valley War aka; the Grahams and the Tewksbury's.

In 1894, Bill moved to Payson and married Carrie Mish Stewart, the daughter of pioneer settlers Ben and Sarah Stewart. They married Sept. 17. Harvey Colcord never married.

Bill and Carrie settled on a ranch in Round Valley, a few miles south of Payson, and lived there until 1910. While living in the area, Bill was active in civic affairs and politics. He served three terms on the Gila County Board of Supervisors, and was instrumental in the building of the county hospital and the county courthouse in Globe. Bill was also a founding member of the Arizona Cattle Growers' Association.

In 1912, Bill bought a ranch near Lake Mary. In 1916, his wife, Carrie, died in Flagstaff, following the birth of her sixth child. This was a blow to Bill and he moved to Sunflower. Bill bought the Diamond a Ranch and Harvey bought the Circle M.

After Bill quit ranching, he built a service station and a store at Sunflower. Later, he owned and operated the Tonto Basin Store. He left the store in 1938. He later married a woman named Lillian and they lived in Tonto Basin. William Clay "Bill" Colcord died on May 16, 1961, in Globe, Arizona.

Bill Colcord along with his mother and his brother Harvey brought cattle into Pleasant Valley in the spring of 1886. They rode the range with both the Grahams and the Tewksbury's, yet remained sufficiently neutral to be placed in charge of the Graham cattle by Tom Graham after Tom's two brothers had been killed and Tom had withdrawn to what he considered the safe refuge of a Tempe farm.

In preparing this narrative of the Pleasant Valley War, Roscoe Willson used the recollections of William Colcord, whom he had been friends with for twelve years, as a primary basis, supplemented by the recollections of Will C. Barnes, who ran cattle on nearby ranges at the same time period, of the misses Ola and Betty Young, whose father ran cattle on an adjacent range during and before the war, and have discussed the matter with Leroy Middleton at whose father's ranch two men were killed, and Judge Walter Shute, who worked in the valley shortly *after the war.*

Roscoe Willson also says he became very familiar with Pleasant Valley and its people in 1909 and the ensuing years as he worked in a supervisory capacity for U.S. Forest Service, and was in charge of the Tonto National Forest, which enabled him to some extent the ability to separate the wheat from the chaff.

The Pleasant Valley War has generally been written in books, magazines and newspaper articles to be a war between sheep men and cattlemen nothing is further from the truth. Although it is probable that sheep brought into the valley accented old hatreds of the two families, the Graham's and the Tewksbury's was a feud, just as big, if not bigger, a feud as the Hatfield's and McCoy's.

According to Bill Colcord, the sheep brought into the valley during the winter of 1886 by the Daggs Brothers, and removed in the spring of 1887, were not, as some claim, run on shares by the Tewksbury's or even under their protection. The fact of the matter seems to be that after the Tewksbury's and the Graham's, who both settled in the valley about 1882 and were friends to start, actually had a fallen out over differences regarding cattle long-roped (rustled) from the herd of James Stinson, the largest cattleman the valley, they became bitter enemies

When the Daggs Brothers suggested to the Tewksbury's, with whom they were friendly, that they would like to drop a band of sheep over the Mogollon Rim, from where their sheep had been grazing, into the north end of Pleasant Valley where the Graham cattle ranged, because they were running out of good grazing ground on the rim and wanted to graze their sheep below the rim for the winter as the winters above the rim were bitter cold in winter and it was not as cold below the rim and they would be able to cut their losses as well as Pleasant Valley was very futile. The Tewksbury's naturally favored the idea since it would injure the Graham's and not them.

Thus it was for a time that outsiders and cattlemen on nearby ranges, looking at the situation from the standpoint of "sheep invade cattle range," were sympathetic to the Grahams, but before the war was over, they came to look with favor on Tewksbury's.

In February 1887 one of the Daggs sheep herder was shot and killed, after which the sheep were taken back to the top of the rim. Although no one knows who actually did the dirty deed, later Andy Cooper bragged, while living in Holbrook that he and John Graham did the deed. The herder was a Basque and the brother in law of James D. Houck, who was also a sheep man and a Deputy Sheriff of the newly formed Apache County, which the county seat was in Holbrook, Arizona. The sheep herder's death was considered the first *death in the Pleasant Valley Feud.*

According to a letter received from Frank Cassanova, who was as a young man, the forest ranger in Pleasant Valley at the time of the feud, in a letter sent to Roscoe Willson, the grave of the sheep herder lies near the Young Road exit and Interstate 260 that connects Payson to Show Low. He goes on to say that the grave of the sheepherder is not far from where Billy Graham was killed.

This author questions the information presented regarding the death of Billy Graham, because Graham was killed while returning from a dance in Globe not in Phoenix, as previously reported by other sources. It happened over the lower Hellgate Trail leading from Pleasant Valley, over the rugged Sierra Ancha Mountains to Globe, that lay about sixty miles south of Young, in Pleasant Valley. It must be noted that Apache County Deputy Sheriff James D. Houck filed his official report indicating that he, in fact killed Billy Graham and not Ed Tewksbury. He was very detailed in his report of the circumstances surrounding the death of Billy. This fact will be discussed in a later article.

The 2nd article written by Willson appeared in the Sunday edition of the Arizona Republic, Days and Ways section concerning the Pleasant Valley war on March 4, 1951;

Outlawry of Era Fans
Pleasant Valley War

Lying at an elevation of about 5000 feet above sea level, Pleasant Valley is enclosed on the north by the Mogollon Rim, on the east by low mesa-like ridges, on the south by the Sierra Ancha Mountain range, while the west and northwest, it is relatively open, except for an occasional intruding butte or ridge. The main part of the valley, near the settlement of Young, where the Graham's and the Tewksbury's lived, lies along Cherry Creek and its branch creeks, which eventually drain into the Salt River north of Globe, Arizona.

The Young sister's ranch house has the settlement post office in a building that is also adjacent to their home. It has been the town post office for 50 years. It was originally one of the Graham ranches. The Perkins store is located just a little over a mile southwest of the store. It was founded by Charles Perkins, who arrived in Pleasant Valley from the East Coast, and who had owned a mercantile store.

For several months after the death of the Basque sheep herder and the withdrawal of the sheep from the valley the ill feeling between the Graham's and the Tewksbury's smoldered, awaiting some untold act to fan the flame. During which time lines were being drawn more tightly between the two factions and their adherents.

On the Graham side of the faction were John, Tom and Billy Graham, Charley Dusha, Louis Parker, Hank Blevans aka: Buscadero Outlaw, Ed and his brother Al Rose, Mart Blevins and his four sons, Andy aka: Andy Cooper, known to be the leader of a gang of horse thieves, along with his brothers Hamp, John and Charles, brother in law, Mose Roberts, Jamie Stott and others. Most of them were killed or left the valley on the run and there were several other men who were not really ever tied directly to the Grahams but definitely were acting on their behalf.

The Blevins family had settled on the property that later became the Ramer, now called the OW ranch, some 20 miles northeast of the Graham ranch. The Blevins men were known to have co-operated with the Grahams in their horse stealing enterprise for some time before the shooting began. They also owned or rented a home in Holbrook, where, Andy, Hamp along with their friend Mose Roberts were killed in a gunfight by Apache County Sheriff, Commodore Perry Owens, who was trying to serve a warrant for the arrest of Andy for the crime of cattle rustling and horse stealing which it must be noted that horse stealing was a hanging offense in those days.

The Tewksbury's had two ranches, one about two miles below the Grahams also located on Cherry Creek, where brother's Edwin, James, John, his wife Mary Ann and their young brother Frank, who suffered from advance stages of Tuberculosis that caused his death at a young age. Tuberculosis took the lives of James and Ed as well. Also living there were John and Mary Ann's two children, Bertha and John Jr. James Dunning Tewksbury, the four brother's father built his ranch house on Crouch Creek, a tributary creek of Cherry Creek, two miles south of his son's ranch, there also lived his wife Lydia and their two young sons Walter and Parker.

According to Bertha Tewksbury, included in the Tewksbury faction were Ed and Jim Tewksbury, John Rhodes, who married Mary Ann Tewksbury after the death of her husband John Tewksbury, Bill Jacobs, Joe Boyer, Jack Lauffer, Jim Roberts and several other ranchers in Pleasant Valley and the surrounding Tonto Basin.

According to Jim Robert's statement to Ed Tewksbury when he arrived at the Tewksbury cabin after getting back his team of horses and his prize stud stallion;

> "It was easy to track the thieves, as they left a trail twenty feet wide that anybody could follow. He told Ed that he caught up to the three thieves just above the Mogollon Rim. He said he sat with them and had a cup of coffee then he walked over to the horses and saw his team. When they asked him what he was doing, he told them they must have made a mistake in taking my horse and that he would just take them back and be on his way. The men then told Jim that there was no mistake, the horses belonged to them. Instead of giving his horses back to him, they drew their guns and Jim said had no choice but to defend himself. He shot all three men dead, got back the horses, and stopped on the way back to his place at Colcord's ranch and gave Colcord his horses, then took his team directly to the Tewksbury ranch, corralled them, then

after explaining what happened he asked to join their side because he knew the Grahams would be gunning for him.

Below is a map of Pleasant Valley that was included in the March 4, 1951 Days and Ways section of the AZ Republic;

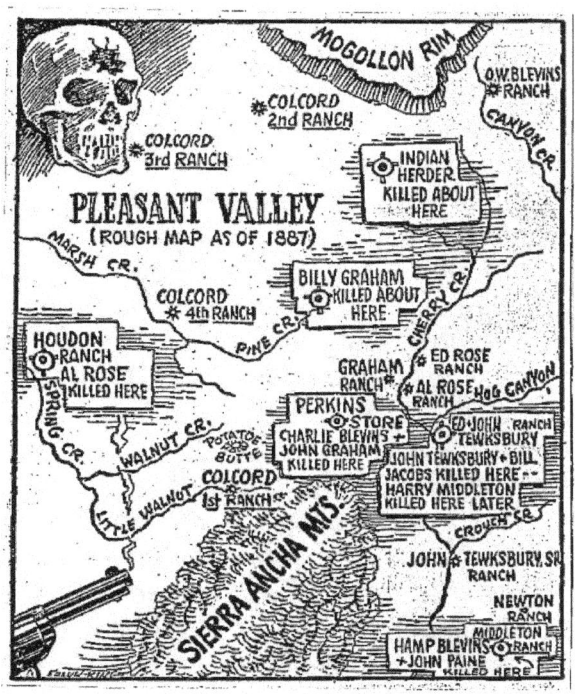

With all this background of mistrust and hatred between the two factions, increased by futile efforts to prosecute each other in the territorial courts, and the outlawry of all sorts prevailing in the Tonto Basin, it's no wonder that devil may care outlaws and cowboys were drawn into the feud. The first killing after the death of the Basque sheepherder

were by Jim Roberts, whether cowboys or outlaws, whether they were associated with the Grahams or 'just for the hell of it were simply horse thieves, decided to start a little war of their own.

Early in August of 1887 Old Man Blevins rode out from his ranch and never returned. His sons hunted high and low for him with no results. They suspected the Tewksbury's of having killed him and hidden the body, but there was no proof.

According Will Barnes, Hamp Blevins was accompanied by John Paine, who had worked as a foreman for the Hashknife cattle ranch, along with three of his men, Tom Tucker, Bob Gillespie and Bob Carrington all well-armed according to Barnes and as they passed through his camp told Barnes, they were going to start a little war of our own. Barnes went on to say the men were well armed as they rode by his camp.

Word spread like wild flowers in those days. The spread in Pleasant Valley that anyone associated with the Tewksbury's better high tail it out of Pleasant Valley or face the consequences. The word that a gang of men were coming for the Tewksbury's spread from Holbrook throughout Pleasant Valley and arrived long before the men ever got to the Middleton Ranch that fateful day. The Middleton family scared for their lives left the valley and moved to Globe.

Hamp Blevins and his men presented a formidable appearance

when they rode up to the supposedly deserted Middleton cabin about midday of August 9, 1887. Seeing signs of life about the cabin in direct violation of their message to residents of Pleasant Valley to get out of dodge, they gave a yell asking the residents of the cabin asking lunch and coffee.

Almost at once a man appeared in the doorway of the cabin, seeing the men were well armed and knowing they were there to cause trouble, he yelled back, 'This isn't no hotel so get the hell out of here. No one knows exactly who fired the first shot butt almost immediately guns blazed from both sides.

The third article in the series written about the Pleasant Valley War written by Roscoe Willson appeared in the Arizona Days and Ways section of the Arizona Republic Newspaper on Sunday March 11, 1951 and follows;

Bloody Battle Fought at the Middleton Ranch

Out in the open, under a merciless fire from the doors, windows and loopholes of the cabin, there was nothing for Blevins and his men to do but shoot and run. They whirled their and shooting as they ran, broke for the cover of nearby trees. They were too late, however. They had prodded a hornets' nest and now the hornets were flying about them.

In the first exchange of shots, Hamp Blevins was knocked out of his saddle and fell to the ground mortally wounded.

John Paine was killed at almost the same moment, while Tom Tucker was shot through the body but managed to stay on his horse until out of sight of the cabin, when he too fell from his saddle to the ground. Carrington and Gillespie received flesh wounds but managed to escape and kept right on going until they were out of Pleasant Valley, never to be seen or heard from again.

The scene of the battle, the Middleton ranch, was owned by George Wilson, who happened to be in Globe at the time of the shootout. It has for many years now been known as the Wilson place. It lies about 15 miles southeast of Pleasant Valley and a couple of miles south of the Newton ranch, which in 1894 became the Ellison place, now called the Q ranch.

The photo below is of the Middleton Ranch, circa 1880's. The photo was supplied by Bill Brown from the Tewksbury family archives.

None of the occupants of the cabin were injured, and apparently they soon rode away, leaving the bodies of Blevins and Paine to be buried later. A short time later the old Middleton ranch cabin was burned to the ground. Edwin Tewksbury reported later that they saw a war party of Apaches on the distant hill and they knew that if they were caught by war party in the cabin they would be burned to death so they got out in a hurry. Edwin believed the Apaches burned the building, which was standard procedure for a war party of Indians. He went on to report that none of them set the cabin on fire.

The result of this killing at Middleton Ranch was to intensify the feeling between the Grahams and the Tewksbury factions, and to bring Yavapai County Sheriff Billy Mulvenon into the valley with a strong posse and warrants for the arrest of the Tewksbury's.

After spending several days in the valley searching for the Tewksbury's that were involved in the gunfight at the Middleton ranch, who were hiding in the mountains, Mulvenon withdrew from the valley and went back to Prescott. Either before he entered the valley or while he was there, James D. Houck, a sheep man and a deputy sheriff of Apache County, carrying a dubious warrant for the arrest of John Graham for the charge of horse stealing but it must be noted that he also held John Graham responsible for the murder of his brother in law the sheep herder.

In his official report filed in Apache County, Houck stated that he was waiting behind a tree in a spot on a trail that John Graham traveled daily, so he could serve the warrant for John Graham's arrest for cattle rustling. (Although this warrant was never located, and it is thought by most historians that it was a means for Houck to bring in John Graham and question him about the murder of his brother in law the Basque Sheep herder.)

Houck claims a rider approached his position, who he thought was John Graham. When he stepped out from behind the tree where he was hiding, to face the rider he immediately noticed that it was not John Graham but his younger brother Billy Graham. In Houck's official report filed, once he noticed that it was Billy, he told the young man that he was not carrying a warrant for him but his brother. Billy told Houck that he was carrying a warrant for him, drew his gun and fired a round at Houck but missed. Houck fired back and hit Billy, who slumped in his saddle but rode away. This author seriously questions Billy Graham's supposed statement that he was killed by Ed Tewksbury. Especially when Houck was so detailed in how the shooting happened, but for sure the Grahams would make up anything to blame Ed Tewksbury, who was blamed for more crimes that he said could have ever committed.

Continuing Willson's story; Billy Graham either was found by someone who helped him or he made it back alone to the Graham ranch but he died from his wounds a couple days later. The death of his younger brother Billy enraged Tom Graham and consequently began an all-out effort to exterminate the Tewksbury brothers and their men, who were apparently keeping to the hills not realizing that the posse after them had left the valley only visiting their ranch from time to time to restock food and water.

It was at about the same time, it was considered a dangerous procedure for strangers to enter the valley. On the one side the Graham's were hunting the Tewksbury's and were suspicious that any newcomer might be of that faction, while the Tewksbury's were likewise on the watch to prevent any new gunmen from joining the Graham's.

Bill Colcord, who lived in the northern part of Tonto Basin just below the Mogollon Rim about 15 miles northwest of Pleasant Valley stated that he and the other ranchers near him avoided riding through the valley in the daytime unless absolutely necessary and never at night for any reason.

An old friend of Willson's, Pierce F. Pius, still living in Pleasant Valley at the time of this article and age 93, told Willson that while on his way from Camp Verde to his ranch above the Mogollon Rim in the summer of 1887, traveling through the western part of the valley, he was stopped by a rifleman who arose from behind a rock alongside the trail and demanded to know his business. Pius went on to state that it was only after arguing the he was allowed to proceed, and then with the admonition from the man; 'keep going and never come back.'

Colonel Jesse W. Ellison told Willson years later that during that same time he attempted to drive a herd of cattle to market through Pleasant Valley and was stopped. Rather than continuing through the valley he drove his herd around the valley, a safer but a longer direction to Holbrook.

William Colcord, who had established his cattle ranch starting at the north end of the valley as his southernmost point and heading north just below the Mogollon Rim, which is now called Colcord Mountain states that he knows it to be a fact that strangers shunned the region, they had good reason to do so.

After the death of his brother Billy, Tom Graham was said to have sent for Andy Cooper (Cooper Blevins) and his so-called gang of horse thieves and cattle rustlers, as he began to lay plans to wipe out the Tewksbury's.

Shortly after the raid at the Middleton ranch that took the lives of two of Graham's friends, Tom Graham orchestrated a raid on the Tewksbury's that took the lives of two men, but in the most revolting incident, that did more than any other feature of the feud to give the Pleasant Valley War nationwide publicity, and to change the sentiment of noncombatants in the surrounding territory in favor of the Tewksbury's.

The fourth article in the Pleasant Valley series written by Roscoe Willson appeared in the Arizona Republic Newspaper, in the Days and Ways section of the paper on
March 18, 1951;

Bloody Ambush Turns Graham Supporters

Just how many of the Graham faction, or just who they were, that surrounded the upper Tewksbury cabin on the morning of September 2, 1887, and waited in ambush for the occupants of the cabin to show themselves, will never be known. But it is for certain that the Graham's were out to kill any and all of the Tewksbury faction who came within their rifle sights.

According to Bill Colcord, who was friends with Edwin Tewksbury, with whom, Bill hunted horses with several years after the war all but ended told him that the occupants of the cabin that fateful day were him, his brother's John and Jim along with his step mother Lydia, John's wife Mary Ann, who was 8 months pregnant at the time, John's two children Johnny and Bertha, Joe Boyer, Bill Jacobs, Jim Roberts and John Rhodes.

In any event, the Graham fighters surrounded John Tewksbury's place so quietly just before dawn, that, all unsuspecting, John Tewksbury and Bill Jacobs left the cabin on foot shortly after daylight to gather their saddle horses that had been kept at a small pasture on Cherry Creek about three quarters of a mile south of the cabin.

Apparently as told by Bill Colcord, the besieger's watched the two men walk down the flat from their positions hiding behind trees and bushes along the trail until the two men passed them and had their back to the Graham men. At a concerted signal, rifles blazed from behind trees and bushes. Before either Tewksbury or Jacobs could draw their guns, they were riddled with bullets the back and fell dead on the flat within sight of the cabin they had just left.

Those folks within the cabin were aroused to the shooting, and prepared to defend themselves. A cautious opening of the front door by Edwin was met by a storm of bullets. Inmates, not daring to leave the cabin, held the attackers in check by firing through Portholes and chinks between the logs of their well- fortified log cabin.

All through the long morning sniping between the attackers and the defenders continued. About mid-afternoon a band of James Dunning Tewksbury's half wild hogs wandered out into the flat where the bloody bodies of John Tewksbury and Bill Jacobs lay. They began rooting at the bodies, ripping and tearing off the clothing to get to the flesh.

From their cabin the Tewksbury's saw the attack of the hogs. They watched in anguish, knowing that if any of them attempted to rescue the bodies *they would be shot down. Finally, unable to stand the sight any longer, Mary Ann and her mother, Lydia, feeling that no man would be low enough to shoot a woman, ran across the flat, sage, scrub oak land in full sight of the attackers, dispersed the hog, rolled the bodies in canvass, tied the canvass and dug shallow graves and buried the bodies. They returned unmolested to the cabin. The bodies of the two men were dug up after the shooting stopped and given a decent burial.*

After this shocking incident the battle died out. There were no more shots exchanged on either side. The Grahams withdrew after witnessing the gruesome hog affair.

Those within the cabin, however, were unaware of the withdrawal of the Graham forces, and maintained their vigilance until late afternoon when John Meadows, justice of the peace from Payson, with several neutral cowmen, rode up to the cabin and at that point the Tewksbury's knew that the Graham's had left the property wanting to have no part of any confrontation with the law.

The ambush at the Tewksbury cabin and the hog incident was the turning point in sentiment of both within and outside Pleasant Valley. Prior to that time the majority had favored the Graham's, but now with the charges against them that would not allow a truce to permit the Tewksbury's to drive away the hogs and permit burial of the bodies of the men they had slain, together with the growling that they, the Graham's, had been working with Andy Cooper (Blevins) gang in stealing horses, sentiment swung strongly in favor of the Tewksbury's.

Whether or not Andy Cooper was with the Graham's in the attack on the Tewksbury ranch cannot be proven. If he was, he certainly made quick time in riding the ninety miles from Pleasant Valley to Holbrook, since within forty-eight hours after the killing of Tewksbury and Jacobs he was in Holbrook, where he and two of his crowd were killed by Sheriff Commodore Perry Owens on September 4, 1887.

According to the Tewksbury family archivist, Bill Brown, it always bothered his grandmother, Bertha Tewksbury, who was in the cabin at the time of the battle and was a young girl of five years of age, but old enough to remember the complete incident, as it was burned into her memory banks. She told Bill many times over and over that the stories told by different authors were totally wrong. Her mother was in no shape physically to run three quarters of a mile to where the bodies lay, as she had been bedridden from her pregnancy, besides the fact that she was so upset about what had happened as well as watching her husband's body being attacked by the hogs, that her mother in law Lydia went to the bodies and did all she could do to save what was left of them and not Mary Ann Tewksbury. .

Upon first hand inspection of the burial site of John Tewksbury and Bill Jacobs with Bill Brown a couple of years ago, it was obvious that an eight-month old pregnant lady was in no way able to crawl under a fence and run three quarters of a mile, then dig a shallow grave in some of the hardest, rock covered earth was very typical of the hard rock and hard dirt of the Sonoran Desert here in Central and Southern Arizona.

> **Below is a photo my son in law Brian and my daughter Christina took on our trip to Pleasant Valley of the gravesite of John Tewksbury and Bill Jacobs that are located on the property of the Cherry Creek Lodge, which was at one time the J.D. Tewksbury Ranch.**

According to this author's research the facts presented previously in this book are that Andy Cooper who had barely arrived in Holbrook the morning he was killed. He went to a local bar and bragged that he killed John Tewksbury, shooting him in the back and that Hank Blevans aka: The Buscadero Outlaw shot Bill Jacobs in the back as they were on their way back from getting the horses that were drinking from the creek. Will Barnes happened to be in that bar at the time Cooper made his admission and who overheard the whole conversation between Andy Cooper and another man at the bar. Will Barnes immediately went to Owen's office. He reported that Cooper had just arrived in town, Barnes having knowledge that Owens had a warrant for the arrest of Andy Cooper for the charge of horse stealing. Barnes also reminded Owens again about the incident at the ranch in Pleasant Valley when he was with a posse following the trail of cattle rustlers to the door of a ranch in the valley at which time Copper informed him and his posse to come on in because he was ready and would not be taken alive.

After going to the livery stable, talking with the owner inspecting the gear, Sheriff Owens confirmed the fact that Andy Cooper was in town by inspecting his mount that was there at the livery stable. Owens knew the Blevins family had a seasonal cottage in Holbrook, so he went back to his office to ready himself for the possible fight that was to come when he tried to serve the arrest warrant on Andy Cooper. It was at that time Deputy Will Barnes volunteered to go in after Blevins but Sheriff Owens wanted no part of passing the buck to his game Deputy Will Barnes. Owens told Barnes that he and Andy had worked together at several ranches punching cows and told Barnes he knew exactly who he was dealing with and what to expect. He thanked Barnes for volunteering but as he loaded his rifle and two pistols he told Barnes;

> *"I have the warrants and it's my job to make the arrest, be sure though, I thank you for the warning but I know exactly what to expect."*

The rest is history. The author has already presented all the facts and diagram drawn by Deputy Will Barnes, who witnessed the incredible shootout, as he stood across the street on the railroad platform from the Blevins home in Holbrook that fateful day and was an eye witness to the gunfight that ensued when Perry stood outside the door and informed Cooper that he had a warrant for his arrest for the crime of stealing horses, that was a hanging offense in those days.

Of course, Cooper being his over confident self, informed Owens that was not coming and invited Owens to come in and get him, which is exactly what Owens did. Blasting through the front door shooting Andy Cooper with one shot, then turning and shooting John Blevins as he entered the room with a pistol in his hand' luckily for John the shot fired by Owens struck him in his right shoulder, he was to be the only male Blevins survivor other John, who was shot in the shoulder and the Blevins women that day. Owens ran outside and hollered to Mose Roberts to stop running, which he did not do. Knowing he was armed or going for a gun, to protect himself, Owens shot Roberts in the back, right then the younger brother, Sam Houston Blevins, age 14 came charging out the front door with a pistol in his hand and when he went to point it at Owens, Owens shot and killed him with one shot through the heart.

The fifth article in the Roscoe Willson wrote about the Pleasant Valley War appeared in the Days and Ways section of the Arizona Republic Newspaper on Sunday March 25, 1951;

Sheriff Trap Ends Pleasant Valley War

> While most writers have included the killing of Andy Cooper, his half-brother Sam Blevins and Mose Roberts in Holbrook, as part of the Pleasant Valley War, it resulted, as a matter of fact from an attempt to arrest Cooper on a horse stealing charge. While it might have led back indirectly to the feud between the Graham's and the Tewksbury's, yet it was not a direct action of the feudists against one another, so it will not be dealt in this

account. Although Bill Colcord feels it ties in with the war, all right, agrees that, for the reason stated above, it probably takes its place as a side drama, incidental to the Pleasant Valley War.

As soon as the news of the attack on the Tewksbury cabin, and the consequent killing of John Tewksbury and Bill Jacobs reached Prescott, Sheriff Mulvenon again prepared to invade Pleasant Valley with a posse to try to bring the war to an end. This time he held warrants for the arrest of both the Graham's and the Tewksbury's. It was not until September 21st, nearly three weeks after the Tewksbury cabin gun battle, that he reached the valley. In the mean-time one more Graham partisan was killed.

A few days before Sheriff Mulvenon arrived in the valley, in anticipation of his arrival, the Graham's planned another attack on the same Tewksbury ranch where they killed John Tewksbury and Bill Jacobs just two weeks earlier.

Like the previous attack it was planned for early morning and the play would have succeeded, as Ed Tewksbury told Bill Colcord later, had not one of the men in the cabin walking around the property that the dew laden grass clearly showed the recent passage of several horsemen. Thus the Tewksbury's were alerted and ready when the Graham's charged down on the cabin just before daylight.

Evil luck seemed to pursue the Graham's all through this war, and this raid was no exception, since instead of killing one or more of the Tewksbury men, as expected, a Graham rider, Harry Middleton, who was no relation to the William Middleton family, original settlers in Pleasant Valley, received a mortal wound from which he died from within a few days after the attack and another Graham that was there that day, Joe Ellinwood was wounded very seriously but eventually recovered from the wound. None of the Tewksbury's received a scratch.

When Sheriff Mulvenon arrived in the valley on the 21st of September with his posse, he and his men hid at the Perkins store in a partially constructed rock addition to the store building. Several riders were sent to scout the situation at the Graham and Rose place's, the Graham place was only a mile and a half northeast of the store and the Rose place about a mile east of the store.

Whether or not these riders were seen by the Graham's is really not known for sure, but they were probably noticed. In any event, John Graham and Charlie Blevins rode over to the store shortly after noon, and as came close to the partly constructed room that concealed the posse, Sheriff Mulvenon exposed himself and ordered the two men to surrender.

Realizing they had run into a trap, Graham and Blevins whirled their horses, and giving spur to them, attempted to escape. It was too late.

> *The posse fired at the first sign of flight, and both men were shot out of their saddles, Blevins was killed instantly and John Graham died within a short time after being shot.*

According to the official report filed by Sheriff William Mulvenon in the Yavapai County courthouse regarding the incident, both John Graham and Charlie Blevins drew their guns and each fired one round at him missing badly as they whirled their horses to run but the posse all fired and the two men were riddled with bullets. Mulvenon went over to John Graham, bent down and asked him;

> *"Why did he have to shoot John? Why didn't you surrender peacefully so we could get your side of the story? Mulvenon went on to say, John never said a word before he died."*

The sixth and final article that Roscoe G. Willson wrote about the Pleasant Valley or Tonto Basin War appeared in the Days and Ways section of the Arizona Republic Newspaper on Sunday April 1, 1951, starts and follows on the next few pages;

Tom Graham Killing in Tempe Ends Feud

> *After the killing of John Graham and Charlie Blevins at the Perkins Store every effort was made to capture Tom Graham, but he had left the valley and gone to live in Tempe, where less than three weeks after the fight at the Perkins store, he was married to Anne Melton.*
>
> *Four days after the shootout he was served a warrant and was arrested in Tempe, then he was transported to Prescott where he was released on bail,*

for lack of evidence, or some other reason, the charges were dismissed.

According to the records in Prescott, Judge Walter Shute states that he was told by a participant of the gun battle at the Perkins Store that a large body of men from the Tonto Basin north of Pleasant Valley led by Captain Watkins, rode into the valley determined to put an end to the widespread horse stealing from which they had all suffered constant losses.

Colcord substantiates this, by saying it occurred before the fighting started. He says that when the Watkins party arrived in the valley, early in 1887, they were unable to catch any of the culprits, but that before departing they left the warning that if the horse stealing was not stopped they would be back.

This warning apparently had little effect, since Colcord remembers that later on, in the fall of 1888, a large committee of outside cattlemen again came through the valley to stop horse stealing, they went up onto a mountain above the rim, where they were joined by cattlemen from farther east. This joint vigilante committee hung Stott, Scott and Wilson as horse thieves on August 8, 1888 at the Stott Ranch.

It was said that these three men were in on the horse running deal and that was Stott's ranch was one of the stations on the horse running route. This has been disputed, and much has been said as to the terrible wrong inflicted on those men. The belief as to their guilt was strong among the old-timers, however, and it is even claimed that stolen horses were found hidden near the Stott cabin. Bill Colcord feels there is little question as to their guilt.

In the valley, after Sheriff Mulvenon took his captives to Prescott, Tom Graham was living with his bride in Tempe, and there was no one left at the Graham ranch to look after the cattle, and most of the time they were left untended.

The fighting in the valley apparently was over, but the fire still smoldered, as was evidenced by the killing of Al Rose, a Graham man, at the Houdan ranch on Spring Creek sometime in late fall of 1887. Still later that year someone winged Jake Lauffler in the arm as he stood in the door of his cabin south of Buzzard Roost.

Contrary to some statements, Tom Graham did not return to the valley until the spring of 1888. Neither did he, according to Colcord, ever bring his bride to Pleasant Valley.

Shortly after the killings at the Perkins store, Tow wrote Bill Colcord from Tempe and asked him to take charge of his cattle. Only once thereafter did Tom come to the valley, and that was for a short consultation with Colcord, in the spring of 1888.

Colcord ran the cattle until the spring of 1889, when through arrangements made by letter he turned the cattle over to S.W. Young. Young soon bought out Graham. His daughters, the Misses Ola *and Betty, who as young girls came into the valley with their father, still own and run cattle on the Graham place.*

After the departure of Tom Graham, and the dismissal of murder charges against him and the Tewksbury's, there was peace in the valley, but apparently old hatreds were not easily forgotten.

Nearly five years had passed since the last killing in Pleasant Valley, and everyone assumed that the feud was dead, when the people of the territory were startled to learn that on August 2, 1892 Tom Graham, the last of the Grahams, had been shot from ambush and killed as he drove his wagon from his farm into Tempe.

John Rhodes and Edwin Tewksbury were charged with the killing, in a preliminary hearing before the Tempe justice of the peace, Rhodes was acquitted of complicity in the crime and freed. During the hearing Tom's widow, Anne, it was said, attempted to shoot Rhodes with a pistol, but was foiled when the gun became entangled in a handkerchief in which she had it concealed.

Ed Tewksbury had no problem surrendering voluntarily three days later in Tonto Basin and was brought to Phoenix for a hearing. He was bound over for trial by the county court, but succeeded in transferring the case to Tucson where on December on December 23, 1893 a jury found him guilty of murder.

A motion for a new trial was made, and after a long delay it was granted. Ed Tewksbury was again brought before a court on January 2, 1895, Judge Sloan presiding. After all of the evidence was presented by both sides, the jury failed to agree and was discharged, and Tewksbury was released on bail never to be tried again and finally all charges were dismissed on March 12, 1896.

This ended the bloody Pleasant Valley or Tonto Basin War, which conservatively caused the death of at least nineteen men, fifteen of whom were said to belong to the Graham faction, while only four Tewksbury men died in the nine yeas the feud existed. Many believe there are others killed on lonely trails and their bodies never found.

Today Pleasant Valley is a serene little community, which gives scarcely a thought to the evil days of sixty and more years ago. Only the ruins of the old cabins inhabited by the Graham's and the Tewksbury's recall that it was once a dark and bloody ground.

The participants in that war are dead to the last man, and William C. Colcord is, as far as is known, the last surviving man whose thread of life intermingled with those of the Tewksbury's and the Graham's during the entire course of the feud. Even though he looked after the cattle of Graham's for a time, he remained friendly with the Tewksbury's, and considered Ed Tewksbury a likeable man. His aid in preparing this article, as *well as that of the others mentioned herein, gives us an approximately true account of the Pleasant Valley War.*

Chapter Seventeen
Willson's letter to Earle B. Forrest

When it is all said and done, historians today, after over a hundred years, can only present bits and pieces of research each one of us finds regarding, the deadliest family feud in the United States history and for sure a huge stain in our Arizona history. With that in mind, while I was researching the Roscoe Willson Collection the author found several letters to the editor from folks around Arizona, who were avid readers of Willson's historical stories over the years. These letters appeared in the Arizona Day and Ways section on Sundays in the Arizona Republic Newspaper which, as a young boy, this author always looked forward to reading every Sunday.

Also with this in mind, the author would like to present the following letters that were written by Earle B. Forrest, the author of the first book written about the Pleasant Valley War called, *"Arizona's Dark and Bloody Ground,"* to Roscoe G. Willson and the letters written by Roscoe Willson back to Mr. Forrest regarding each separate article. These letters are very interesting and simply need to be shared with the reader, to help put together a few more pieces of the puzzle surrounding the Pleasant Valley War. In the authors estimation, it doesn't get any better than disagreements between two very knowledgeable, passionate historians than these letters. There are some interesting facts that come out in these letters.

The first letter I found was written by Roscoe G. Willson to Earle B. Forrest on May 1, 1951, commenting on Forrest's book after Willson read Mr. Forrest's book, "Arizona's Dark and Bloody Ground," for the second time after completing his research and writing his six-part series on the Pleasant Valley War, also known as the Tonto Basin War and the Graham-Tewksbury Feud;

Mr. Earl B. Forrest
Care Washington Observer
Main Street
Washington, PA.

Dear Mr. Forrest:

Having some years ago and recently read your book "Arizona's Dark and Bloody Ground," and having also met your old friend and schoolmate, R. Trevor Ferguson, who with his wife is spending the winter at the Shelly Apartments in Glendale near here, I am at Fergy's suggestion sending you a condensed story of the Pleasant Valley War as it appeared in six successive Sunday issues of the Arizona Republic, in my column in the Arizona Days and Ways section, that I have now been writing for over three years.

There are a few minor corrections on your story, but nothing that detracts from your book's being the best and most exhaustive one on the subject to date, as most old-timers agree.

It was difficult to get Bill Colcord to talk, even after all these years, and had not the Young sisters, Lena Ellison and Judge Shute urged him in the matter I would not have gotten the history.

There is one outstanding point that disagrees most accounts, and that is that in actuality Tom Graham, while outwardly much more the gentleman than any of the Tewksbury's, was in the horse stealing ring that involved the Blevins family. Not only Colcord, but also Franz Cooper, who was in and out

> of the valley at the time, swear to this. Colcord says; 'I know damn well he stole four of my horses as well as my Tonto Basin neighbor rancher, Jim Roberts' horses.
>
> I know am in the possession of the inquest records on the killing of the Blevins boys by Commodore Perry Owens and I will write that up for my column soon. There will be little change from your story except possibly some minor details. I will also write the Stott, Scott and Wilson story before too long.
>
> Fergy and I became acquainted when we were both working for the Forest Service in Montana from 1914 to 1920. His wife, Lavonia, is in poor health just now. I shall be glad to hear from you and I hope you will look me up if at any time you come out here again.
>
> Sincerely,
> Roscoe G. Willson

As to be expected after receiving the letter from Willson, Mr. Forrest sent a letter to Willson explaining his position, on May 10, 1951. A copy of the letter Mr. Forrest wrote to Roscoe Willson is below and on the following pages. Along with the copy of the letter Willson sent to Forrest, letters that the author has in his possession along with copies of all the newspaper articles that Roscoe G. Willson wrote;

> Mr. Roscoe G. Willson
> 925 West Heatherbrae Street
> Phoenix, Arizona
>
> Dear Mr. Willson,
> I was certainly delighted and surprised to receive your letter of May

1st and especially, to hear indirectly from Trevor Ferguson. Be sure and give the old so and so my very best, and tell him I smiled when I called him that. He was here with his brother about a year ago. It was first time I had seen him in years, but I knew him right away. He was the same old Trevor. I did not meet his wife at that time, but had the pleasure of meeting her once when they were here years ago. I am certainly sorry to hear that she is in poor health. I hope that the Arizona climate will restore her health. It should, for there is no better climate in the world. Tell him to go to Flagstaff in the summer to get away from that hot weather of southern Arizona.

I have read with much pleasure your story of the Pleasant Valley War. You have a lot of good facts and I congratulate you. I cannot agree that Tom Graham was mixed up in the horse stealing ring. I have never found anything that corroborates that. On the contrary, the old-timers I knew in Flagstaff years ago did not think that he was a horse thief, but he and his brother John were involved with the Tewksbury's in rustling cattle, especially from Jim Stinson.

It would have been hard to convince those old-timers at Flagstaff; the Babbitts, John Francis, Bill Houdan, John Weatherford and others that the Tewksbury's did not agree to guard the Daggs sheep and were to have a share as payment for their service. They all knew the Daggs brothers and the

Tewksbury brothers. William Colcord undoubtedly did lose some horses, and Jim Roberts lost his special horse, but it was blamed on the Blevins clan and not Graham.

Horse stealing at that time was not nearly as bad as cattle rustling. There was not a good market for horses. There were plenty of wild horses on the ranges and at $5 to $10 a head when you could sell them unbroken was simply not a profitable business. A good broken horse, of course was a different proposition, but in most cases they were well marked and hard to dispose of in any quantity.

I well remember when I was riding for the Babbitts' CO Bar Ranch, horse stealing was never a problem. In fact there were so many that Bill Babbitt would have liked to have killed a lot of them. They were a real nuisance. In fact several cowboys quit their jobs and went to horse hunting. The old Circle S range south of Flagstaff was alive with them, and they ate so much of the range that there was little left for the cattle to eat.

The cowboys trapped the wild horses by the dozen and shipped them unbroken east. Fred Volz, an Indian trader who ran the trading post at the Canyon Diablo railroad station used some good Hopi runners to run down horses on foot trapping them with great success.

Cattle rustling though was a different matter in those later days in the early years of the present century. We had a good deal of trouble with rustlers.

I, too, secured the records of the inquest at Holbrook, and from that and Sam Brown's account to me, I wrote the story of the killing. I found that the lynching of Stott, Scott and Wilson is still a touchy subject even to this day. Jim Houck seems to have been the worst villain in the play. According to Sam Brown, Houck wanted Stott's ranch to raise sheep.

Stott's worst mistake, according to Brown, was that he bought horses with blotched brands. This may have had something to do with the lynching of the three men, for there was a belief at the time that the so-called vigilance committee was composed of some rustlers who had sold him the stock.

The heat was being put on them and they were afraid that Stott would disclose their names. No matter who was in the crowd, Jim Houck was the leader. I have a large number of letters written by Stott, his mother, and others at the time, bearing on this case. Furthermore, D.G. Harvey, Justice of the Peace at Holbrook, wrote to Stott's father. This letter clears young Stott of rustling. At any rate, neither Jim Stott nor Jeff Wilson had any hand in cattle rustling. I have been informed that Jim Houck committed suicide in 1918. Could there have been remorse?

I have plated your story in my Pleasant Valley scrap book, and I would be very glad to receive anything else that you write on the subject. If the old

> graveyard in Phoenix is still there it might pay you to visit it and hunt up Tom Graham's grave. I think you will find something to surprise you.
>
> Well, I'll close for tonight and go to bed. Be sure and give my best to Trevor.
>
> With Best Wishes, Sincerely,
> Earle R. Forrest

The reader must remember that stealing a horse was considered a capital offense in those days, all across the country and punishable with a death by hanging in the courts or by lynch mobs. Rustling cattle was not considered a capital offense. Sadly, though our cattle ranges were overcrowded with wild horses, the cowboys hated them because they ate up the range and the cowboys spent most of their time digging post holes from the horses knocking down their fences which they still do to this day. Cattle will go up to a fence and stop but horses will jump the fence and kick it down tearing out swaths of fencing. Now back to the letter from Earle Forrest to Roscoe Willson;

On May 10, 1951, Roscoe Willson sent another follow up letter to Earl B. Forrest basically asking Mr. Forrest for permission to use a picture of Jamie Stott in his upcoming story about the lynching of Stott, Scott and Wilson. The letter is following in its entirety;

> Mr. Earle B. Forrest
> Care Washington Observer
> Washington, PA
>
> Dear Mr. Forrest;
>   Since writing you and enclosing a copy of my sketch of the Pleasant Valley War, I have received the manuscript coroner's inquest testimony on the Commodore

Owens killings at the Blevins' home in Holbrook, as well as some other previously unused data in the matter and have just finished writing the story, which, when published shortly, I will send to you. There are practically no differences in our versions; possibly a small addition or two to your story, and a different commentary.

Now I am preparing the story of the Stott, Scott and Wilson hanging, and, frankly, I am arriving at a somewhat different conclusion than you did, as to Stott's guilt based partly on old-timers' beliefs and knowledge and partly on records of the time.

After telling you this I may be nervy in asking you know of any way in which I might obtain permission to use the Stott photo that appears in your book.

By the way Fergy just left for Great Falls. His wife, Lavonia, is not at all well.

Sincerely,
Roscoe G. Willson

On May 15, 1951, Roscoe Willson wrote another follow up letter to Earle B. Forrest of which the author has a copy of in my research material for this book;

Earle B. Forrest

205 North Main Street
Washington, PA

On August 5, 1951, Earle B. Forrest sent his final communication letter to Roscoe G. Willson regarding his position concerning the questions and research the two historians pondered in the letters sent to each other. This letter from Forrest to Willson was the last communication between the two men that the author could find in

Willson's research files, letters and newspaper articles. Below and on the following pages is word for word this letter of which the author has a copy in my research files;

> 205 North Main Street
> Washington, PA
>
> Dear Mr. Willson,
> Your letter of July 31st, with enclosures of your stories of Commodore Perry Owens fight and the hanging of Stott, Scott and Wilson came Friday. I was deeply interested in both accounts. I think between us we have a pretty good account of the gun battle at Holbrook that day. If Andy Cooper wasn't in the attack on the Tewksbury cabin on September 2nd he certainly knew of it because he boasted of being the in re when he got to Holbrook, and it is hard to imagine Andy not taking part in such an affair if he was in the neighborhood
> Yes, I knew that "The Honorable." Jim Houck served a term in the territorial legislature, and that Osmer D. Flake was a deputy with McKinney with Sheriff Mulvenon's posse at the Perkins store. McKinney says nothing about him or anyone else riding around the valley while the main posse remained at the store before the killing of John Graham and Charley Blevins, but several of the posse did make a round of the ranches after the shooting.
> Deputy McKinney says it was the wounding of Jake Lauffer that aroused the people of that vicinity, and was the

cause of the hanging of Stott, Scott and Wilson. He also says that Lauffer was on the side of the Tewksburys and that Stott was a Graham sympathizer but took no part in the fighting. He did not know Wilson, but he did know Scott and speaks highly of him.

The reason he was there was that he was after a horse that he had loaned to Louis Neglin which had not been returned. Here is something that corroborates the statement that Houck was the leader of the gang that did the lynching. McKinney says that the reason Scott was hanged was that of he incurred the enmity of Houck when he called Houck's hand one night in Holbrook, when Houck was shooting his head off recklessly. Houck backed down and refused to go, but forever afterwards had an awful grudge against Jamie Stott. McKinney also says; Jim Houck was the cause of Stott's demise.

McKinney says nothing about any of the three being accused of horse stealing. From what I have gathered it seems clear to me that Stott's worst offense was that he did associate, as you say, with some questionable characters. I also know that he was warned about this by Sam Brown and Harvey. There is one thing to remember that most of the residents in that section of Arizona (the Pleasant Valley and Mogollon region) were not too law abiding themselves.

To my mind the fact that Stott did keep books is proof of his innocence.

Rustlers just didn't keep books. It would be like a burglar of highwayman keeping books of his transactions. Stott was no fool, and to place on record in books from whom stock was stolen would be to put a noose around his neck or send him to the penitentiary, and well he knew it. He may have recorded the brands and from whom he purchased horses, which was proper and according to law, but as for placing on record from whom they were stolen, well, it is hard to believe. As I have said, rustlers just didn't keep books.

Houck had made his boasts that he would have Stott's ranch for his sheep. I do not recall whether I told you in my former letters or not that James Houck committed suicide about 1918. As for Barnes, I have been at a loss at time to know just how much credence to put on his statements. I still have letters from him in which he made statements that were afterwards found to be false, one of which is the story of exhuming the remains of Jamie Stott and sending them back to his parents in Massachusetts.

Did you ever run across a photo of Mulvenon? I would like to get one for my collection. There was one taken by a photographer in Prescott, but I was never able to locate one.

Of course you know about the death of Mrs. Mary (John) Tewksbury Rhodes last December. If in your research among old times you ever run across that Winchester rifle I raffled off at

Oracle in 1903 please let me know if it can be bought. It is a 30-30 model 1894, checkered walnut forearm and pistol grip stock, take down. On the side of the receiver is engraved a buffalo and a big horn on the other. John Rhodes, who was on a ranch somewhere near Mammoth won it.

Well, I guess I have rambled on enough for this time. Again, you have certainly done good work on your Pleasant Valley stories.
My very best wishes.

Sincerely,
Earle B. Forrest

Even though the hangings of Stott, Scott and Wilson probably had little to do with the Pleasant Valley War, because in one of the stories presented, Stott and Scott were at the Tewksbury ranch that fateful day that John Tewksbury and Bill Jacobs were killed. The man who told the Tewksburys who was present was most probably James Pearce, who turned on the Grahams after this despicable deed. His statement took place again in an interview he had with the author Maurice Kildare as stating to Tom Graham;

> "When Tom Graham told Stott that he need not get involved in the affair, Jamie Stott replied to Tom, if they do something wrong to my friends then I am in!"

Obviously as both Willson and Forrest have discussed, the word amongst folks that supposedly were there, simply have to be questioned, when talking with one person who was supposedly at the affair and getting his story, then another person who was supposedly there and has different version, we must simply deduct that it is very difficult to ascertain the real truth.

With this in mind below the author is presenting the story that Roscoe G. Willson wrote about this affair in column, the Arizona Days and Ways section of the Arizona Republic newspaper because Earle B. Forrest was in complete agreement with Willson's findings. The lynching's took place over 130 years ago and unless some amazing research comes to the surface the will never know, other than James D. Houck, Osmer D. Flake, Tom Horn and Gila County Sheriff Glenn Reynolds, who else was present at the brutal lynching of Stott, Scott and Wilson is still a mystery. The first article appeared in the Arizona Days and Ways section of the Arizona Republic Newspaper on July 8, 1951;

"Mystery" Lynching is Controversial Subject

For some time following the blaze of gunfire that burst forth in the blood-letting year of 1887, during which 10 or12 men of the Graham and Tewksbury factions had been killed in Pleasant Valley and three of the so-called Blevins gang killed in Holbrook by long haired Apache County Sheriff Commodore Owens, there was a lull in death dealing activities in the Mogollon Rim Country.

In Pleasant Valley most of the Graham faction had been killed and Tom Graham, last of the Grahams, had left his cattle in care of William Colcord and retired to his farm in Tempe. With the killing of the Blevins men, in September 1887, who were said to be associated with the Grahams in horse "running." It was generally assumed that the days of the "disappearing horse" were over and that only "the ordinary run" of violent deaths would again possess the land.

For a short time after the Blevins affair there were almost no losses from horse stealing, but gradually complaints began to be heard that "runners" were at it again. Freighters up in the Mormon settlements reported that wagon stock turned loose to graze at night failed to show up in the morning. Ranchers as far as Safford and Phoenix also found horses unexplainably disappearing from their pastures. Even in nearby Tonto Basin, Payson and Pine country, horses were here today and gone tomorrow.

There were, of course, many footloose and "full of hell" cowboys and outlaws still in the land and many of them under suspicion, but for a time no particular person, any rendezvous or holding station, could be satisfactorily tied in with illicit trade in horses.

Finally, however, suspicion fell upon Jamie Stott, a young Easterner about 25 years of age, who after a couple years of cowboying in Texas, had come into the rim country around 1885 and located a horse ranch at Bear Springs, just above the Mogollon Rim about 12 to 15 miles north and East of the Blevins ranch, later known as the Ramer ranch.

Stott had been suspected as a receiver of stolen horses for some time, while it was never charged that he himself actually had stolen any, yet according to Will C. Barnes in his book

"Apaches and Longhorns."

The livestock association, of which Barnes was a member, employed a detective, Carl Blasingame, well known by Osmer Flake, who reported back to Flake, that, "Stott's ranch was the headquarters of a well-organized band of horse thieves." Also by the summer of 1887 most of the ranchers in the Tonto Basin region and the Mormon settlements to the East of Stott's ranch were convinced that Stott was in the game up to his ears, if not the actual head of the organization.

The records of events leading to the climax and the manner in which the final act was carried out, as well as the names of the persons involved are very much confused and even contradictory, in that it is practically impossible to give a report that will not be subject to criticism and correction.

One fact, however, is clear and undisputed. Jamie Stott, Jim Scott and Billy Wilson were taken from the Stott ranch on the morning of August 11, 1887, by a body of men, whether a vigilant committee or a posse and hanged until they were dead; In other words, lynched, and their bodies left suspended from the execution tree. Two or three days later, found by two Esperanza cowboys, Broadbent and Johnson.

Prior to the necktie party, Stott, even though suspected of having dealings with known horse thieves, had made himself fairly well liked in Holbrook, and among nearby ranchers. As Osmer Flake, who lived at Snowflake, relates, Stott had a pleasant man and liked to participate in sporting events.

On the other hand, Stott apparently at times was inclined to be somewhat cocky and to swagger a bit as a gunman who gunman who could take care of himself. Will Barnes states in his book Apaches and Longhorns, that when he tried to warn Stott that he was playing a dangerous game, Stott replied by slapping his six-shooter in its holster saying, "I can take care of myself any day, I'd love to see the color of a man's hair who could get the drop on me"

Osmer Flake substantiates this devil attitude in Stott. Presumably Stott was making a living from his horse herd and a small herd of cattle. Also it was shown later, that occasionally he received money from his father in the east and had no need to participate in horse running. If he was tied in with horse thieves it was probably because of his high spirits and sporting disposition caused him to take a gamble that had an element of dangerous risk in it.

Just how Jim Scott and Billy (Jeff) Wilson got into the picture and came to be hanged with Stott is somewhat obscure. One story states that Scott was a cowboy who, having loaned a horse to Louis Naeglin, a Graham supporter, living in Pleasant Valley, had ridden into the valley to reclaim his horse, and was simply on his way back to his outfit, and just happened to stay overnight at

Stott's place. Other reports indicated he may have been involved in the horse running business.

Billy Wilson (sometimes called Jeff) was said by Will Barnes and Osmer Flake to have been a cook in the employ of the Hashknife, but for some time previous to the hanging, he had, according to the St. Johns Herald, been seen about the Stott ranch and in Pleasant Valley. He was supposed to have been working for Stott. According to Earle B. Forrest's book "Arizona's Dark and Bloody Ground," Willson was a prospector just passing through on his way from Colorado to the mining camp of Globe.

Also at the Stott ranch at the time Stott, Scott and Wilson were hanged were two consumptives, a Mr. Clymer and a boy named Alfred M. Ingram who had been invited by Stott to stay at his place until their health improved.

This then, is the setting for the most widely discussed lynching that ever occurred in Arizona, the details of which will be narrated in this column in next Sunday's Republic.

The second article or the last one in this series about the facts and Willson's research about the lynching of Jamie Stott, Jim Scott and Billy Wilson that was published in the "Arizona Days and Ways Column," in the Arizona Republic newspaper on Sunday July 8, 1951 and follows over the next few pages;

Triple Hanging Is Subject of Mystery

Just how the seizure and hanging of Stott, Scott and Wilson was brought about probably will never be known, since the records, newspaper accounts, and personal recollections are confusing and in most cases are contradictory.

Only one person involved in the affair, Jim Houck, a deputy sheriff of Apache County, made a direct statement for publication, which first appeared in the Yavapai Democrat and was reprinted in the Apache Review on August 22, 1887, a transcript of which was furnished the writer through the courtesy of C.R. Zaring, secretary of the Holbrook Chamber of Commerce, as were other newspaper accounts.

While Deputy Houck's actions have been questioned by some persons, I can see no reason for not accepting a part of his statement as a guide to action leading up to the hangings regardless of the fact that he may have been blamed in the matter.

Houck stated that on August 5, 1887, someone fired at Jake Lauffer, breaking his arm, and that later the same day two men, Coleman and Cody, also were fired on as they passed through Pleasant Valley from the Lauffer ranch. Both men escaped unhurt, although Cody's horse was killed.

According to Houck, Justice Haigler then gave him a warrant for the arrest of Stott, Scott and Wilson, as the parties suspected of the shooting. At the same time Bill Voris, an Ellison cowboy, was deputized to assist in making the arrests

It is well to observe that since Houck was out of his jurisdiction, it is probable that Bill Varies was given the warrant and that Houck was either also deputized or simply went along with Voris.

In any event, since the seizure was made within Apache County, Houck was within his jurisdiction when it occurred, although it would also seem that Justice Haigler's warrant would be void in Apache County since he lived in Tonto Basin, which was in Eastern Yavapai County.

Houck states that accompanied by a posse, he went to Stott's Circle D ranch and effected the arrest of Stott, Scott and Wilson, he started back toward Pleasant Valley with the prisoners, when he met a party of about 40 masked men, who took the prisoners away from him and his posse and "invited them to go on their way."

Houck does not say what disposition he made of himself and his posse, but does state that two days later two men came into Wilford and reported they had seen the body of Jamie Stott hanging to a tree."

Alfred Ingram, the young consumptive staying at the Stott ranch is quoted in a communication to the St. Johns Herald on August 30, 1887 as saying;

"On the morning of August 11, 1887, before daylight, before anyone had arisen, an armed party of 38 men, headed by James D. Houck, came to the house of Mr. Stott; I talked to Mr. Houck and asked him if he had warrants for the parties; Houck seemed to hesitate, and finally said 'Yes, but I left them in my coat at the cabin where we stopped last night.' The weather was quite chilly, the altitude being high and it struck me as strange that he would travel during the coldest part of the night without a coat."

Since this communication was signed, "One who Knows," obviously was written by someone who put the words in Ingram's mouth, and had him relate only a fragment of the happenings at the Stott cabin, it cannot carry much, if any, more weight than Houck's story.

Regardless of whether Houck's posse seized the three men and the prisoners were then taken from it on the trail by about 40 masked men, or whether the 38 men led by Houck came to the cabin and took them away, the fact remains that two or three days later the bodies of Stott, Scott and Wilson were found hanging from trees. All signs indicated that they had been handcuffed, ropes thrown over the limbs, a noose place about their necks as they sat on their saddles, and the horses simply let out from under them, leaving them to strangle slowly to death.

W.J. Flake states that the limb of the tree from which Stott hung showed several grooves, indicating that he had been raised and lowered several times, probably in an effort to make him confess his activities and associations.

At once, on the discovery of the bodies, a furor arose in the press. The St. Johns Herald and the Apache Review of the same place, at first were s vociferous in denouncing the hanging as a mob law not in which innocent men were hung. Later probably after having heard from the settlers in the vicinity, they grew less assured of the innocence of the men, the Apache Review stating in its issue of August 12, 1888;

"Whether J.W. Stott was a horse thief or not, it is stated to be a fact that his ranch was the headquarters of men, known to be thieves, and that he acted as a go-between."

Stott's parents shortly came to Holbrook, were taken to their son's ranch, and also interviewed some of the local settlers. Since they were aged people, and Mr. Stott was a cripple, with both arms amputated, they were extended highly unusual courtesies and considerations.

Apparently Stott's ranch holdings were sold to William Flake of Snowflake, since Osmer D. Flake, a son of William, who was 19 years old at the time, records in a biography of his father;

"Jamie Stott's father, mother and sister came out and that they of course felt awfully bad and kept boy, when repeating, they killed an innocent boy, when they hanged our son, Jimmy."

According to Osmer Flake, his father had in his possession young Stott's books, which told from whom the stock was stolen, and not wanting him to go a that way with the feeling that innocent men can be murdered here without the people doing something about it, took the elder Stott to a retired place and left him to look over the books. Osmer Flake recorded in his father's biography the following when Mr. Stott returned;

"In a couple of hours, he came in and said, I will say again that again, but he did not need to do what he did. I am wealthy, and sent him money every time he wrote for it, and the books show just what money I sent him. Flake told him; 'I was sorry to do this, but I wanted you to know the truth, but do not tell his mother and sister.' Young Osmer Flake, himself, looked through the books and states that it clearly showed thefts."

In some way the books evidently came into the hands of Justice of the Peace D.G. Harvey of Holbrook, and according to Earl R. Forrest, in his book, "Arizona's Dark and Bloody Ground," Harvey wrote Stott's parents;

"I am fully convinced after a thorough inspection of Jamie's books and papers that he purchased and paid a good sound price for every head of stock on his ranch. But I do think he was imposed upon by designing parties and through his kindness he had to suffer; and I believe this opinion is proven by every law abiding person in the country."

Now how, let me ask, can Flake's and Harvey's statements be reconciled. They cannot. There's something wrong somewhere. Flake wanted to protect the good name of the Arizona people and he was an honorable man, a leader in his community. Did Harvey wish to soften the blow to his parents? Did Flake or Harvey misinterpret the books?

The answer will never be known, and I cannot take it upon myself to decide upon the question of young Stott's guilt or innocence. It is pretty clear, however, that young Stott associated with the wrong crowd and left himself open to suspicion. He was warned by Apache County Deputy Will C. Barnes, Flake and others, and in the end lost his life.

Those who were in the crowd that did the lynching and there are a few still living, will never tell. The records are lost men but it is remembered by a few persons still living that three of the men who were accused of participating in the lynching were arrested and held for a hearing at St. Johns.

Osmer Flake remembers that during the hearing a party of 20 well-armed men suddenly appeared on the outskirts of Snowflake and camped there for several days, keeping a torch with the proceedings at St. Johns by runner. When the three men were released for lack of evidence the campers disappeared as suddenly as they had arrived. Evidently these campers had been prepared to effect a jail delivery had the three men been convicted.

The crumbling bones of Stott, Scott and Wilson still lie in the earth among the whispering pines above the Mogollon Rim near the settlement of Forest Lakes, and nothing now remains

> to indicate the exact spot where this drama of Arizona pioneer days was played. The players have departed and the stage is bare.

At this point it is important to share the biography of William Colcord since he was the main source for Roscoe Willson's interviews and writings;

William C. "Bill" Colcord was born in Louisiana in 1867. His father, Col. William Rogers Colcord, returned home from the Civil War and found his Louisiana sugar plantation in ruins, so he moved his family to Oklahoma Territory. After the death of his father, Bill, and his younger brother, Harvey, moved to Arizona Territory. They arrived in Flagstaff in 1885 with a herd of cattle. There, Bill worked for Babbitt Brothers Cattle Company, and Harvey tended the Colcord cattle. After a year, they moved to Walnut Creek, west of Pleasant Valley. When he was 32 years old, Wayne Colcord married Pauline Merritt of Prescott. While in Pleasant Valley, Bill and Harvey became acquainted with both factions of the Pleasant Valley War, the Graham's and the Tewksbury's.

In 1894, Bill moved to Payson and married Carrie Mish Stewart, the daughter of pioneer settlers Ben and Sarah Stewart. They were married on September 17 of 1894. Bill's brother Harvey Colcord never married.

Bill and Carrie settled on a ranch in Round Valley, a few miles south of Payson, and lived there until 1910. While living in the area, Bill was active in civic affairs and politics. He served three terms on the Gila County Board of Supervisors, and was instrumental in the building of the county hospital and the county courthouse in Globe. Bill was also a founding member of the Arizona Cattle Growers' Association.

In 1912, Bill bought a ranch near Lake Mary. In 1916, his wife, Carrie, died in the Flagstaff hospital, following the birth of her sixth child. This was a blow to Bill. He picked up and moved to Sunflower. Bill bought the Diamond-A-Ranch and Harvey bought the Circle M. After Bill quit ranching, he built a service station and a store at Sunflower. Later, he owned and operated the Tonto Basin Store. He left the store in 1938. Bill Colcord died May 16, 1961 in Globe.

Below is a photo of Bill and Carrie Colcord the day they were married. This photo was found in our National Archives and is public domain.

Chapter Eighteen
Deputy Sheriff Joe McKinney

There have been many versions told about the Pleasant Valley War that in have shared in this book *"Tonto Basin War Revisited,"* and with this in mind the author is going to share a story of the Pleasant Valley War from the perspective of Apache County Deputy Sheriff Joseph T. McKinney, that he related to Roscoe Willson a few years before he passed in 1948. Just like all of the stories that this author has shared, the author finds this one very interesting as it is just another little piece of the puzzle. McKinney's personal experience in the Pleasant Valley War, as one of the members of the Apache County Sheriff's posse that met Yavapai Sheriff William Mulvenon at the Perkins Store and his involvement in the most brutal and deadly feud in United States history, the Graham-Tewksbury Feud aka the Pleasant Valley War.

Joseph Thomas McKinney was born in Falcon, Columbus County, Arkansas on June 20, 1858. McKinney was a pioneer and law enforcement officer in the Arizona territory. He arrived in Arizona around 1885 and worked for the Wabash Cattle Company near St. Johns in Apache County for about a year. In 1886 he was appointed undersheriff *(next man in line to become sheriff)* of Apache County by Apache County Sheriff Commodore Perry Owens. After he left the sheriff's office the Board of Supervisors appointed McKinney a Constable for Winslow, Arizona. He left Winslow in 1888 and spent several months at Fort Apache before moving on to San Carlos where he herded cattle. Joseph T. McKinney ranched in Fort Thomas until he moved to Bowie in 1896. In 1905 he relocated to Yuma where he became a guard at the Arizona State prison. He died at the age of 90 in Wilcox, Arizona on September 29, 1948.

In the fall of 1887 a Santa Fe passenger train was robbed at Navajo Springs, or rather, it was robbed at the water tank about three miles west of the community of Navajo Springs. The news came to Deputy McKinney while he was working at his office in Winslow, Arizona. McKinney immediately put his saddle and his mount on a special train which he boarded and he was on his way to Navajo Springs, where he met two local men that he wired ahead to meet him and they all left from there to the O. B. Little ranch, where the two men that were with him obtained mounts.

The next morning at daybreak they took the trail after the robbers that led across the high desert country southwest toward Pleasant Valley. The robbers' tracks were easy to find because there were three men in their party, so McKinney says they lost no time, as the trail was easy to follow. They crossed the Little Colorado River on a direct line to the town of Snowflake, Arizona.

> Navajo Springs at that time was an unincorporated community located on the Navajo Reservation, but it was near the town of Holbrook, Arizona near the reservation border.
>
> The community is almost exclusively Native American, and a permit is required from the Navajo Nation for off-road travel in that area. During the time of the Old West, this area was frequented by notable western characters, such as Apache County Sheriff Commodore Perry Owens, along with his deputies Will Barnes and Joe T. McKinney. Navajo Springs was a stopping place for travelers to water their horses and themselves.

The Beale Wagon Road, a precursor of the transcontinental railroad built through the area in 1882 as well as the," "Arizona – California Trail," known later as U.S. Route 66 and now Interstate 40 that ran through the community of Navajo Springs. The Arizona territorial government was organized here, and later a monument at the springs was erected to commemorate the event. At the insistence of the Santa Fe Railway Company, all Navajo were forcibly moved away from the Navajo Springs area, and by the 1930s. They had all been allotted lands within the area but the government pulled the plug and they were forced to vacate their land. But by the late 1890's, the lands were once again occupied by Navajos, this time by Navajo "refugees" from the Navajo-Hopi land dispute

Deputy Sheriff Mckinney goes on to say that they rode at a trot all day and they reached Snowflake at dinner time. After eating their dinner, they got a change of horses, as their horses were getting tired and they knew they had some hard riding ahead of them. McKinney goes on to say that they also picked up two more deputies to go with them. That made the posse five strong. From Snowflake, they traveled west following the trail until they struck the foothills of the mountains. A shower had fallen and they were having trouble following the trail.

It was getting late and one of the boys said there was a seep spring and dugout that would get them out of the rain and it was just over the ridge not far away. The posse decided to go there and stop for the night. McKinney goes on to say; as we approached the dugout we saw a very small fire and one man sitting next to it. We got down from our horses and camped with him.

One thing was for sure and that was we were hungry and none of us thought to pack anything to eat but the man we found in the dugout shared what little food he had with us. After we finished eating what consisted of no more than a snack, McKinney writes that he asked the man if he had seen any men in his travels earlier that day. The man said he had seen some fresh horse tracks up a little north of where we were camped. Of course that was the trail of the men we had been following. McKinney asked the man where he lived. The man replied that he had a horse ranch about ten miles south of there and he was out looking for some of his horses that had strayed from his ranch. McKinney had a strong feeling that the man may be one of the men they were following but they were following three men and not one man. McKinney resolved himself that they would continue the search for the three outlaws the next morning anyway.

McKinney writes that they slept comfortably and hobbled their horses for the night so they would not run away. The next morning, they went to get their horses. All were close at hand except his horse. We followed his tracks for about three miles when they finally caught up to his horse. He set the saddle on the horse, mounted it and rode back to their camp at the dugout. The man that they camped with had a bite to eat, while McKinney was gone and left right after eating. The man proved to be one of the men they were following. His name was *"Kid Swingle."* McKinney felt he had let a bird fly the coup, but he was not sure enough at the time to follow the man.

We went to the spot where we lost the trail of the robbers that we were following until we got into a heavy rain storm. While we were looking around the area to intersect the robbers trail again, Jim Houck, another Apache County Deputy Sheriff came along.

He told them he had just come from St. John's and was carrying warrants for the arrest of all the outlaws in Pleasant Valley. We figured that in all probability our train robbers had gone the same way and we felt we might get them by going with Houck as well. Houck told McKinney that Yavapai County Sheriff Billy Mulvenon was on his way there to meet them with warrants for a general roundup of the outlaws in Pleasant Valley.

Deputy McKinney went on to say that his posse consisted of John Scarlett, Lon Hawes, of Navajo Springs along with Osmer D. Flake and Joe Hershey Apache County Deputy Sheriff's from Snowflake, Arizona. They rode with Deputy Sheriff James Houck from there directly to Haigler's ranch, just north of Pleasant Valley in Tonto Basin, where they watered and rested their horses. Then from there the posse traveled a few miles north of Haigler's place to a cozy little nook where they found Yavapai Sheriff Mulvenon's camp. By this time though, it was late in the afternoon. Sheriff Mulvenon was glad to see Jim Houck and myself and our three special deputies. We all sat by the fire drinking coffee and eating biscuits as we discussed our plans. McKinney told Mulvenon that someone had seen him and his men on the trail of the robbers and went toward Pleasant Valley in a hurry as far as he could tell by the tracks the man left. McKinney told Mulvenon he thought they would be on their guard and looking for a posse. Mulvenon replied:

> "Five or six men won't bother these fellows."

Sheriff McKinney told Mulvenon that he had been in there a short time ago with the same number of men in his posse and the outlaws came right into their camp and made their big talks of what they would do. McKinney said they he knew that he and his men were very much outnumbered so he denied having any warrants for their arrest.

After talking things over McKinney, Houck and Mulvenon decided to move into Pleasant Valley that evening. Sheriff Mulvenon told them that he and his men would hide their mounts in back of Perkins Store, which was the only place in the valley to buy supplies. Mulvenon told Houck and McKinney that he and his men would secrete themselves in and around the store building and wait for their prey to come to them. Mulvenon directed McKinney and Houck to take their posse early the next morning, and cross over the foothills on the south side of the valley.

McKinney said that Mulvenon instructed them to ride through the valley in broad daylight to keep the outlaws guessing as to who we were and why we were in the valley. McKinney and his men were told to avoid any difficulty if possible, then to come back within three or four miles south of the Perkins Store, then ride up to the store dismount and tie their horses, then we were to walk around there, so the suspected outlaws could see that a posse was there. He said they would get their army together and soon come down to interview us and make us explain our business in Pleasant Valley. Mulvenon told McKinney that was exactly what he wanted them to do. McKinney went on to say that they were there for quite a while when Mulvenon realized the men whom he held warrants for were not coming, so he put a man on McKinney's horse and the six men that were in his original posse rode away on the trail in the same direction that they had used to come into the valley.

McKinney writes they didn't have to wait long when they saw two riders approaching from the East. They came to a stop about four hundred yards from the store, then they spirited their horses to the right, which was in a northerly direction and they rode all the way around the store and approached it from the southwest corner. McKinney said Sheriff Mulvenon and the large posse were all lying down in the half built walls of the new Perkins store building, as it was in the construction process at that time. The walls were made of stone, the highest part of the walls at that time was about six feet and it had places for doors and windows to be installed later.

When the two riders were within fifteen or twenty feet from our position, Sheriff Mulvenon stepped out from behind wall of the half-built building and came around the southwest corner of the building and said;

> "Put up your hands boys, I have warrants for your arrest for cattle rustling."

Both men put the spurs to their mounts. And at the same time one of the men, John Graham, pulled his pistol from his holster but an immediate charge from Mulvenon's shot gun in his horse's neck brought Graham's horse to the ground. Mulvenon then turned his shot gun on the other man, Charlie Blevins and his next shot from his double barrel shotgun hit Blevins in the back as he was drawing his Winchester rifle from it scabbard, the rifle being partially out of the scabbard when he was hit by the fatal shot from Mulvenon's other barrel killing Blevins outright. Jim Houck started after Blevins, and McKinney said he went after Houck because he was afraid Houck was going to finish off Blevins. McKinney said he ran right up to Houck and asked him not to shoot Blevins as Houck was reaching down to Blevins body. Houck turned to McKinney and told him he was not going to shoot unless Blevins made the first move.

McKinney went on to say that he and Houck turned over Blevins on his back and the pallor of death could be seen on his face. We carried Blevins to under the shade of the big trees that were in front of the house. Nothing but the buckshot from

Mulvenon's shotgun had hit Blevins. John Graham was hit with a rifle ball. It hit his left arm a little above the elbow and went straight through his body. He lived for a little while. McKinney said he got Graham some water and gave him a drink. Graham said nothing that McKinney heard. Mulvenon said to him;

> *"Johnny, why didn't you put up your hands when I told you too; Didn't you know me?"*

Graham shook his head indicating he did not know the sheriff. Sheriff Mulvenon said;

> *"He knows me, he is a damn liar. He knew me. That was cruel. I didn't like that."*

The men that they sent to ride out around the valley must have heard the shooting because they were soon there at the Perkins store riding their mounts. From the Perkins Store, Sheriff Mulvenon, Apache County Deputy Sheriff Joe McKinney, Apache County Deputy Sheriff Houck and all the combined posse force went directly to John Graham's ranch, which was about three miles east of the Perkins store. Once there they put a line of men one hundred feet long about fifty feet in front of the house. With the combined force in our posse there must have been close to fifty men with them at that time.

No more than they had stopped and lined up, when a woman came out of the house carrying a baby in her arms and a little child holding on to her dress. When she reached Mulvenon she dropped down to her knees on the grass. Mulvenon dismounted and walked up to where she, the baby and the child were positioned and she said to him;

> *"I will tell you all that are in the house. My husband, Joe Ellinwood, is in there and he has been wounded and not*

able to move about. Also our hired hand, Miguel, is in there too. They are all that are in the house."

Sheriff Mulvenon told her to return to her home, and that he did not have warrants for either of them. As they approached John Grahams Ranch they saw two riders making their getaway, they were recognized by posse members as Louis Parker and James Bonner. Since Mulvenon did not have warrants for either of them, he let them go. They were never seen in Pleasant Valley or Tonto Basin again. As far as McKinney knew one of the men was living somewhere in eastern New Mexico under another name and had a good working cattle ranch and the other man, McKinney writes, he has no knowledge on his whereabouts.

After they made their rounds to the different ranchers in Pleasant Valley looking for the men Sheriff Mulvenon was carrying arrest warrants for, the posse returned to the Perkins Store, the place where the ranchers congregated. John Graham died while the posse was away. From there the posse went to the Tewksbury ranch, where they found all of the Tewksbury party. Sheriff Mulvenon told McKinney that the Tewksbury's would be there and ready to surrender.

When the posse arrived at the Tewksbury ranch, they found Ed and Jim Tewksbury there, along with Jim Roberts, George Newton and Jake Lauffer. There may have been others but it was so long ago that these are all the men that McKinney could remember as being there at the Tewksbury ranch that day. An incident that happened there though, McKinney says he remembers well; Jim Roberts was shoeing a horse while Jim Tewksbury was holding the horse by its reins. Jim Roberts was a jolly fellow and kept up some merriment while he was working. While he was hammering away on the nails, shoeing the horse said;

> "I guess Tom Graham will come home and take charge of the country when they take us away."

Jim Tewksbury turned all kinds of colors and seemed very upset. One could see all kinds of desperation in his eyes as he looked down at the ground, shaking his head back and forth before he spoke with his voice cracking;

> "No damned man can kill a brother of mine and stand guard over him while the hogs eat his remains and live within a couple of miles from me."

McKinney wrote that he saw more desperation in Jim Tewksbury's face that day than he ever saw in Ed Tewksbury; more than I think was ever in Ed. Sheriff Mulvenon was also carrying an arrest warrant for Tom Graham but he was not able to serve the warrant because Graham had been killed at the Perkins Store. McKinney said he knew nothing about the trouble, but for sure the feelings between the Tewksbury's and the Graham's had become very desperate, to say the least. All McKinney said was that he heard that Ed Tewksbury and Tom Graham had at one time been very good friends.

After the posse gathered up as many of the men that Mulvenon carried warrants for, their work was done in Pleasant Valley. Sheriff Mulvenon had his prisoners in hand, and McKinney said he started back to his office in Holbrook. Deputy Apache County Sheriff McKinney said he was instructed by Yavapai County Sheriff Mulvenon to wire his office in Prescott and report what had happened in Pleasant Valley, and that he would file an official report upon his arrival and that he, his posse and most of the men he was after were in custody and they would expect to arrive in Prescott in a couple of days. McKinney went on to say that he looked into all of the ranches along his route back to Holbrook for the other men that they were carrying arrest warrants for but they found none of them;

> "The arrest of the men we had in custody was pretty much the end of the outright war in Pleasant Valley, but one of the participants said that there will be quiet assassinations going to happen in the valley for some time to come."

The next tragedy in Pleasant Valley was the shooting of Jake Lauffer from ambush by some unknown party. Lauffer was wounded in the arm but in time fully recovered from the injury. This shooting incident aroused the people of Tonto Basin and Pleasant Valley, who armed themselves again, thinking trouble was on the way. The ambush of Lauffer was in all probability related to the hanging of Stott, Scott and Wilson near Heber, Arizona, just above the Mogollon Rim north and east of the valley. Jake Lauffer was a sheep man and a friend Jim Houck and also the Tewksbury's. Scott was a friend of the Graham's, but he was never as far as McKinney knew, ever involved any fighting. He was simply known to favor the Graham's. McKinney says that he never knew Wilson or heard anything about him ever being involved in the feud.

Jamie Stott was working on the ALC ranch in New Mexico before he arrived here and settled on a small horse ranch near Heber where he built a cabin, corral and dug his well. McKinney says Stott was a friend of his. At the time he was hung, Stott was working as a cowboy for Henry Hunning in Snowflake. His ranch was small and could not support him so he worked for different ranchers as a part time cowboy when they needed help.

> *This is where the story of Jamie Stott's being involved in the Pleasant*

> *Valley War or Graham-Tewksbury Feud differs from all other accounts concerning his demise. The author of this book, knowing that Apache County Deputy Sheriff Joseph T. McKinney was neutral in the feud, who later served a one-year contract as an Arizona Ranger. The author believes this to be an interesting and a real possibility of the actual account of why Jamie Stott was hung with Scott and Wilson.*

Apache County Deputy Sheriff Joe McKinney says the reason Scott happened to be in Pleasant Valley the day he was hung was to pick up one of Stott's horses and rig that he had loaned Louis Neglin, who worked for Tom Graham and was absolutely aligned with the Graham's during Graham-Tewksbury feud. Stott loaned Neglin his favorite pet horse and rig a couple of weeks earlier, but Neglin had not returned the mount.

McKinney believed that the real cause of Jamie Stott's demise was due to the fact that one night in Holbrook, Stott called out Jim Houck, when Houck was shooting off his mouth recklessly. Jamie Stott had a reputation of being very fast and accurate with a pistol and practiced everyday honing his skill. In any event Houck backed down and refused to fight but forever afterward, Houck held a grudge against Jamie Stott.

Jamie Stott was not a small man, probably close to six feet tall, thin but muscular and about twenty-eight years old at the time of his death. Stott had a light complexion and was a handsome young man. The characteristic that McKinney most remembered about Stott is that he had one brown eye and one blue eye. McKinney says that Stott was a hard working good cowboy and was never out of work. McKinney says he also had a very agreeable disposition but was far from being cowardly if he thought he was right. There is no question in McKinney's mind that Houck was the cause of Stott's demise.

McKinney believes the shooting of Jake Lauffer also played a part in the death of Stott, Scott and Wilson. By McKinney's count the men who lost their lives on account of the Pleasant Valley War, Tonto Basin War or the Graham-Tewksbury feud were the Basque Sheepherder, who by the way was the brother in law of James D. Houck, "Old Man" Mart Blevins, John Paine and Hampton Blevins, Billy Graham, John Tewksbury and Bill Jacobs, John Middleton, John Graham, Charlie Blevins, Sam Houston Blevins, Mose Roberts and Andy Cooper (aka; Cooper Blevins), Al Rose, Stott, Scott and Wilson, George Newton and finally in 1892, Tom Graham was the last man from the Pleasant Valley War to die. Not much was known to McKinney about the Middleton family other than they migrated to Tonto Basin from Texas, where John Middleton Senior worked for the Defiance Cattle Company that was located at Navajo Springs and had his own small herd of cattle at his family ranch in the north end of Pleasant Valley.

McKinney said that he and John Rhodes were trailing an outlaw with arrest warrants in 1906 while they both worked as deputies as members of the Arizona Rangers and one night by a campfire they got talking about the Pleasant Valley and Rhodes told him;

> "I moved down to Salt River Valley in early 1888 after I married John Tewksbury's widow Mary Ann to get out of the valley that brought so much death and despair and I went to work for a large rancher taking care of some cattle while we built up our own spread because I wanted to live in peace.

According to Rhodes, he went on to tell McKinney that he didn't even carry a pistol and only took his rifle out when he was going deer hunting. He said he did not carry any guns at all with him when he moved to Tempe, in the Salt River Valley.

Everything went along for about four years, and then people started telling him that Tom Graham had sent for a man to kill him. Rhodes said he refused to believe the reports and just went on about his work. He had also run into Tom Graham from time to time as Graham also lived in Tempe, but there was never a cross word between them, and at that time Tom Graham also never carried a weapon. Rhodes said he heard that the assassin was in town but still did not believe the stories and continued about his work. Then one day Rhodes said they were all at the Grain Mill in Tempe and he saw Tom Graham point him out to Charlie Duesha, who was Tom's best friends and served as his body guard. Duesha looked straight at Rhodes and said with a smirk on his face; "Don't you think that was long enough?"

John Rhodes told McKinney that he went right home after the incident and wrote a letter to Ed Tewksbury and asked him to come at once, and that it was very important and that their might be trouble brewing with the Grahams again. Rhodes said that Edwin Tewksbury had been living quietly in Pleasant Valley, without any trouble but

Ed still carried a tremendous hatred for Tom Graham for murdering his brother John and he blamed Graham for the death of his young half-brother Frank. He just needed a good reason to finish Tom Graham.

When Ed arrived at Rhodes's home in Tempe, Rhodes told him what should be done. Rhodes told Ed that he would shoot Graham and he wanted to make sure that Ed would protect him from Charlie Duesha. According to what Rhodes told McKinney, Edwin Tewksbury killed Tom Graham but Rhodes was right there with him when the deed was done because Charlie Duesha was not with Graham that morning.

Getting back to the event at the Perkins store; According to McKinney an attempt was made to indict Sheriff Billy Mulvenon for the killing of John Graham and Charlie Blevins. McKinney said that he was subpoenaed to go before the grand jury in Prescott regarding the case. McKinney said that when he arrived in Prescott he met all of the Tewksbury clan and heard that Tom Graham and his clan were also in town and the whole town was on high alert with both factions of the Pleasant Valley War in town at the same time. But to the credit of Tom Graham and Ed Tewksbury there was no trouble.

This concludes the presentation of Roscoe G. Willson's newspaper articles and letters concerning his research on the Pleasant Valley War. I believe he did a great job in his work to research to support these stories. He has presented a different view and should be presented along with all of the other folk's work that I have presented in this book.

Below is a photo of Roscoe G, Willson, the author found on the rear cover on the back of Willson's book, "No Place for Angels,' a compilation of short Arizona historical stories, that Willson wrote and was published on January 1, 1958 by Arizona Silhouettes, Tucson, Arizona

Barry Goldwater, deceased United States of America Senator and Presidential Candidate in 1964, now deceased was quoted;

"What a valuable service Roscoe Willson has rendered all Arizona. Having been an avid student of Arizona history all of my life, and a collector of Arizona memorabilia, I have followed

> with the deepest interest, Roscoe Willson's stories, and it delights me to know that I will have the opportunity of adding his written collection to my personal library."

Carl Hayden, United States of America Senator, now deceased and who was once the Phoenix city Marshal was quoted;

> "By his writings Roscoe Willson has performed an invaluable service for all who are interested in what happened before the kind of an Arizona that we enjoy today was achieved. It is good to know that his stories are available in newspaper and book form.

Chapter Nineteen
Summary of Author's Research

There really is no conclusion, just a summary of this author's research. The author again went into this story with a complete open mind. Although, the author's research has brought out some very startling evidence, it must be noted that every historian and researcher could very possibly take a different approach depending on each author's research.

Jamie Stott, James Scott and Jeff Wilson

At this juncture, the author would like to thank Lee Hanchett for his diligence in going back to New Basilica, Mass., and obtaining the letters that Jamie Stott wrote to his mother and two sisters, most of the letters went to his sister's Hattie and Hannah. Then publishing them in them in his book called Back Mesa. Sadly, though, according to Jamie's sister Hannah, she was so upset with Jamie's death, that she burned most of the letters. The letters that Hanchett received from the Stott family may not have been all of the letters that Jamie sent his family during his trek from Texas to Arizona. Sadly though, one of the contents of one of these letters is very suspect.

Jamie had moved to Castroville, Texas from his birth home in North Ballerica, Massachusetts and settled at the Circle Dot Ranch in West Texas. Two months had passed and he still had not heard from his father, his financial backer, concerning his desire to buy some horses from his boss Judge Noonan. Concerned that his father might be having financial problems, Jamie turned his thoughts to looking around the western part of Texas for a possible place to settle down. Still, he knew that without the monetary support from his father, there would be little chance for success. So the first letter the author will present was sent to Stott's sister Hattie;

May 26, 1884

*Circle Dot Ranch,
Castroville, Texas*

Dear Sister Hattie,

It is some time since I have heard from you, although it is probably not your fault. I have sent for my mail that is at the ranch where I used to work at Coleman, Texas and I expect it soon. It is getting warm again and I think I shall have to skip this part of the state and go further north. There has been considerable rain around here lately and last week it hailed in great shape for about a half hour. The hail stones were sort of flat and about as large as a half dollar. I was out when it began but got under cover as quick as my horse could take me there.

Judge Noonan is out of here for a week or so and he is keeping us stepping about in great shape. He sold all of the best saddle horses a week or so ago, so we have only the old ones to ride and they are not so good. I wish I could send a pair of horses to you all to use for I could send some nice ones, and may bring one home if it doesn't cost too much. What are you and Hannah (His other sister) going to do this summer? I expect to work stock of all kinds and may take a trip through the western part of the state and see what I can find for a place to settle.

Father has not informed me since I have got in connection with him again about what he thinks about my buying some stock from Judge Noonan. I wish he would decide favorably. I hope Father has not had losses, but I am of the opinion real estate is as safe an investment as anyone can make, and whenever I have the funds to lay by till a rainy day, (if such a time ever comes), shall try to find enough ground to invest my cash in.

I suppose you and Hannah are growing rich very fast the way you both talked about last year. I cannot say I have made much money in the last year but, still I have gained much in experience and knowledge of my work. I intend to make a business of what I have started in, although I may not much more than pay expenses for a year or two. I am determined to make it pay in the end if I can but live long enough.

Remember me all to my cousins and friends and tell them to write to me although, I do not have time to write often. I will close now with love to all.

Your brother,
Jamie

Jamie's sister Hattie was disturbed by this letter. What could Jamie possibly have meant, *"if I can live but long enough!"* This wasn't the Jamie we knew. Jamie was young and to our knowledge not sick in any way. Why would he be concerned about how long he might live? Perhaps he was just trying to make us laugh at such a foolish notion. Yes, that must have been his meaning.

By the spring of 1885, Jamie was preparing to move to Arizona. His first move was to collect all of his horses, which were scattered from Castroville, San Antonio to Coleman. Two hundred miles further north. Second, and most important, he must wait for a check from his father to finance his trip.

Jamie wrote his sister's Hattie and Hannah regularly. He was planning on going to work for the Aztec Cattle Company in Arizona, while he looked for a place to settle down and start his stock ranch. After collecting his stock, Jamie was on his way to Arizona with his horses, and planning on working for Aztec, arriving in Holbrook, the headquarters of Aztec in October of 1885.

Without a letter of recommendation, Aztec did not hire Jamie, so he worked around the Holbrook area for different ranchers. While working in the area, Jamie settled on two ranch locations that he spoke to his father about, and who sent the money to Jamie to purchase both ranches, one at Bear Springs and the other at Aztec Springs. Jamie settled on the Aztec Springs ranch and built his home and corrals in February of 1886. Both locations had running springs and meadows to raise his stock.

In February of 1887, Hattie received a letter from Jamie that left her and the family perplexed. Was Jamie getting in with a crowd who operated outside the law?

> *February 8, 1887*
> *Taylor, Arizona*
>
> *Dear Sister Hattie,*
> *Yours received last night and think you were right in saying it is a long time since you wrote. I received a letter from our sister Hannah Louise the other day and will answer it soon. It has been snowing here, about ten inches, but the*

> sun has come out now so warm, it will mostly be gone in a few days. I never enjoyed such fine weather in my life, and when you were telling me of the big snows up there, everything was like fall here.
>
> I just returned from Tonto Basin last night (which lies about seventy-five miles southwest of here), where I had been to recover a horse that someone had taken over there and did not want to give up. I got him however, and if they want him again they will have to get him in a hurry, for I will dispose of him as soon as possible.
>
> There is some fine country down that way but it is too dry. Water is scarce about this country, but I have plenty and am likely to continue so. I want to close now for I am in a hurry to hunt some of my saddle horses. I would advise you not to come to this country this winter, but would be glad to see you anytime in the Spring, Summer or Fall. Love to all and excuse the haste,
>
> Jamie

A month later young Jamie was arrested by Sheriff Commodore Perry Owens of Apache County on the charge of horse stealing. Needless she says in a letter that the family was beside themselves with worry. Was this the beginning of something even worse?

Jamie had no problem coming up with the bail money required to assure his appearance in court, the date set for late March of 1887. The complaint had been filed by a close friend of the Tewksbury family, Jake Lauffer. The complaint filed by Laufler was never substantiated by the finding of his stolen horses although it was thought that he simply got rid of the stolen horses before he was arrested.

Jamie was never brought to trial. The judge in Globe felt there was not enough evidence to hold him over for trial. The charges of horse stealing were dismissed and the warrant for his arrest was squashed.

To add to the story, Apache County Deputy Sheriff James Houck had a couple of incidents with Jamie Stott. Stott was a boastful young man but had a very fast draw with his pistol and was an accurate shooter. He backed Houck down one evening in a Holbrook Saloon and on another occasion told Houck flat out that he would never sell either of his ranches to Houck at any cost. No question about it, Stott made his first real enemy in the person of James Houck, who was absolutely a Tewksbury faction member.

Upset about the fact that the charges of horse stealing on Jamie Stott had been dismissed, Houck set out to prove Stott's ranch was a holding place for stolen horses from a very organized group of horse thieves in Colorado. Then buyers from Southern Arizona and New Mexico, would arrive and remove the stolen horses. There was never any real proof that Stott was paid but the fact that he was associated with the Graham faction of the Graham vs Tewksbury feud and was present along with Jim Scott and Billy Wilson at the Tewksbury ranch the day that John Tewskbury and Bill Jacobs, no doubt played a huge part in their demise.

Gila County Sheriff Glenn Reynolds and his stock detective deputy, Tom Horn, carried warrants for the arrest of James Scott, and visited several ranches in Tonto Basin gathering evidence. When they had enough evidence they arrested Scott, who claimed he was in Pleasant Valley to pick up a horse that Jamie Stott had loaned him. The brand on this horse was very dubious. Scott was being held at the Perkins Store, until arrangements to move him had been secured.

So on the morning of August 11, 1887 Reynolds and Horn proceeded up the North Hell Gate trail to meet Apache County Deputy Jim Houck at the intersection of the Hellgate and Verde Trail, who would have Stott and Wilson under arrest also for stolen stock who would stand trial in Holbrook, while Wilson would be transported from Holbrook to Globe, where he would stand trial for stealing the horse found with him at the Perkins store. Horn and Reynolds found stolen stock at Stott's ranch, but his ranch was out of their jurisdiction, which was why Houck and Flake were there to arrest the two suspected horse thieves. By the time later that morning when the two posses' met at the intersection of the Verde and Hellgate trail, both posse's numbered twenty-five members.

This has all been verified by Chip Carlson in his book Tom Horn, Blood on the Moon, in which Horn admitted to John Coble, his employer in Wyoming where he worked as a stock detective that he had been involved in the lynching of three horse thieves and the disappearance of, in Horn's words, a rough old crusty son of a bitch. (Mart Blevins)

On the morning of August 11, 1887, Deputy of Apache County led a posse *(including Osmer D. Flake, who recorded the event in his memoirs)*, appeared at Jamie Stott's cabin. They found Jamie and Jeff Wilson at the cabin, along with two guests staying with Stott, Lamore Clymer and Alfred Ingham, who were convalescing from their Tuberculosis. Stott was a very kind and generous man and had opened his doors to these two men, who had been staying with him for a month.

Houck along with Osmer D. Flake who was a deputy that was with him at the time, placed Jamie

Stott and Jeff Wilson under arrest, stating that he had warrants for their arrest for horse stealing. But, when the arrest warrants were challenged by Stott's guests, Houck just laughed and he did not need to have them with him to make the arrests.

At that point, believing he was innocent or at minimum, felt the charges would never stick, Jamie Stott suggested they all go inside and have breakfast. He and his guests made a healthy breakfast for all, *(Also mentioned in Osmer D. Flake's Memoirs)*. After breakfast the posse took Stott and Wilson on horseback and led them away.

Later that morning, Houck and his posse with his two prisoners ran into Reynolds and Horn coming up from Pleasant Valley on the Verde Trail. It is thought by this author that when Houck and his posse met Reynolds and Horn, after discussing the situation decided that the three men would probably end up being released and the charges squashed, a spur of the moment decision was probably made by Reynolds, Horn and Houck to simply lynch the three men and be done with the situation. According to Osmer D. Flake, it all happened so quick that none of the deputies had a chance to say ya or nay. Also according to Osmer Flake in his memoirs;

"it was one of the most brutal hangings he had ever witnessed."

Whether the men were guilty or innocent, one thing is for sure, according to Apache County Deputy Sheriff Will Barnes, Jamie Stott had breakfast with him two days before he was hung, at which time, Barnes warned Stott that he was involved with the wrong people and that the shit was going to fly. Barnes wrote in his book, Apaches & Longhorns that there was a lot of evidence indicating the Grahams and their friend Jamie Stott were involved in a wide spread horse stealing ring and that the members felt they were above the law. Barnes said:

> "Jamie, would always pat his pistol and say, let them come and try to take me."

Sadly, we will never really know the whole truth for sure, but we must consider the fact that Deputy McKinney was a good friend of Stott and that Deputy Houck was a bitter enemy. The man in the middle was Deputy Will Barnes, who was simply neutral and he indicated that he knew that Stott was involved in either horse stealing or hiding horses for a Colorado Gang of horse thieves waiting buyers that came from New Mexico and Southern Arizona. Then there was Osmer D. Flake, who was also a Deputy Sheriff of Apache County under Sheriff Perry, who had to have been with the posse, when they hung the three men in order to have recorded his version of the affair from the arrest to the hanging.

The reason Stott's parents left so abruptly the next day after Will Barnes took them to the hotel. The next day he sent Louis Johnson, the young man who found the bodies to their room to take them to the grave site but after talking with Louis, they decided not to go to the gravesite.

Below is young Elias "Louis" Johnson's statement that that was he recorded and was provided by his great granddaughter Sandra Barnhart, of the facts surrounding the lynching of Stott, Scott and Wilson. Young Louis Johnson writes;

> I was out working the range and my horse stepped through a juniper clump, I saw three human bodies hanging by their necks from the limbs of a pine tree, my horse snorted and leaped back through the trees with such alacrity that this sixteen year old cowboy was almost unseated. I had only got a fleeting

glimpse of the three men before my horse jumped back with fright. So when I was able to stop him, I dismounted and hobbled the horse so I could go back and take a better look at the gruesome scene. He said he recognized each of the blackened, swollen faces of the remains of James W. Stott, who had recently established a ranch at Aztec Springs, that was located about twelve miles to the northeast of his current location. The other men were James Scott, a Former Hashknife cowboy and Billy Wilson who was employed by Jamie Stott. Johnson figured by their condition that they had been dead for at least five days.

The location of the lynchings was at the crossing of the Heber-Young and the Verde roads on the Mogollon Rim, in Apache County, Arizona Territory. The date was August 9. 1888. Louis left the bodies hanging and says he rode to Snowflake, the headquarters of the Flake Ranch, and reported the discovery to his employer, Jim Flake.

This is where there is a little conflict with this report. According to Will Barnes, young Johnson was working for him and when he found the bodies and he came rushing back to his ranch and reported the incident, telling Barnes where the bodies were so he could go and inspect them himself. Barnes writes in his book, Apaches & Longhorns that he sent Johnson to Holbrook to report the incident to the Sheriff Commodore Perry Owens. This writer is not sure which account is correct but it does not seem to matter, because the rest of Johnson's account is verifies all the facts.

Stott was the son of a wealthy Boston Couple, as mentioned previously and had left home to seek adventure in the West. He drifted to Apache County, where he found work as a cowboy for the Hashknife Ranch. His job was riding bog on the Little Colorado River. Jamie was a pleasant, sociable young man, who disliked being alone. He became active in the social life of the young people around nearby Woodruff and also in Holbrook, and fancied himself as a singer, and would entertain at parties at the slightest suggestion.

Soon the young man financed by his parents, left the hashknife ranch to establish his own place at Aztec Springs on the Mogollon Rim. He engaged in buying and selling horse and cattle. The new rancher would buy horses from the nearby Navajo reservation and then trail them through Phoenix, along the way he would steal more horses along the drive.

In Phoenix, he would sell the horses and buy cattle that he would trail up to his ranch. Along the way he would steal more cattle and in addition, Stott branded every calf he could catch along the trail. Now there were some very tough men in Apache County in 1888. Some of these men assembled on the night of August 3, 1888 north of Heber and rode to Stott's Ranch. They planned to hang him and his companions for horse stealing and cattle rustling.

Early on the morning of August 4, 1888, while it was still dark, they captured Stott and Wilson while he slept, and took them twelve miles southwest from Stott's ranch and hanged them.

There is a little confusion here in Johnson's statement because Osmer D. Flake, who was an Apache County Deputy Sheriff, who was also the Mormon Church historian at that time, claimed that he along with another Deputy, J.D. Houck had arrest warrants that they were going to serve to Stott and Scott. There is strong evidence that they met Tom

Horn at Stott's ranch, who had an arrest warrant for cattle and horses that had been stolen in Gila County, that he found on Stott's ranch. Osmer D. Flake also mentioned that there were two other men with them but never recorded their names.

According to Johnson, he claims that William J. Flake led a burial party to the hanging site on August 11, 1888 but the ground was so hard that graves could not be dug, so they carried the bodies in tarpaulins in the back of a buckboard about a quarter of a mile from Black Canyon, where the three men were buried.

James "Jamie" Stott's parents were notified of their son's death, and immediately came west. They wanted a full scale investigation made, that would prove their son innocent, because, they would not believe their son was a thief. Also they wanted to return the body to Boston for internment in the family plot.

Jamie Stott's parents arrived by train to the nearest railroad station that was located in Holbrook. From there they hired a livery rig and drove to Snowflake. There were no men present at the Flake Ranch headquarters when they arrived. The women there tried to detain the distraught couple until some of the men returned, but they would not wait. After getting a fresh team, they drove on in the direction of their son's grave site.

Louis Johnson was riding west of Snowflake on the road and saw the buckboard on the Snowflake-Heber road. In it were an obviously well to do, middle aged Eastern lady and gentleman. When Louis rode toward the strangers, who stopped and introduced themselves as the parents of the late Jamie Stott, the young boy felt terrible. He did not know what to say, therefore he gave his name to them, resolved to say as little as possible. Then the woman asked with her voice trembling and close to tears:

"Did you know our son?"

Young Louis hesitated of a second and then spoke;

"Yes ma'am."

Mr. Stott spoke next asking;

"Did you know that our son was hanged?"

The couple gasped, then clasped hands and stared intently at each other before the man spoke;

"Is there any evidence indicating our son was guilty of horse stealing?"

Suddenly young Johnson's horse was too big, his boots, chaps and hat were too small. There was a dull pain in his chest and his eyes hurt. He could not even think. Then with the anxious pleading face of the elder Stott's before him, he heard a voice he did not recognize but had to be his own saying;

"Sir, I regret to inform you and the lady, your son was guilty of stealing both horses and cattle."

Below is a photo of Elias "Louis" Johnson and his wife Caroline Flake Johnson that was taken the day Louis and Caroline were married.

Stott's parents, without saying a word, turned their buckboard around and returned to Holbrook where they caught the next train and went back to Boston.

Louis Johnson, who went by Louis at that time passed away in 1955. He claimed the most difficult thing he ever did in his long life was the act of telling Jamie Stott's mother and father that their boy was a thief.

There is also no doubt in this author's mind that the Tewksbury brothers were probably involved in the lynching of these three suspected horse thieves but there is no definite proof that they were at this affair. Again according to Maurice Kildare from his interview with James Pearce, Stott, Scott and Wilson were friends with Tom Graham and were with the Graham's, when they held the Tewksbury's at bay for three days after the Graham's and their faction bushwacked John Tewksbury and Bill Jacobs, shooting them in the back and then letting the bodies lie were they were died and allowed wild hogs feast on their bodies. The whole thing was very brutal but for sure, with Ed and Jim Tewksbury not about to let anyone involved in the death of their brother, their friend Jacobs and also the mysterious death of their friend Jake Lauffer, get away with these murders and all that were present would be held responsible.

It is also thought by this author that James Pearce, who Maurice Kildare interviewed in 1932, and who related the story of the murders of John Tewksbury and Bill Jacobs was with the Graham's the night before the three day stand but there is no proof that he was with the Graham's the morning of the killing of the two men on September 1, 1887, that took place at the site of J.D. Tewksbury's cabin.

Three days later Pearce became a Tewksbury follower and if he was there he was probably so sick about what had happened and either left or went to the Tewksbury's after telling them he had nothing to do with the murders and relayed to Jim and Ed Tewksbury all of the folks who were involved and were present. For some reason Jim and Ed must have known that Pearce was being honest, because he had no reason to come forward and tell the Tewksbury's unless he was very remorseful. Let's be honest, the whole thing was a very sorted, brutal killing of these two men, one by Hank Blevans and the other by Andy Cooper.

The Blevins Family

With Tom Horn admitting to his employer, John Coble, who was also his closest friend while living in Wyoming, many years later, that he was involved in the disappearance of "crusty old bastard," referring to Mart Blevins in Arizona during the Pleasant Valley War, with this in mind, we can finally put a name to the man who killed Old Man Mart Blevins, who in fact was the first Graham Faction of the Pleasant Valley War, the head of Blevins family, to bite the dust and who was considered a ornery old man by the citizens of Pleasant Valley and nearby Tonto Basin.

The next of the Blevins clan to bite the dust was Hampton Blevins, who was killed along with John Paine at the Middleton Ranch, while out looking for Old Man Mart Blevins. Hampton Blevins may or may not have known that Paine announced in Holbrook that he was heading to Pleasant Valley to start, *"A little War of our Own."* Hamp may have just been with the wrong company, we will never know for sure.

There is no doubt about Charlie Blevins, who was with John Graham at the Perkins store, when Sheriff Billy Mulvenon tried to serve a warrant on John Graham for being a suspected horse thieve. Both men decided to shoot it out, rather than be arrested, an obvious admittance of their guilt.

The next of the Blevins family to die were at the shootout at Holbrook with Apache County Sheriff

Commodore Perry Owens. At this fight, probably caused by Andy Cooper, killed were Andy, his young fifteen-year old brother Sam Houston Blevins and their brother in law Mose Roberts, leaving just John Blevins, shot in the shoulder, the last and only Blevins to survive the Pleasant Valley War.

Old man Mart Blevins obtained ownership of their ranch form the Adams Brother who were about to go on their Mormon mission but there is some question on how he obtained the ranch. It is thought that he was coerced to sell the 160 acre ranch for $40. Mrs. Blevins sold the ranch to James Ramer in 1888, then she took what was left of her family back to Texas. James Ramer built the first home on the property. The same home that Larry and Patty Boeshling, the ranch caretakers live in that is pictured on the next page. Then he built the barn in 1893 that is still on the premises and being used to this day.

Ramer sold the ranch to a man by the name of Frank Wallace. The ranch had two other owners before Ed and Margie Delph bought it in 1977. Ed and Margie have owned the OW Ranch longer than any other owner.

With all of the Blevins men dead but John, Mrs. Blevins just wanted to get as far away from Arizona as possible. She lost her husband, four sons and a son in law so she was happy to get back to Texas with what family she had left. This history is according to Larry Boeschling, the caretaker of the ranch since 1992, along with his wife, Patty Boeschling,

Also according to Ed Delph, the Blevins family never built a permanent home on the ranch. One has to wonder if they really lived there or did they live in Holbrook all along, and it is possible the ranch could have been just used to keep stolen stock.

Larry Boeschling went on to say the Ramer family along with building the home below, the barn along with building the blacksmith shop, still in use today and a storage building that is also still used to this day. Larry and his wife Patty live in that same home that was built in 1893. Below is a photo of their home that was taken by the author on a recent visit and tour of the ranch. The home is a lot larger than it looks in this picture.

The Meadows Family

Some authors have indicated that Justice of the Peace John Meadows may have been on the Tewksbury's side. This author has found no evidence to support this statement. Let's take a look at the death of William Graham. There is no reason to believe that James Houck's written confession and filed report to Apache County Sheriff, Commodore Perry Owens would be a lie and made up just to protect another person. There was an investigation started from the Sheriff of Yavapai County into the death of young Billy Graham, started from a complaint filed by Justice John Meadows. But after investigating the death of Billy Graham there was not enough evidence to proceed with an indictment as it was officially ruled to be self defense by Apache County Deputy Sheriff J.D. Houck.

Tom Graham believed that Justice Meadows should have investigated his brother's death as a murder and not self defense, which is exactly what Justice Meadows did. It was not his job to pass a judgment because he was simply a Justice of the Peace. Whether Houck was carrying warrant, which is still unclear or not, the fact that Billy Graham claimed that he was killed by Ed Tewksbury does not make sense. Along with the fact that J.D. Houck's official report stated that he shot Billy in self defense, he could never have gotten an indictment and would absolutely never get an indictment against Edwin Tewksbury based on Billy Graham's statement to his brother Tom that it was Edwin Tewksbury who killed him, if in fact he even told his brother Tom this or Tom made it up to fuel his hatred for the Tewksbury's. Tom Graham thought Justice Meadows was in cahoots with the Tewksbury's that was the reason John Meadows was on Tom Graham's hit list. This was as far from the truth as possible. There has never bee any proof that Justice John Meadows was anything but an honest, straight shooting officer of the court.

Why would Justice Meadows proceed to arrest a man with an alibi, who supposedly killed William when he had a written filed report from a lawman explaining how and why he killed young Billy Graham? Especially since it was not his job, who also started an investigation by notifying the Sheriff of Yavapai County. There is no doubt that Jim Houck had a vicious hatred for Tom Graham, who he felt was responsible for the death of his sheepherder brother in law, the Basque who was murdered bringing the Daggs brothers sheep from Flagstaff to Pleasant Valley and there is also a lot of doubt that Houck was actually carrying warrant for the arrest of Tom Graham. That warrant has never been found and is very suspect, but in his official report Houck claimed Billy drew first, shot and missed and he returned fire with a barrage of shots mortally wounding young Billy Graham, who rode away from the scene, definitely mortally wounded.

As far as "Arizona Charlie Meadows," involvement with the Tewksbury factions, again this is conjecture that is totally unsupported by any facts. "Arizona Charlie," as he was later known as while riding in "Buffalo Bill's Wild West Show," while they toured Europe in the late 1890's. His only involvement was that he participated in the Payson Rodeo, or then called "August Doins," as well as other cowboy events held in Payson, Globe and Prescott with the Pleasant Valley cowboys, with some of the Tewksbury cowboys. According to all the records, he was never involved in any shootings, killings, rustlings or hangings. To try to involve him in any of these events is simply conjecture and is totally unsupported. He was simply the brother of Justice John Meadows and that is the beginning and end to that story.

Below are two photos found in our National Archives of Justice of the Peace John Meadows on the left, and his younger brother Arizona Charlie Meadows on the right.

The Daggs Brothers & their involvement in the Pleasant Valley War

The five Daggs brothers came from Missouri and arrived in Flagstaff in 1875 with a band of 1500 sheep, became prominent Flagstaff businessmen. The Daggs brothers primarily grazed their sheep in the high meadows of the Flagstaff area, but also grazed bans of their sheep in the Phoenix and Tempe area.

The brothers were Peru Paxton (P.P.), William (W.A.), John (J.F.), Robert (R.E.) and Jackson (A.J.). Their sheep business extended from northern Arizona to New Mexico and southern Colorado. At one time the Yavapai County Records report they had over 50,000 sheep grazing in just northern Arizona.

Individually and as partners they had interests in ranching, real estate, land development, mining, a butcher shop, an ice plant, railroads and banking. JF Daggs owned a Flagstaff Brewery which turned out, "Fine Beer," according to add they placed in the Coconino Sun Newspaper and R.E. and A.J. Daggs were prominent Flagstaff Attorney's.

In the February of 1887 the Daggs brothers decided to move their herd into Tonto Basin to graze because of the warmer winter weather of the lower elevation. The Tewksbury's were to receive a share of the sale of wool and meat in the following Spring for their work and guarding the band from any harm.

Tonto Basin and nearby Pleasant Valley were considered cattle country and sheep had been forbidden to come into the area. This event was thought to have triggered the violence that would become known as the Pleasant Valley War.

A Basque sheep herder for the Daggs brothers and the brother in law of J.D. Houck, was the first person murdered allegedly by the Graham brothers, a cattle ranching family in Pleasant Valley.

In March of 1887, through the efforts of P.P. Daggs and his attorneys, the Arizona Territorial Legislature had the two mile limit law repealed. This law prohibited sheep owners from passing or grazing their herds within two miles of established stock ranges. The Daggs lawyers convinced th legislature that the law was unconstitutional. This gave them some legal status to graze their sheep on open ranges. The Daggs were believed to have armed the Tewksbury's and provided them with money for legal defenses for any of the Tewksbury faction that was arrested. The Daggs also used their political connections with lawmen, attorney's and judges in Yavapai and Apache counties. Lawmen from Apache and Yavapai counties with the Tewksbury faction members were known to have killed fifteen and wounded five of the Graham faction.

During the same year, the Aztec Land and Cattle Company sued the Daggs brothers over a ranch house, grazing land and water rights at a place called Pine Spring in northern Arizona. The cattle company was also known as the Hashknife Outfit. They were cowboys, many of them from Texas, that had a reputation of being tough and not afraid to use violence to force ranchers to give up their land. Some of them were known cattle rustlers. The Daggs brothers wer not the type to back down. The lawsuit ended with the Daggs winning the decision and getting the property. Some of the Hashknife cowboys participated in the Pleasant Valley war as part of the Graham faction.

In the 1920's, P.P. Daggs responded to a letter from the Arizona Pioneers Historical Society in Tucson who asked him about the Daggs Brother's involvement in the Pleasant Valley War. He would only say that it cost them $90,000 and then quoted General Sherman; "War is hell." The Graham faction shot and clubbed to death large herds of the Daggs brothers sheep bands and drove some over the cliffs of the Mogollon Rim. The Daggs lost so many sheep in 1887 that they decided to move what was left of their band of sheep down further to the Salt River Valley.

By the year 1892, the Pleasant Valley War had for the most part subsided. Tom Graham, the last surviving member of the Graham family was murdered in Tempe. He had moved out of Tonto Basin a few years before, to get away from the violence. He was driving a buckboard loaded with grain on his way to the Hayden Mill and was unarmed when he was killed, allegedly by Edwin Tewksbury and John Rhodes. Rhodes and Tewksbury were arrested and charged with his murder. John Rhodes again was the brother in law of Edwin Tewksbury. Ed's brother John had been killed by the Graham's in the early days of the war and Rhodes married John's widow Mary Ann and adopted John Tewksbury's son, also named John and gave him his Rhodes last name. Ed Tewksbury was the duly elected constable of Globe at the time of the murder. Ed was popular in the Globe area and Globe was known as a Tewksbury sanctuary.

P.P. Daggs also admitted in the 1920's that they bankrolled Rhodes and Tewksbury's defense, hiring some of the best lawyers in Arizona to represent them in their trials. A few weeks before Tom Graham was murdered, John Rhodes had met with the Daggs brothers in Tempe, but there is no evidence that has been presented that linked them to the shooting of Graham. Rhodes had been staying at the Tempe hotel that was owned by Robert Bowen. Bowen was at one time the foreman of the Silver King Mine that was owned by the Daggs brothers and was a partner of the Daggs in some other business ventures. Ed Tewksbury had stayed at the same hotel a few weeks earlier and had been seen in the hotel bar earlier the same morning that Graham was murdered. Robert Bowen was also a stockholder and board member of the Bank of Tempe along with two of the Daggs brothers, W.A. and P.P., who were also stockholders in the bank and board members. Bowen owned several ranches in Pleasant Valley and Tempe. John Rhodes had been working for him at his Tempe ranch.

During Rhodes' preliminary court hearing, Bowen and some of his employees supplied an alibi indicating Rhodes could not have been at the scene of the murder at the time it was committed. On the third day of the hearing Tom Graham's widow Anne smuggled a gun into the court room. She approached Rhodes and placed the gun in his back and pulled the trigger. The pistol failed to fire. Family and friends pulled her away. She was not charged with any crime over the incident. She testified that her husband before he died told her that he had seen Ed Tewksbury and John Rhodes fire at him. Others would testify that they witnessed Tom Graham tell them that he had looked behind him when he heard the sound of horses approaching. He saw Rhodes and Tewksbury aiming their guns at him. Before he he could jump from the wagon they shot him. They then rode up next to him as he lay helpless on the ground. He said Ed Tewksbury pointed a gun at him but was satisfied that Graham's wound was mortal so he did not fire. Then according to Tom Graham, they rode away.

After ten days of testimony, Rhodes was released and the charges were dropped, because of the alibi provided for him. The judge's decision was not popular and there was talk in Tempe of lynching Rhodes and maybe hanging the judge in effigy. Friends of John Rhodes greeted him upon his release from jail. They were armed and prepared to defend Rhodes as they escorted him back to Pleasant

Valley. Rhodes would later become a stock detective as an Arizona Ranger from 1906 to 1908.

John Rhodes later moved to Pinal County where he worked on a ranch near Mammoth. His stepson John (Tewksbury) Rhodes became a well known working and rodeo cowboy around Mammoth and the lower San Pedro Valley. Johnny as he was called became a world champion team roper in 1936 and 1938. Even in his later years Johnny Rhodes was considered a premier team roper and often competed with his son Tommy. Tom Rhodes became a world champion steer roper in 1943 and 1944. Later in life Tommy was one of the owners of Don Juan's Tavern in Oracle, Arizona. Johnny and his son Tommy Rhodes are listed in the Pro Rodeo records as being from Sombrero, that is located near Mammoth, Arizona.

Edwin Tewksbury was finally charged with the murder of Tom Graham. The trial was moved to Tucson for Ed's protection and because it was felt that the furor over Rhodes' release, that Tewksbury would not receive a fair trial in Maricopa County. Tewksbury had some high quality and expensive lawyers defend him. There is nothing concrete as to where the money came from to pay for these high power attorneys but it was believed that the Dagg's bankrolled the defense for Edwin Tewksbury. One of the defense attorney's for Tewksbury was Tom Fitch, aka; "The Silver tongued Orator of the Pacific Slopes." Fitch and come from California to join the defense team. He had defended the Earp brothers an Doc Holliday after they were charged with murder following the Gunfight at the Ok Corral. In 1871 Fitch successfully defended Brigham Young and other members of the LDS Church over polygamy charges brought by the Federal Government.

Even the best legal defense possible did not help Edwin Tewksbury, who was found guilty of the murder of Tom Graham. However, an appeal was quickly filed and it was discovered that there was no record of Tewksbury ever being allowed to make a plea during the preliminary hearing. Somehow the court records regarding the plea failed to show that a plea had been made. Due to this technicality, Edwin Tewksbury was granted another trial. The second trial resulted in a hung jury, probably due to the fact that Tom Graham's widow, Anne Melton Graham had moved to California and due to illness was not able to attend the trial even though she had been called as a witness.

Over $20,000, thought to be Daggs money was spent on the two trials of Edwin Tewksbury, which was an unheard of sum for a trial back in those days. It was decided by the court not to try Tewksbury a third time. After spending two and a half years in jail, Edwin Tewksbury was a free man. He moved to globe were he became a deputy constable and worked at the Old Dominion mine. Edwin Tewksbury, like his brother Jim, several years before, died from the effects of tuberculosis in 1904.

In May of 1895, R.E. Daggs along with his brothers W.A. and P.P. were arrested in Phoenix and charged with embezzlement in connection with the failure of the Bank of Tempe. Seven indictments alone were charged to P.P. Daggs. His bond was set at $12,500. Bonds for R.E. and W.A, Daggs were $6,000 and $8,500 respectfully. A.J. Daggs and W.M. Billups, a cousin of the Daggs secured the bonds and were released from custody. The Graham Guardian Newspaper published out of Safford, Arizona said that the Daggs brothers along with P.B. McCabe and W.L. Van Horn had also been indicted for embezzling $50,000 and 1,000 head of sheep from the now defunct Bank of Tempe. In June of 1895, three of the seven charges against P.P. Daggs were settled out of court. Later in the month of June 1895, P.P. Daggs was acquitted of all charges. In June of the following year the rest of the Daggs brothers were acquitted of all charges stemming from the failure of the Bank of Tempe.

R.E. Daggs was charged with grand larceny in 1897. The Arizona Central Bank accused him of stealing $860. The trial was held in Flagstaff in April of 1897 and ended with a hung jury. A petition was filed with the court to have a second trial that was transferred to Navajo County. In October the trial was held in Holbrook and R.E. Daggs was acquitted.

In 1905, A.J. Daggs wrote a book titled, "How to run a Corporation," and it was still being reprinted as late as 1988. A.J. and his brother R.E. Daggs had other business interests including real estate, banking and mining. They also sold stocks and bonds and were partners in a number of corporations. They were the biggest incorporated business in the Arizona Territory. In October of 1905, newspapers carried the story on the front page about R.E. and A.J. Daggs being indicted for assaulting two sisters, Esther and Marie Power. R.E. Daggs had also been indicted for assault and rape of 16 year old Esther Power.

The brothers allegedly threw the two women out of their office in the Monihan building in Flagstaff, hurting them when they fell down the stairs. It was also alleged that A.J. had brandished a gun. The sisters said they were there to collect $2 that was owed Esther for work she had done at their office. The Daggs brothers said that the Power sisters were attempting to blackmail them over Esther's allegation that R.E. had thrown her on the floor and supposedly tore her dress trying to get at her. R.E. admitted to kissing and hugging Esther with her consent but said nothing else happened.

R.E. Daggs was convicted of the attempted rape charge having to do with Esther Power and sentenced to 18 months at the Yuma Territorial Prison. He filed an appeal with the Supreme Court and was allowed out of prison on $5,000 bail. After being found guilty, the Daggs brothers asked for a change of venue for the assault charges to Yavapai County, which was granted. The Yavapai Board of Supervisors then asked the County Attorney to dismiss the charges due to the unusual costs that would be incurred. Charges were dismissed and R.E. waited for his appeal with regard to the assault with intent to rape charge. In March of 1908, the Supreme Court overturned his conviction and returned his bond.

This ends the story of the Daggs brothers, their involvement in the Pleasant Valley War and their monetary relationship with the Tewksbury faction of the famous Graham vs Tewksbury feud.

Bill Brown, the Tewksbury Family historian

After presenting all the stories, written by different authors, newspaper articles, research material, written accounts by survivors and information provided by Bill Brown from his Tewksbury family archives, this author leaves it up to the reader to make their own decisions. None of us were there from 1883 through 1892, so we can only present our research from those folks who recorded the events. The most deadly time was between 1887 and 1889, with that being said, this author is presenting his research. These were real people; it is up to historians to present their story as well as possible, which is why there are so many different directions different authors have taken.

This author is also presenting the views of this terrible stain on Arizona history, according to stories Bill Brown's grandmother Bertha Tewksbury and his great grandmother Mary Ann Tewksbury-Rhodes along with the other research the author was able to obtain. Over the years while he grew up with his grandmother who lived with his family all of Bills life. It's not surprising that Bill has retained all of this information, since it is all about his family. On many occasions over the years something would jog his grandmother's memory and she would share the story with young Bill about his family's involvement in the Pleasant Valley War or the Graham vs Tewksbury feud provides us with another view of a person whose family was directly involved in this feud. Mary Ann Tewksbury and Bertha Tewksbury's personal knowledge is very valuable as they were two of the last survivors who was directly involved in the feud.

According to Mary Ann, she told Bill time and time again, that the Tewksbury's were willing to let the whole thing end but they heard through the grapevine that Tom Graham paid to have George Newton, the jeweler and their friend from Globe, killed, and when he disappeared on his way to Pleasant Valley to inspect his cattle herd, they were worried that the Grahams were not going to let it go.

John Rhodes, who with Mary Ann his wife and family were living in the Tempe area, where Tom Graham and his family were also living, would see Tom Graham from time to time, but the fact that neither one of them was wearing a gun, convinced Rhodes that the war was finally over between the two families But right after the disappearance of Newton in early 1892, John Rhodes saw Tom Graham with Charlie Duesha near the grain mill in Tempe.

While the two men were talking, John saw Tom Graham point him *(John Rhodes)* out to Charlie Duesha and when Duesha looked over at him, he saw Duesha just nod his head up and down with a very sheepish smile on his face. Rhodes being one of the main men associated with the Tewksbury faction immediately knew there was something sinister up. With the disappearance of George Newton, he thought he might be the next man to disappear, as it appeared the Grahams were not letting go of the feud, they had just taken a different approach rather than outright fighting it appeared they were simply either hiring assassin's and Tom's dark alley murdering associate and body guard, Charlie Duesha, was carrying out death sentences.

By that time, Ed Tewksbury was working his ranch in Pleasant Valley and also was a Deputy Graham County Sheriff. Bill Brown's grandmother told Bill that when his great uncle Ed came to their home, during the conversation they decided that with the disappearance of their friend and supporter, George Newton that the Tom Graham, even though not wearing a gun, had taken a different more sinister approach, and that the war was not over. This all happened out of the clear blue it seemed because they had all been living in peace for four years after Tom Graham moved out of Pleasant Valley to Tempe.

Ed had heard some small talk around Pleasant Valley while he was working his cattle, to the effect that the feud was not over, so they decided that as long as Tom Graham was alive the war would never end. Sadly, the two men realized that even though they did not want any trouble, it appeared trouble had found them again in the person of Tom Graham and his assassin partner, Charlie Duesha. Bill's grandmother Bertha Tewksbury was just a young girl at the time her Uncle Ed and her father John Rhodes met that day at their home, both men very upset and concerned for their lives, and they made plans to end the feud once and for all by killing Tom Graham. Bills grandmother Bertha Tewksbury told Bill many times over the years;

> *"If Tom Graham had just let it lie, he would still be alive."*

It is for sure that both the Tewksbury's and the Graham's were blamed for a lot of crimes they never committed. The fact that there were so many outlaws, killers and rustlers working in the area that had no affiliation with either faction probably had more to do with the trouble than either the Tewksbury's or the Graham's. As previously mentioned in this book, after the bridge was finished over Canyon Diablo by the Atlantic & Pacific Railroad, the gambling, drinking and partying with sporting ladies was over in 1883. That bad element simply moved on to Pleasant Valley, the White Mountain towns of Show Low, Snowflake and Greer and set up for business again.

Whether it was by accident or design, a lot of really bad men seemed to gravitate to Tom Graham and his faction along with his underhanded moves regarding buying up the loan papers of the Wells family and then forcing them to take his side in the feud or just the fact that he seemed to attract known killers, rustlers and outlaws, were probably just looking for a cause and Tom Graham's vengeance was good enough reason. In any event it was a sad state of affairs.

Yavapai County was the largest county in the country, extending from Black Canyon City on the south to the Utah border on the north and then from Mohave County on the west all the way to the Navajo Indian Reservation on the east. The lack of lawmen was the only constant in the territory at that time so the area was swamped with outlaws and rustlers. There was no way that the Yavapai County Sheriff located in Prescott, more than a hundred miles away from Pleasant Valley, could cover the whole territory.

It was probably Jim Houck, that was the deputy who spent the night at Horton's home, and after, told Horton and his wife that he was a Deputy Graham County Sheriff at that time, soon to be a deputy sheriff of the newly created Apache County. Houck inquired if Horton knew John Graham and Ed Tewksbury. Horton told Houck that he knew both men because he had worked with them both as a freighter. When Horn asked him if he knew how to find John Graham, then he told them that he was carrying a warrant for Graham's arrest for horse stealing, Horton told him that John Graham rode down the Hellgate trail every evening at the same time and told the deputy a place nearby where he might possibly intersect Graham on his ride, but warned the deputy that he would be taking his life in his hands if it went into that country alone, so he volunteered to help the deputy find a couple of stolen horses that were along the trail but told the deputy in no uncertain terms that he was on his own from that point on and that he was taking his life in his own hands if proceeded into Graham held country. The deputy thanked Horton and went on his way.

Horton wrote that Deputy Houck stayed in the barn with his horse and after breakfast the next morning after breakfast Houck inquired if Horton knew where he might find John Graham. Houck listened to Horton and went to the spot on the Hellgate trail to intersect John Graham but instead of John, it was Billy Graham who showed up and the rest is history. There is no doubt that Horton knew both Ed Tewksbury and John Graham and that there was no way he would mix up the two men he knew so well when he told the deputy where he could find John Graham. So, with this in mind, although the deputy never showed Horton the arrest warrant, which was very dubious, there is no doubt it was not Ed Tewksbury who killed Billy Graham.

Again Horton gave Houck directions where the deputy could probably find John Graham. This incident makes it clear that Deputy Houck killed Billy Graham just like he reported and Ed Tewksbury, who Billy Graham said killed him was either mistaken or Tom Graham decided it was Ed Tewksbury who killed his brother to light a fire under his faction. There is some doubt about the presence of a very dubious arrest warrant that Houck never showed Horton.

Whether he actually had a warrant is suspect but in any event it was not Edwin Tewksbury who killed Billy Graham, supposedly thinking it was John Graham riding up the trail.

This Author believes that Edwin and Jim Tewksbury were no choirboys, but Edwin Tewksbury was blamed for more crimes than he could possibly have committed unless he figured out how to be in two places at one time. Being half Indian and half Irish though, in those days they were considered half breeds. They were treated as outcasts. There is no question there was an agreement between James Stinson and the Grahams to eliminate the damn blacks, when referring to the Tewksbury's.

In point of fact half-breed Indians and white were considered the lowest form of human being in the Old West. Absolutely the Tewksbury's were major victims of racism. They were not allowed in most saloons, bars or social events with the "good white folks," in fact a half breed was looked upon as a lower class than a person that was of African, Hispanic, or Chinese races. Because of bigotry and the general way they were treated, they became hard men. They carried a chip on their shoulders and justifiably so. The Old West was a tough place to live and required men with tough hides. John, Ed and Jim Tewksbury needed to be tough men to survive.

John Rhodes, Bill Brown's great Grandfather;

According to William MacLeod Raine, a famous author and personal friend of John Rhodes, and who accompanied Rhodes on a cattle drive, in the early 1900's, Rhodes relayed his side of the story to Raine as follows, while camping and trailing the cattle on the drive;

> "After the battle at the Tewksbury Ranch in 1887, at which time John Tewksbury and John Jacobs were

murdered, the feud was all but forgotten by Ed and Jim Tewksbury. Tom Graham left Pleasant Valley right after the gunfight in 1887 along with his bodyguard and friend Charlie Duesha. Tom bought a farm in Tempe, Arizona. Then in July of 1892, he decided to go back to Pleasant Valley and drive his cattle to Tempe, consequently at the same time, George Newton, the friend of the Tewksbury faction disappeared, his body never to be seen again, which may have been a coincidence but not to John Rhodes and Edwin Tewksbury. Had Graham not foolishly boasted about his exploits, according to Rhodes, he would still be alive today. He insinuated that the Tewksbury's were afraid to attack him.

Six weeks later, on August 2, 1892, while driving to the mill in downtown Tempe from his home in the Buttes area, hauling a load of grain, Graham was shot close to the Cummings Ranch. He lived till the next morning and told Charlie Duesha and others that Ed Tewksbury and John Rhodes were the assassins, who shot him in the back while he drove his crop to the mill.

John Rhodes married Mary Ann Tewksbury, the widow of John Tewksbury and had been identified as with that faction of the feud since the trouble began to brew in 1883. Rhodes was arrested and taken into custody and jailed in Phoenix with his trial starting almost immediately on August 4, 1892. During the trial that lasted over two weeks, the prosecution presented their eye witnesses and the defense presented their witnesses. On August 19, 1892, the jury came back with the verdict that they could not come to a conclusion either way with regard to Rhodes guilt or innocence. Rhodes was set free because of a hung jury and was never tried again.

During the trial many witnesses swore positively to having seen Rhodes near the Cummings ranch on the morning of the killing in the company of a man who wore a scarlet ribbon tied around a white sombrero. As the trial progressed, the widow of Tom Graham, Annie Graham, a woman of strong conviction was convinced as testimony piled up against Rhodes, overcome with hatred, drew a pistol, but her father caught her in his arm and the hammer caught on her scarf and did not fire. She was escorted out of the courtroom, never to return.

Edwin Tewksbury was tried later. The scarlet ribbon around his white sombrero ended up being the item that convicted him after two weeks of both the prosecution and defense presenting eye witnesses swearing they either saw him at the scene or a hundred miles away in Pleasant Valley. Edwin Tewksbury was granted a new trial and released on bail. The case against him was finally dropped. According to Rhodes, Ed Tewksbury was a man of iron nerve, of wonderful physique and a dead shot. Rhodes went on to say that his 45/70 repeating rifle was so heavy that no other man in Pleasant Valley could handle it.

Raines went on to say that he personally knew John Rhodes who became a respected cattleman, a school trustee, and one very well thought of by his neighbors and acquaintances. Raines went on to say that it is hard to believe that such a jovial, warm-hearted man, the best cowman in Pinal County, could be guilty of such a cowardly assassination. Raines said in his book that Rhodes was a man to tie too. He was a man of splendid physique and he threw the longest lasso of any cowboy he had ever met. It was characteristic though that nearly all of the men engaged in this feud from the Tewksbury faction were in general good citizens but in a rough way. Even the Tewksbury's were usually quiet men of friendly and generous disposition unless they were riled up from persecution or when they had too much to drink."

William MacLeod Raine was the author of twenty-eight books of which the above statement is found in his book, "Famous Sheriffs and Western Outlaws," Incredible True Stories of Wild West Showdowns and Frontier Justice, published by New Home Library, New York, NY in 1928.

It also must also noted that John Rhodes was contracted by the Arizona Rangers from 1906 until 1907 as a stock detective. Rhodes was just another example of a Tewksbury Faction member who after the feud ended became a lawman.

Below are pictures of Bill Brown's great grandma & grandpa that given to the author to use in this book.

John Rhodes, 1930   Maryann Rhodes, 1940

This author would like to thank Bill Brown, the Tewksbury family historian, his grandmother, Bertha Tewksbury and his late great grandmother, Mary Ann Tewksbury's for all of their efforts to help Bill keep solid records from their own recollections, and along with the two amazing books, one written by Will Barnes, "Apaches and Longhorns," and the other written by Frederick Russell Burnham, "Scouting on two Continents," both very credible individuals who were directly involved in the Pleasant Valley War, this author would not have been able to present so many interesting and factual content. And of course credit must be given to Maurice Kildare aka; John Winslowe, who also wrote several magazine articles used in this book that included his personal interviews with some of the folks that were involved in this feud. Each one of these resources offers a little different look at this horrible stain on Arizona and United States History. There really can be no summary. Each reader will come up with their own conclusion.

When this author started researching the Pleasant Valley Feud, he was completely neutral, knowing nobody involved or related to those folks involved, with no ties to either family or any other person involved in this Range War. The author finds it interesting though that two of the last survivors on the Tewksbury faction, John Rhodes became one of the 26 men to serve a term as an Arizona Ranger and Jim Roberts was the first deputy sheriff that Buckey O'Neill chose when he became the Sheriff of Yavapai County in January 1889 stating;

> "I want the best shot on both sides of the Pleasant Valley War and the fairest, most honest man I ever met to represent my office and keep peace in the Tonto Payson Area of Yavapai County."

In the end there will always be a lot of mystery as to the facts and deaths in Pleasant Valley with many questions still unanswered as none of us were there and lived during this incredible range war, we have to rely on new research and maybe someday it will all come together.

Again this author went into this project knowing nothing about either family and took no sides. This Author's research indicates the Tewksbury faction of the Tonto Basin or Pleasant Valley War were not the bad folks, but in fact were live and let live down home Arizona folks, that simply wanted to live their lives in peace, raise cattle and grow crops and just enjoy a quiet pleasant life the beautiful Pleasant Valley. On the other hand, the only survivors on the Graham faction, Hank Blevans, Charley Duesha and John Blevins

Below is a photo of Bill Brown the Tewksbury family historian pictured on the left with the author pictured on the right. This picture was taken by our friend Bob Carpenter just behind the gravestone of John Rhodes that was recently installed by the Arizona Rangers.

Below is a picture of an old abandoned home in Young, that was used for the cover of this book was taken by the author.

Below is a picture taken by the author of what remains of Jim & Ed's ranch.

Below is a photo of the well that is in the middle of what is left from Ed and Jim Tewksbury's ranch, seen above.

The picture below is the Perkins Store, now a museum, which is where Bertha Tewksbury, Bill Brown's grandma lived most of her life until moving in with Bill Brown and his family.

Bibliography

Chapter One

"Osmer Flake Family Journals," by Osmer D. Flake, published (1897)

"Canyon Diablo," by Zeke Crandall, published (2013)

"Commodore Perry Owens," Wikipedia, the Free Encyclopedia (July 29, 1852 – May 10, 1919)

Chapter Two

"Arizona's Dark and Bloody Ground," by Earle R. Forrest, University of Arizona Press, Tucson, Arizona. (1984)

"Osmer Flake Family Journals," by Osmer D. Flake, published (1897)

"War in Pleasant Valley," by Clara T. Woody and Milton L. Schwartz, the Journal of Arizona History. (Page 43)

"The Pleasant Valley War," by L. J. Horton, the Journal of Arizona History. (Page 49)

"Apaches & Longhorns," by Will C. Croft, the Ward Ritchie Press, Los Angeles, California. (1941)

"The Tonto Basin War," By Marc Peterson, published in the Summer edition of Old West Magazine (1965)

Chapter Three

"Osmer Flake Family Journals," by Osmer D. Flake, published (1897)

"War in Pleasant Valley," by Clara T. Woody and Milton L. Schwartz, the Journal of Arizona History. (Page 43)

"The Pleasant Valley War," by L. J. Horton, the Journal of Arizona History. (Page 49)

"Apaches & Longhorns," by Will C. Croft, the Ward Ritchie Press, Los Angeles, California. (1941)

"History of Arizona Territory," by Joseph Fish, (1840-1926) (published in 2009)

"Arizona's Secret History," by Daniel J. Herman (April 2012)
 "History of Arizona Territory," by Joseph Fish, (1840-1926) (published in 2009)

"History of Giesla," by Jane Peace (1949)

"Arizona Cultural Inventory Project," William MacLoed Raine collection, Arizona History Museum (1871-1954)

"Apaches & Longhorns," by Will C. Croft, the Ward Ritchie Press, Los Angeles, California. (1941)

"Canyon Diablo," by Zeke Crandall. (published in 2013)

Chapter Four

"The Pleasant Valley War," by Maurice Kildare, Real West Magazine, November of 1967 issue.

"Long Remember," by Maurice Kildare, True West Magazine, February 1969 issue.

Chapter Five

"War in Pleasant Valley," by Clara T. Woody and Milton L. Schwartz, the Journal of Arizona History. (Page 43)

"The Pleasant Valley War," by L. J. Horton, the Journal of Arizona History.

Chapter Six

"The Pleasant Valley War," by L. J. Horton, the Journal of Arizona History.

"Letter from Gwendolyn Kimmell to Ed Tewksbury," March 1st, 1904, Supplied by Bill Brown from his family archives

"The Hoof and Horn," by Buckey O'Neill, Published in Prescott, Arizona. (November 15, 1888)

Chapter Seven

"Charley Duchet (Duesha)," by Bill Roberts, the Traveler Magazine. (September 1993 Edition)

"Lynching's In Pleasant Valley," by Bill Roberts, the Traveler Magazine. (September 1991 Edition)

Chapter Eight

"Buscadero Outlaw," by John Winslowe, Westerner magazine, (July-August 1970 issue)

Chapter Nine

"Those Were the Days," by Doctor Robert K. Hilton, the Camp Verde Historical Society.

"Last of the Old-Time Shooting Sheriffs," by Cleveland Amory, Jerome Historical Society.

"Who shot the Bank Robber," by Herbert Vernon Young, The Old West Magazine. (Fall 1982 Edition)

"1928: Bank of Arizona Robbery in Clarkdale, Arizona," by Glenda Farley, the Verde Independent newspaper, Cottonwood, Arizona. (December 8, 2013)

Chapter Ten

"Century Old Feud Commemorated," by Claudette Simpson, the Prescott Sun Newspaper. (July 11, 1990)

"Encyclopedia of Frontier Biography," by Dan L. Trapp, University of Nebraska Press, Lincoln, Nebraska. (1991)

Chapter Eleven

"Apaches & Longhorns," by Will C. Croft, the Ward Ritchie Press, Los Angeles, California. (1941)

"Will Croft Barnes and the Apache uprising of 1881: Adventures of A Soldier and Versatile Citizen of the Southwest" by Paul J. Scheips, U.S. Army Center of Military History, "Meteorological Mettle helps Barnes to Medal of Honor" by Nancy Kirkpatrick Wright. (2003) "William Croft Barnes," Wikipedia Online Encyclopedia

Chapter Twelve and Chapter Thirteen

"Apaches & Longhorns," by Will C. Croft, the Ward Ritchie Press, Los Angeles, California. (1941)

Chapter Fourteen

"The Remarks of Major Frederick R. Burnham," The Historical Society of Southern California, 13 (4) pages 334-352 (1927)

The foreword, "Six Horses," by William, Banning & George Hugh, New York, New York. (1930)

"The Howl for Cheap Mexican Labor," by Charles Stewart Davison, Galton Publishing; New York, New York, pages 44-48. (1930)

"Scouting against the Apache," James E. West, The Boy Scout's Book of True Adventures; Their own story of famous exploits and adventures. New York, New York. (1931)

"Taps for the Great Selous," by George Bird, Kermit Roosevelt Cross, W. Redmond; Trails on Three Continents; a book of the Boone and Crockett Club, the Derrydale Press. New York, New York (1933)

"Madison Grant (Eulogy)," Boone and Crocket Club, pp 29-31. (1931)

"Taking Chances," By Haynes, Los Angeles, California (1944)

"The Fire that shall never die," Boys Life (Boy Scouts of America) 7, 35. (1945)

According to James McClintock, Arizona's first historian and other sources, Burnham's father was a Congregational minister, Burnham later wrote on his father as a Presbyterian preacher. At that time Burnham was young, Presbyterians and

Congregationalists cooperated in establishing many new congregations in the Midwest, USA. Burnham was drawn into the Pleasant Valley Feud by his association with John Middleton and his family. Another historian says the name of the family was Gordon. In his memoirs, "Scouting on Two Continents," Burnham never states the name of the family, but in the undated manuscript he mentions his friendship with young Tommy Gordon and his family from Globe, Arizona.

"Aids to scouting for non-commission officers and men," by Baden-Powell, Robert, Gale & Polden. (1899)

"Reconnaissance & Scouting." A practical course of instruction in twenty plain lessons, for officer and non-commissioned officers, Baden-Powell, Robert, W. Clowes and Sons, London, England (1884)

"Scouting for Boys: A Handbook for Instruction in Good Citizenship," by H. Cox, London, England. (1889)

"Filming the Boer War," Beginners of the Cinema in England, Bishopgate, London, England. (1894)

"Last of the Scouts," the Boys' own book of Adventures, Chapter 3, Macmillan, New York, New York. (1923)

"Organizations Defending Wild Life," California Game & Fish, by H.C. Bryant. (1915)

"Shangani Patrol," by Frederick Russell Burnham, Westminster Gazette, London, England. (1895)

"Northern Rhodesia," by Frederick Russell Burnham, Simpkin, Marshall Hamilton, Kent & Co, pp 177-180, London, England. (1899)

"Modern Mine Valuation," by M. Howard Burnham, C. Griffin and Company, London, England. (1912)
"Burnham, the Scout," Pearson's Magazine, by Curtis Brown, London, England. (1901)

"Borrego Desert Park," by Frederick Law Olmsted, Sierra Club Bulletin. (April 1933)
"Major Burnham, Chief of Scouts." by Richard Harding, Real Soldiers of Fortune, Charles Scribner & Sons, New York (1931)

"Veteran Scout." by E.B. DeGroot, Boys Life Magazine, Boy Scouts of America. (July 1944)
"Major Burnham-The Scout." by V.L. Ehrenclou. Union Oil Bulletin, Union Oil Company of California, Los Angeles, California. (May-June 1925)

"Battles of the Nineteenth Century," by Archibald Forbes, Arthur Griffiths and George Alfred, Castle and Company Ltd, London, England. (1896)

"Frederick Russell Burnham," by James E. Homans, The Cyclopedia of American Biography, The Press Association Compilers, Inc. PP 249-251, New York, New York. (1918)

"Foes of Our Own Household," by Theodore Roosevelt, George H. Doran page 347, New York, New York. (1917)

"Arizona National Wildlife Refuges". (Arizona Department of Transportation) 17. (1941)

"Chief of Scouts Major Burnham's Adventures," the Times (44450) (London). (December 9, 1926).

"Frederick Russell Burnham Papers, Manuscripts and Archives." Yale University, at the Wayback Machine. A large collection of Burnham's documents: Correspondence, (1864–1947). Subject Files, 1890–1947. Writings, (1893–1946). Personal and Family Papers, 1879–1951. Photographs, California. (1893–1924)

"Frederick Russell Burnham Papers," (1879-1979). The Hoover Institution Library and Archives, Stanford University. A large collection of Burnham's documents

"Frederick Russell Burnham," Wikipedia Online Encyclopedia

Chapter Fifteen and Sixteen

"Scouting on Two Continents," by Frederick Russell Burnham, Garden City, New York; Doubleday, (1926).

Chapter Seventeen

"Pleasant Valley War Witness Talks," By Roscoe G. Willson, the Arizona Days & Ways section in the Arizona Republic Newspaper, February 25, 1951

"Outlawry of Era Fans Pleasant Valley Feud," By Roscoe G. Willson, the Arizona Days & Ways section in the Arizona Republic Newspaper, March 4, 1951

"Bloody Battle Fought at Middleton Ranch," By Roscoe G. Willson, the Arizona Days & Ways section in the Arizona Republic Newspaper, March 11, 1951

"Bloody Ambush Turns Graham Supporters," By Roscoe G. Willson, in the Arizona Days and Ways section of the Arizona Republic Newspaper, March 18, 1951

"Sheriff Trap Ends Pleasant Valley War," by Roscoe G. Willson, in the Arizona Days and Ways section of the Arizona Republic Newspaper, March 25, 1951

"Tom Graham Killing in Tempe Ends Feud," by Roscoe G. Willson, in the Arizona Days and Ways section of the Arizona Republic Newspaper, Published on April 1, 1951

"Letters from Earle Forrest to Roscoe G. Willson and letters from Roscoe G. Willson to Earle Forrest," Found in the Roscoe G. Willson Collection, in our Arizona Historical Archives.

Chapter Eighteen

"Sheriff Tells of Range War," By Roscoe G. Willson, in the Arizona Days and Ways section of the Arizona Republic Newspaper, published on April 29, 1973 and May, 6 1973

Chapter Nineteen

"Famous Sheriffs and Western Outlaws," by William MacLeod Raine, New Home Library, New York, NY. (1928)

"The Daggs and Not so Pleasant Valley. The Copper area Newspaper, July 13, 2013

"Tonto National Forest Trail Map," United States Department of Agriculture, Tonto National Forest

Supervisors Office, 2324 E. McDowell Rd, Phoenix, Arizona, 85006

"Mary Ann Tewksbury-Graham," her conversations and statements made to Bill Brown, her grandson with whom she lived with until her death.

"The Tewksbury family archives," including pictures, letters and other statements. Bill Brown, curator, Tempe, Arizona.

"Black Mesa," written by Leland J. Hanchett, Jr, Pine Rim Publishing, Phoenix, Arizona 1996

"Personal interview and Larry Boeschling" with the Author.

Additional books to read on the Pleasant Valley War aka the Graham-Tewksbury Feud;

"Arizona's Dark and Bloody Ground," written by Earle R. Forrest, The University of Arizona Press, Tucson, Arizona, published in April 1984, ISBN number 928-0816508532.

"A Little War of our Own," written by Don Dedera, The Northland Press, Flagstaff, Arizona, published in 1988, ISBN number 978-0873584630.

"Famous Sheriffs and Western Outlaws," written by William MacLeod Raine, republished by Sky Horse Publishing, New York, New York in 2012, the first publication of this book was in 1903. ISBN number 978-1-61608-542-1

About the Author

William "Tom" Vyles aka Zeke Crandall was born in London, Ontario, Canada. The family moved to Phoenix, Arizona February of 1956. Suffering life long battle with asthma and several bouts with pneumonia, along with being in an out of hospitals the first nine years of life, the family was instructed to move to Arizona for the hot dry climate, that would be the best way to prolong the life of the author

With no family in Arizona, they Vyles family adopted their elderly neighbors as our Arizona grandparents. , who also had no family in Arizona. Kenny and Mary Harris moved to Arizona from Cincinnati, Ohio also in 1956. They also had no family in Arizona. .

Kenny worked in the stockyards in Cincinnati as a brand inspector for cattle coming from Arizona. He became friends of John Wayne, who brought his cattle through the stockyards in Cincinnati. The Duke talked Kenny into moving to Arizona. Kenny was a professional fiddle player, along with his friend Rudy McDonald, who played banjo, they toured Arizona playing gigs. The author fell in love with Arizona.

The author went with them on most of the out of town gigs. It was his job to set up their instruments and listen to the first set to make sure they sounded good. The carrot so to speak for his young boy was that the two men would take the lad quail hunting.

www.ingramcontent.com/pod-product-compliance
Lightning Source LLC
Chambersburg PA
CBHW071313150426
43191CB00007B/604